Southwest
Gardening

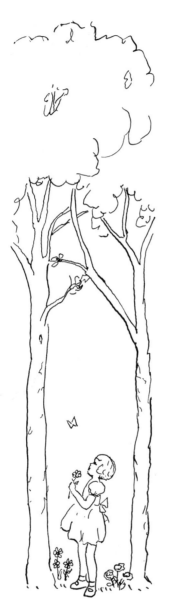

Newly revised edition

DRAWINGS BY ROSALIE DOOLITTLE

Southwest Gardening

ROSALIE DOOLITTLE

in collaboration with

HARRIET TIEDEBOHL

A BOOK WRITTEN IN SIMPLE LANGUAGE FOR THE
GARDENING NOVICE RESIDING IN THE SOUTHWEST —
NEW MEXICO AND THE STATES SURROUNDING IT.

THE UNIVERSITY OF NEW MEXICO PRESS

Library of Congress Catalog Card No. 52-11535
Clothbound ISBN No. 0-8263-0026-x
Paperbound ISBN No. 0-8263-0027-8

COMPOSED, PRINTED, AND BOUND AT
THE UNIVERSITY OF NEW MEXICO PRINTING PLANT
ALBUQUERQUE, NEW MEXICO, U.S.A.

For all who
love a garden

Preface

THE SOUTHWEST, including the Rocky Mountain area, presents to the gardener many problems which are not found elsewhere in the country. The solution of some of these problems for the average novice gardener is the purpose of this book, which is the result of many years of experience by the author. It represents her personal conclusions gleaned from this experience. The book is intended to guide such gardeners through the technique of planting and tending a garden plot, and to give such instructions as are necessary for them to avoid the costly mistakes made by gardeners unfamiliar with the conditions encountered in the Southwest.

New Mexico, Arizona, Colorado, and Texas comprise most of the area discussed, but parts of Utah, Nevada, Oklahoma, and California also could be included. Such portions of the area as are extremely high and cold or extremely low and hot should be excluded.

Special problems, such as high alkaline content of the soil, protection against hot, drying winds, and the need for irrigation, are discussed here, and this book will apply to any locality where these conditions are found.

The trees, shrubs, and flowers listed are the plant items most easily grown in this locality. There are enough of these to fill whole estates to overflowing, for most plants that thrive in the temperate zone will grow here. Thus, this book is directed not toward "specialty" plant culture, which requires extra care and attention, but at gardening made easy. Instructions are included for the preparation of the soil for flower beds and lawns, on how to transplant, and how to care for trees, shrubs, and plants within the garden.

Only the simplest terminology has been used, in deference to the novice gardener. The common names of nearly all plants have been used, and some botanical names have purposely been omitted from the text.

Preface to the Revised Edition

SINCE this book first was written, gardening has become a more exciting hobby than ever before. Hybridizers are at work bringing out new varieties so fast it is difficult for the specializing hobbyist to keep up with new introductions. New plants from other parts of the world are becoming available. I believe that sometimes new irises, roses, and daylilies are put on the market too hurriedly, and that it is wise not to get these until they are tried and approved by the public. I have in mind a rose that was "ballyhooed" from one coast to the other. Practically every rosarian succumbed to the praise and now, after a few years, the rose has not proved itself. It even winterkilled in a severe late freeze. However, most garden hobbyists would rather have new plants than a new dress or suit—this is one of the things that makes gardening fun.

Certainly garden designs are improving, and America finally has a type of garden all her own, made to fit the city lot of the vast majority, and designed for outdoor and family living. The enclosed, walled gardens with attractive fences in various designs, and planned illumination for night use, make it more and more a perfect outdoor living room. Trees are being carefully pruned to produce a trim sculptured look in silhouette and shade pattern, thereby aiding the things growing underneath. Large, paved areas of flowing or modern design with lawn islands reduce upkeep, but here let me sound a little warning—arrange for *enough* shade because paving can act as a furnace in our hot sun. My own design adds trees to reduce the heat given off by the large patio area. Many attractive louvers of wood, or two-by-fours, put together in square block fashion, give some shade and protection from sun in patio or outdoor living areas.

New flowering trees appear each year and these can give great pleasure. In the spring I have two months of constant bloom and beauty from flowering trees, and my garden has not suffered, because these small trees are not avaricious enough to rob my flowers of food and water.

Specialist hobbyists are finding more and more varieties—irises by the thousands, daylilies (hemerocallis) in many varied colors, pinks and maroons being added to the old oranges and yellows. Both irises and daylilies are found together in many growers' catalogues, perhaps because they are good companions. For both these hobbies plenty of space is needed. Peonies, if well fed, are being grown more successfully in the area, and whole catalogues are devoted to them—the single and Japanese types being as beautiful as the big doubles. Among the roses, the floribundas are increasing at a rapid rate and are better and better. A new race, the Grandiflora, is producing some of our finest bushes and flowers, such as Queen Elizabeth, Carrousel, and Montezuma. Tuberous begonias are more popular now since the discovery that they are not as difficult to grow as formerly was believed. However, as often happens, troubles develop with popularity —mildew, wilt, and failure of the tuber to leaf out. Chrysanthemums, as always, offer a challenge, with more Japanese and English varieties on the market. Their growing season has been lengthened with varieties that bloom earlier and with those that withstand some frost. In the fiftieth annual chrysanthemum show staged by the French people in Geneva, Switzerland, I saw wonderful varieties that I hope may reach this country.

An almost Oriental devotion to arranging flowers has been a popular trend brought about through flower show schools whose trained teachers take five courses in arrangement. The arranger is ever searching for unusual and odd materials to give line and originality to flower compositions. Seed pods and line material such as Bells of Ireland are grown for this purpose.

Where lawn failures occur, I am more convinced than ever that few persons prepare the soil well enough. Some of the finest lawns I have seen used double the amount of farmyard manure generally recommended. Lack of feeding (particularly in the fall) is far too evident. One well-managed lawn is fed every seven weeks except in high temperatures. Irrigating lightly and too often, as well as cutting too closely, causes worm-eaten and fungus-ragged lawns. New grasses are not needed as much as proper management.

The introduction of a balanced foliar food for various plants has been of the greatest help to the gardener in recent years. When used properly, its ease of application even in the heat of summer without causing leaf burning, has made it especially valuable to arid areas.

Garden clubs are growing at a rapid rate. Flower shows are multiplying in number and beauty. Competition in growing fine specimens is more of a challenge. The over-all gardening activities in the Southwest are expanding and with this comes greater beauty in our modern living.

The author is proud that shortly after the publication of the first edition of SOUTHWEST GARDENING, she received a National Council of Garden Clubs award "in recognition of distinguished service in compiling and publishing material of extraordinary value in the advancement of gardening."

ROSALIE DOOLITTLE

Acknowledgments

WE WISH to express our grateful appreciation to the following persons who have furnished the inspiration for the work leading to this book: Dr. E. F. Castetter, Academic Vice-President and Dean of the Graduate School of the University of New Mexico; Cecil Pragnell, former Bernalillo County Agent in New Mexico; Mrs. R. Fred Pettit, an old friend and gardening colleague; Mrs. W. H. Long, one of the early professional landscape gardeners in this area; Mrs. Earl Mount, with whom we have exchanged ideas on chrysanthemum and iris culture; Mrs. Alice Gilliland, who was among the first to encourage new garden materials in Albuquerque; and the late Mrs. W. C. Reid, who planted the seeds of garden clubs in New Mexico. To this list also are added the names of the late Chester T. French, L. C. Bolles, and Lake S. Gill of Albuquerque, and Pamela Edwards of Santa Fe.

Farther afield, the collective friends in the American Rose Society, with whom Mrs. Doolittle has met and worked, including Dr. R. C. Allen, author of *Roses for Every Garden;* also the late Mr. Hugh Bryan and Mrs. Bryan of Salt Lake City, Utah; the late Mr. William Jonson and Mrs. Jonson of Pasadena, California; and Mr. and Mrs. Fred Walters, of La Canada, California.

Appreciation is expressed also to the late Fred E. Harvey, formerly of The University of New Mexico Press, who supplied the necessary encouragement when the book was just an idea; the late James P. Threlkeld, Emily Ramage, Elizabeth Bright, the late Mrs. George Bryan, Mrs. Frank H. Scheck, and Mrs. J. R. Miller, who comprised a committee to meet and discuss the book and the need for such a work before it was started.

Mrs. Miller, in particular, is mentioned since she was the "guinea pig" at whom the book was aimed. Mrs. Miller moved to the Southwest from Ohio three years earlier and was attempting to establish a garden at the same time she managed a home and took care of her three very young children and husband.

SOUTHWEST GARDENING was slanted at all the Mr. and Mrs. Millers and their families, to give them the required information on gardening as they worked together on long summer evenings to have a beauty spot around them.

The author and collaborator express gratitude for the patience of their husbands during the three years it took to get this work together, and for the understanding of family and friends who were badly neglected in the interests of "the book."

Taylor's *Encyclopedia of Gardening*, Bailey's *Manual of Cultivated Plants*, revised edition, and *Standardized Plant Names*, prepared for the American Joint Committee on Horticultural Nomenclature, have been used as authorities for spelling and definition of plant names and terms.

Table of Contents

Look at Your Thumb

LOOK at your thumb. It isn't green.

The desirable green thumb comes from knowledge of good gardening principles and the putting of these principles into practice.

The person with a so-called green thumb is the one who loves flowers with the same sort of love one feels for his family, dog, riding horse, or any other thing that lives. It all wraps up into one attitude, appreciating life about us. Because of this love, there is the desire and willingness to work with the live beauties of nature.

To those who wish to extend their activities into garden work, let me warn that the grounds about the house are very much a part of the home. Untidy housekeeping and slovenly habits indoors repeat themselves for all the world to see. A weedy, half-dead lawn, shrubbery struggling against the odds of no food and little water, trees dying inch by inch, are the reward. Even those with money to spend on gardening find many little chores that must be performed at odd moments personally. For those who do not wish to do these things, the cactus-studded front yard, with a few chamisa and yucca stuck in here and there, plus rocks and boulders for accent, might be the solution.

Those who love their family pets wouldn't think of letting them go hungry, or without water, and housing is planned for suitability to the animal's needs. To be a good gardener the same needs of the plant must be considered. A plant's home is the earth. In this earthly home there must be food, water, light, air, sunshine, heat—just as in providing for the human family.

Plants must be protected from extremes of heat and cold. Their homes must be well ordered and well kept. Nothing alive can exist without food.

Nature will supply food up to a certain point, but in our area we must constantly replenish the supply. And, plants cannot go out foraging for themselves. They must have their requirements brought to them.

The question of water in our arid Southwest is most important. When your child asks for a drink, he gets it. But in your garden are many baby plants that cannot ask for water. You must learn when the drink is needed.

This attention to the plant when attention is needed probably is the most important factor toward acquiring that envied "green thumb." I believe that flowers, plants, and trees respond to human love and the touch of the human hand in affection, just as surely as will your pet dog. You can see the wag of the tail, the devotion in the eyes of the dog. So it is with the flowers in your garden.

Often a plant, tree, or shrub comes to me from a long way. Out of its native habitat, and, perhaps, upset in its travels, this plant shows the shock. Each day I will go out to look at it, I'll touch it and fuss around it. Oftentimes the response is magical. It's almost as if it knows the love and prayer in my heart that goes out to it in addition to its physical needs of water, shelter, and food.

All of this attention does not require as much time as it may seem from the telling. It is the thoughtfulness behind what you are doing that brings the extra dividends. Not the hours brought into garden work, but the day-by-day regularity of chores is what brings the added results of splendor. When I go into the garden to move the hose, I'll stop and pull out a weed along the way. Should I be out in the late afternoon to pick flowers for a bouquet, I'll snip a little twig that has grown out of line and needs pruning, or put a bit of compost or fertilizer about a plant that seems to grow timidly.

These constant attentions take up little time and are very important. Almost anyone can give fifteen minutes a day to the "extras" in the garden. With the occasional half-day that you will want to spend in it on gorgeous days, your garden will thrive.

Doing the chores at the right time is important, too. When winter keeps you indoors, list your seeds and other needs for the approaching season. Have them on hand when planting time comes. In the fall think of your early spring garden. Order your bulbs. Plan new beds.

There is much fun in keeping a garden diary. Thus you can check with yourself on the progress in the seasons to come by looking back over previous performances.

Since the average home lot measures 50 to 100 feet in front, with depths of 100 to 150 feet, many home owners feel they can do little in the way of gardening.

When I left one home, which measured 75 by 120 feet, with 2,000 square feet of it taken up by the house and garage, plus an additional space going into the driveway, paths, and service areas, I counted plants and flowers into the hundreds. Within two years I had planted and enjoyed the beauties of 85 rose bushes, 12 climbing roses, 75 varieties of iris, 50 varieties of chrysanthemums, 4 evergreens, 12 trees, 15 shrubs, many bulbs, and an additional 75 varieties of annual and perennial flowers.

Perennial borders in my gardens always are crowded, with several "blooming" crops growing in one spot but at varying degrees of development. A cutting garden and vegetables stand in the service yard. Extra marigolds, petunias, zinnias, and chrysanthemums stand by. As the tulips die away, or the early oriental poppies have blazed across the bed, plants from the "spare" garden go in close enough to hide the worn-out plants.

A blooming chrysanthemum can be moved in to replace a hardy aster that has been cut back after it bloomed in August or September. This close planting method is very desirable in the Southwest as it tends to keep the ground well-shaded and cool. Very little cultivating is needed with close planting, since the ground does not have a chance to bake in the sun. Irrigation is not needed as frequently, and weeds won't compete under those conditions, either.

All children love beauty, and in talks before parent-teacher groups I have stressed the fact that a beautiful yard is just as important as an attractive living room to the sensitive mind of a growing child. Children are outdoors more than inside during the year and mothers should be educated to fill their need of serenity and beauty of surroundings. Children accustomed to a lovely garden never are destructive in one, and never consciously do damage when visiting another garden.

Dogs, too, can be taught not to destroy a garden. Chica and Penny, the black cocker spaniels we had for fifteen years, respected the flower bed areas as much as I do. They had their own area for romping and their necessities. Now a toy poodle is being trained.

So, let me preface our actual gardening instruction by saying that after learning "how to" in a garden, get busy and do. With this simple prescription, I am sure you will succeed in having a beautiful garden setting for yourself, your family, and your friends.

Why Are We So Different?

GARDENING "back home" was such an easy chore. One slipped a seed into the ground, nature watered and fed it, and up popped the most beautiful flower imaginable. But now you have moved to the Southwest—the Land of Enchantment. Behind you are the damp, foggy, luscious hills and dales of California or the East. The abundant green shrubs and tall, gracious trees are gone.

The very absence of vegetation, the stark strength of mountain and desert thrills us, but, for our own little corner in this new land, we will want a garden spot scented with familiar blossoms; bright with the flowers we held dear "back home."

What are the differences, then, between gardening in the Southwest and in other localities, and what can be done to reconcile these differences?

Soil quality, irrigation, altitude, and high winds are the chief differences. The make-up of our soil is greatly on the alkaline side in most areas excepting in mountainous localities. Some valley areas are exceptions and have much natural growth from a well-balanced soil condition.

Soil in this area of the country is of several types and, for the most part, lacks humus. One kind is the heavy adobe, which the natives depended upon for building material. Another is pure sand, or gypsum resembling snow, as in the White Sands area of New Mexico, but heavy "caliche" (almost cement-like and heavily limed) is the real problem soil. Regardless of the type of soil encountered, it can be taken for granted that it lacks humus.

Flower beds back home were made like this to insure drainage.

In this area beds need to be four inches lower than the soil at lawn level in order to hold water.

Irrigation is a necessity in all but a few sections of the area. Some mountain areas do have more moisture, but even here come periods when a flower garden needs additional water. Every garden or field must be planned to hold water. In our home gardens this may be done by lowering the beds several inches, and the wise gardener plans to mulch to conserve moisture. But in our modern cities a sprinkling system is a part of the cost of every home and is planned along with other modern conveniences.

High altitude does not greatly affect what we grow as far as I can find. The difference is in too hot daytime temperatures and very cool nights.

Of course, we can't grow tropical plants or those requiring high humidity. Such plants as azaleas and camellias can be grown in a very protected, shady spot if the gardener will baby the plants summer and winter. Even then an unusual freeze or high wind might mean death to these species. Irrigation must be handled with care in this land of contrasting night and daytime temperatures. Plants must "dry off" before the cool night approaches.

One of my desires would be to grow the exotic broad-leaved plants found along the West Coast and in Florida; but I find that these plants require a high humidity and above-freezing temperatures. Rhododendrons are in the same class. They fail to thrive, not because of the temperature but because they like acid soil and damp air. Soil can be made to fit most special situations by additions, but it is impossible to keep it acid where the water we use is greatly alkaline, as is the case here. The constant irrigation required by these specialty plants defeats our very aim to make soil more neutral.

Winds, in most of our area, present a big problem. To me, it is the most irritating problem of them all. I can easily improve the soil; I know what to plant that will grow easily and happily; I can irrigate when needed. But there is very little I can do to battle the wind or counteract it beyond the planning of roof lines, walls, and other windbreaks. Roof overhangs are important.

My new home was planned as much as possible to deflect wind from important garden areas, shielding the inhabitants of the house as well from these seasonal furies. I always feel a little uneasy when talking to gardeners in isolated places on the plains where nothing protects them from the blasts. Probably the only advice to these plains dwellers is to plant as many trees for windbreaks as possible, using tamarisk hedges (which, however, will drain water away from other plants), Russian olive, pussywillows, or similar standbys. This is where the maligned Siberian elm fits our planting scheme, as it is a hardy tree that withstands heat and dryness well.

In valleys and near rivers, the cottonwoods grow well. Surrounding a town they are beautiful indeed, with their dense summer green and their autumn mints of gold. People in small rural towns in the plains areas could get together in community planting to benefit entire localities by the use of these two trees alone.

Sunshine is a problem throughout the Southwest, and "sun-loving" plants should be numerous in our garden. Gardeners will discover that here they flourish in the shade as well. The sunlight imparts, even to our shade, enough brightness to cheer these plants on to astonishing endeavor. Shade has never been a problem in my garden, since so many more plants grow in the shade than the average gardener realizes. In fact, my shady garden spots are treasured, for it is there that I tuck away the begonias, columbine, hydrangeas, and even delphiniums. This last plant, which does not grow well in the southerly sections of our area, can be grown on the north side of a house. Korean hybrid chrysanthemums growing on the north side of my house were among my nicest.

Once the gardener new to the Southwest understands the underlying differences in soil, watering, altitude, and winds between his old home and his new, the greatest garden problems have been solved.

Flatow and Moore—architect

Dream House

RIGHT in the middle of writing this book came the planning and building of our new home. My family needed a larger house, and this was to be the dream house, the goal of every heart's desire. Since nearly everyone, at some time or other, has the desire to build a dream house, my experiences may be of help to those who are about to fulfill that desire. It generally takes a year or two to establish a lawn and garden around a new house, but I was able, by careful planning, to have a landscaped home almost from the time we moved in.

I loved my old home, particularly its four-year-old garden, and my affection for the garden made me somewhat regretful at first. However, as plans took hold for the "dream garden" along with the dream house, the backward looks changed to eager anticipation, and I realized that now was the time to put into being the home we long had planned. Then, when I learned that the new occupants of our old home would love my four-year-old dogwood, just then coming into bloom, as much as I did, the last qualms vanished.

This was my real opportunity to integrate house and garden plans until the two became a blend of one master plan. Inside and out the house would reflect the beauty of the garden, would beckon the outdoors to be shared by us through picture windows. Every window was to be planned to frame a garden picture. There would be little "warm" flower beds here and there so well protected by house and garden wall that they would catch the sun all day and would reward us by the earliest blooms of all in the spring. Then there would be the "cool" beds protected against the sun by the wall of the house, where my beloved begonias would grow.

Planning against the wind was important, too, and for sunshine in the garden through the summer and into the house in the chill of winter.

No unsightly spot should mar the beauty of house and garden while waiting several years to grow a protective screen about clothesline or compost box, the log pile for the fireplace, or the collection of garden stakes and other impedimenta.

Flowers would harmonize with the color of the house itself. The patio would be truly an outdoor living room most of the year. There would be warmth in winter and shade in summer in our patio, and its floor would be so simple that leaves and papers swept in by the wind could be easily swept out again.

This house, too, would have to be planned for making housekeeping a minimum job, so that its gardener-owner could spend more time in her beloved garden.

What an opportunity!

The first blow fell when we learned we had to vacate our old home immediately for the new owners. The new garden wouldn't be ready for the "starts" of plants from my old garden.

But, just a minute! Why not? After realizing I had a half acre I thought, "surely in my future garden I can have a tiny slice that the workmen won't trample while they are building the house."

My background planting went in against the walls of neighboring properties. A virtual nursery row came into being at the base of these walls. About six feet away I set out stakes connected with heavy twine as a suggestion of protective fencing against all those workmen that soon would be swarming about.

Even before house plans were completed, climbing roses were planted. One of the mistakes I had made in my previous garden was the neglect of background climbers for the formal rose plantings because of the expense of doing both at the same time. Had the climbers gone in first, the second year would have seen a much more handsome garden.

Trees and shrubs went into the new location. Perennials and iris at the old garden needed dividing anyhow, so I could take some of each of these for the house in the valley without a guilty conscience. In fact, I saved the new tenants a lot of work by this garden housekeeping.

Almost a ton of compost went into the new nursery strip, along with my nice new redwood compost bin, which was moved to the new location, to stand exactly where it was to be permanently. Thus, when the house was completed, dozens of budding and blossoming plants left this nursery for their new beds in the patio. In this way, the new house never had the bare look of a just completed residence.

Many seedlings were started in flats small enough to be carried about easily. Here were begonias, pansies, delphinium, pyrethrum, columbine, veronica, and the little border plant with its bright flowers, called the anagallis.

As soon as the wall was built about the service yard down at the new house these little seedlings were transplanted close together in rows. This service yard was to be the permanent home for my exhibition chrysanthemums. In August, while the thermometer registered in the 90's, I placed these plants in rows, staking them for support. Thus, in October, when we moved in, I was rewarded with fairly good blooms.

Vegetables, too, were started in this yard, and even before we moved in I was able to gather carrots, beets, lettuce, radishes, parsley, and a few others.

Before the house was completed the interior colors and decorations were planned. The patient decorator who worked with us was helpful and understanding of my idea to carry the garden indoors. No drapery or furniture was to detract from my garden. Colors inside and out were to harmonize to actually become a part of the garden setting.

Perhaps I might mention that, as a small reward, the following year when we were entertaining with an early evening reception, some of the guests wandered through open doors into the floodlighted patio thinking they actually were entering another room.

In the walnut-paneled sun room facing the patio where we would do most of our "living" I planned a niche for flower arrangements in the wall of book shelves.

Every room was to frame a picture, each view showing a color theme that predominates inside the room as well as outdoors. Thus the flower border under the living room picture window would have blue columbine to add to the indoor blues of rug, chair coverings and wall tones. Tuberous begonias were to match the strong colors of drapery and give contrast to the blue-gray walls and the gray sash curtains.

Off the dining room a bed of yellow roses harmonizes with the gauzy yellow glass curtains. Roses of another color and shade, a "rose" color, pick up the color tones of the rose-patterned wall paper in the same room. A flowering plum tree just outside the breakfast-nook window will be a thing of joy when it blooms in the spring, contrasting with the yellow-walled nook and kitchen, and the blue-gray cabinets.

Remembering all the while that these special beds of color in flowers will look well against the blue-gray walls and yellow trimmings of the house, I reveled in the general planning.

The house itself is low and rambling, somewhat like a distorted shallow "U," with thick shake roof. I know there will be many plants I would like to include in the landscaping, but I will always have to remember the height limitations. I'll not want formal evergreens, for they will not be right for this type of house. Low and simple planting will be the answer, with contrasts in color. And lots of roses.

We all have ambitions for our hobbies. One of mine is one day to buy and plant 1,000 tulips all at once.

So you see, where it appears that the end of the road lies near, with the dream house completed and encircled by its garden, my gardening experiences actually are continuing and taking on new aspects. The knowledge collected through the years will be used only as it is coupled with the advances being made continually by horticulturists everywhere to further intrigue me into experimenting with and adding to the beauty already contained in my garden.

This edition of the book finds the dream house sixteen years old and there have been many changes. With the family gone there is less interest in the vegetable garden so this area has been changed completely and now rhododendrons are being tried in shade. They were planted in a mixture of peat moss, compost, and sand, and all food given to them is acid. They are sprinkled often to keep the area around them moist. I am very encouraged over the results so far. This is the fun of gardening—making changes. With redecorating and colors changed, plants are needed to meet the inside color scheme.

Do not cover a picture window with heavy planting which will cut off a view beyond the garden wall.

Landscaping

THE TYPICAL Southwestern home is of Pueblo or Spanish architecture, small and one-storied; with the ranch type and modern style finding their way into our growing communities. Many houses are constructed without much thought of design, and it is this type that can be made attractive or ruined by the planting about it.

All home owners cannot be garden architects, but we all can follow a few simple principles. Not only should the owner of the small home seek information on the locality in which he lives, but estate owners as well can better direct garden employes toward the effects they want if they acquire knowledge regarding the flowers, trees, and shrubs that will surround their homes.

Should the home owner feel completely at a loss in planning landscaping to match the residence, and if he can afford the service, a professional garden architect should be employed to provide at least the over-all design. These architects also will supervise the actual putting together of the garden.

The most common fault is literally to hide a house by planting a solid line of shrubs and evergreens about the foundation, with no thought of over-all design. All line and character of a house is removed with such heavy base plantings, and in later years they will outgrow the building. Plants will then have to be removed, and possibly the whole landscaping plan rebuilt. Constant pruning might control such a situation for a time, but how much better to plan proper plantings in the first place.

NATIVE PLANTING

Part of the breathtaking beauty of our great outdoors in the Southwest is the variety of unusual and colorful native plants. Great carpets of desert plants cover the mesas at times, literally matching the burst of a sunset in the sky. A half-hour walk across the desert when plants are in bloom can result in a collection of as many as twenty-five blooming varieties of flowers. Truly the desert is generous when it is given the slightest encouragement with the barest spring rains.

Naturally the impulse is to bring this beauty home, to plant it in the garden about us, and a few gardeners make the attempt. Native-type homes lend themselves in particular to this type of planting. The chamisa (rabbit brush), with its gray-green upward sweep topped in late summer with yellow blossom, is a favorite. Cactus in several varieties, from the long, thin, ungainly spines to the tubby, low types, are seen lining driveways or are given a corner of their own.

Although no general book is available on the culture of desert wild flowers and plants, a number of botanists have made important contributions to their description and growth habits. No doubt the beauty and attraction of desert plants will result in more widespread experimentation until a number of varieties will be "domesticated" enough for the garden. It is to suggest the obvious to remark that our most refined flowers at one time in the past were "native" in their habitat. In the meantime, to transplant most wild flowers in our Southwestern areas results in failure of these plants in our own gardens. They are accustomed to drought, and we water our lawns and flower beds generously. They have learned to like the alkaline, parched soil of mesa and mountain, while we add food and chemicals to our soil to encourage bigger and better plants and blooms.

Recent years have seen some very artistic gardens designed for the Southwest that have been inspired by Japanese gardens. These must be done with skill and restraint. Native material such as gnarled piñons have been combined with rock groundcovers and other suitable plants. One problem remains unsolved—keeping weeds from these rock or gravel floors. When plastic or roofing paper is used the weeds will not appear until enough "blow sand" will allow some windborn seed to germinate. If the area is poisoned a sudden rain may carry poison to the trees or plants and kill them. When large rocks are used in the design they should be placed as in a natural outcrop. If a neighborhood is all grassed and planted in a traditional manner some grass should be used in the design so that this Southwest garden will not stick out like a sore thumb.

The desire to protect native plants against vandalism and careless destruction by the traveling public has led to the passage of laws and regulations against digging up specimens in some states. It would be wise for those who contemplate acquiring specimen plants to check on what is permissible in their locality.

PLANTING FOR NATIVE-TYPE HOMES

Southwestern-type homes—the Pueblo, Spanish, and territorial colonial adaptations of architecture—as well as the ranch type home, can have distinctive plantings about them. Usually these can be brilliant in color, strong in line, and tend somewhat toward what is called indigenous or native. Among these are the flowers introduced to the Southwest long ago from Mexico and other regions.

Cacti, in their many shapes and varieties, head the list for newcomers who are intrigued by these strange plants on their arrival. For the same reason, yucca and chamisa are popular.

Cottonwood trees, any flowering or fruiting trees, the Russian olive, weeping willow, and tamarisk or salt cedar, seem "made" for our adobe colors and our pueblo lines.

Red-twigged dogwood, photinia, pampas grass, Spanish broom, mahonia, forsythia, rambling and shrub type roses, poinciana, or bird-of-paradise, grape and trumpet vines, santolina, succulents, cosmos, hollyhocks, geraniums, castorbeans (poisonous), and pyracantha, combine easily with the distinct Southwestern architecture. All ground covers and most annuals and perennials may be added to the list.

Most of our native architecture should be surrounded by landscaping with natural effects. Formal planting has no place in Pueblo architecture or about a ranch-style house, since the designs themselves are rustic and natural.

In New Mexico, Santa Fe and Taos gardeners have been most successful in planting not only in keeping with their homes and their own plan of living, but in extending their planning to include the unique historic atmosphere of their communities. These artists who turn to landscaping their own homes have, in many cases, used native plants and shrubs in place of lawn. Their patios follow the old Spanish custom, adopted by the early Americans, of a secluded garden behind high walls. Landscaping in the more modern cities, such as Phoenix, Albuquerque, El Paso, Roswell, Denver, and Colorado Springs, generally follows a more conventional plan.

Since New Mexico and the Southwest are so vivid with what nature has given us, color about the native type house is imperative against our brilliant skies, fleecy white clouds, the blue of our mountains, and the purple shadows of mesa land.

Should an occasional house bid for evergreens, severe plant designs still are out of place. Much less formal but more desirable winter greens come to mind. These are the junipers, piñon, some spruces, photinia (a gracious evergreen shrub), the mahonia or Oregon grape, and the almost too popular berried pyracantha.

Color in wintertime is introduced into the garden with the bark of shrubs and the less formal evergreens. Sometimes the structure of shrubs and trees presents lacy and interesting patterns of branches, trunks, and twigs that contrast against our Southwestern skies. Spirea and forsythia bushes, generous with blooms in the spring, retain qualities of attractive lines and stem colors through the entire winter.

Nearly every native-type house should have a little patch of flowers to connect the landscape directly to the house. Hollyhocks and zinnias do this well.

Do not neglect the indoor approach to your outdoor landscaping. What is planted on the outside will show inside, through the window. Coloring should harmonize with drapery and furniture. Rose-colored drapery in the living room suggests floribunda roses just outside. The Permanent Wave variety could be a good one here, perhaps deeper toned than the color selected for the curtains.

By planting too much shrubbery in front of your attractive windows, you destroy the purpose of those large expanses of glass meant for light and air and to admit the view of your garden and the distant hills and mesa. Frame a picture with your window, but be sure that beyond it there *is* a picture, not the purposeless promise of a great window area. Suppose the window does overlook a neighbor's garage. Trail a climbing rose on its wall, or plant a tall and colorful shrub before it, making an asset of what could be an annoyance. Contrast the building with the color of your climbing rose or shrub.

Keeping in mind that trees give shade, when planting near the window on the east or west side of the house, plant the trees somewhat to the north to hold back the intense rays of an August sun, since the sun is farther to the north during those hot summer months.

Remember that our flat houses do not require the large trees that could easily overshadow the house itself. Consider your neighbors, too. Often trees are planted with no thought that too much shade will extend to your neighbor's garden and obstruct his view as well.

In olden days homes were two-storied and demanded the gracious old trees as handsome groupings about an acre of garden. Big trees send out big roots to steal into your neighbor's garden and sap the plant food put there for his prize rose bed, or his perennial borders. The thefts are just as bad and worse from your own favored garden spots.

Newer sections in our Southwest, with its fast growing communities, do sometimes look like "row house" buildings, with no thought toward block landscaping to beautify the whole area. Neighbors who would work out plans together should consider the thirty or forty varieties of smaller trees in their area, so none need stray outside home territory. Such a plan would provide over-all effective landscaping—each neighbor planting several of the tree species until all are represented in this "block planning" system.

Everyone falls for the tall and stately avenue of trees glimpsed in old pictures, down the roads leading to great estates, or lining one side of a country home. Too many of those entranced by such a vista plant a row of poplar trees along the back or side of their town property. Poplars require much root space and are fine for windbreaks on the farm, but they can overshadow the long, low, and flat lines of our modern homes and may cut off a neighbor's cherished view.

Poplars planted too close to the house seem to "hang" over it. The roof line has been lost, architecturally speaking, and the overall effect of what could have been a graceful picture has been ruined, along with the individual appeal of house and garden.

From a distance, three or five poplar trees grouped at one side can be effective, if you must plant poplar trees on a small town lot; but put them in a far corner, or behind a chimney. I filled a long, narrow space at the side of my first home, where only five to eight feet were available, with a line of poplars. The subsoil was sandy, and roots, as they grew to robust

Yes

No

proportions, found it easy to slip under house foundations and crack the plaster of walls. We blamed the cracks and "settling" of the foundation and walls on construction faults until a thorough inspection by an experienced contractor disclosed the real reason.

Another fault is to plant evergreens in groups at the street corners of properties to loom up, deep and dark and forbidding, as they take their stand. They actually become traffic menaces. Where the vision is obstructed, the clump of evergreens on which the owner looks with pride may be the cause of the death of a youngster wheeling his way along to school.

When residing for a brief time in Washington, D.C., it seemed to me no place was as beautiful in the spring. I know now it was the flowering trees that made it so. Not all varieties grow in this enchanting land of ours, but many will. Why not bring this topic up when you are with a group of gardening friends and mention it to the city fathers when new park areas are being discussed?

Most flowering trees not only give dense shade, but in winter the beauty of their trunks and bare branches surpasses that of many other trees. Most artistic in their winter state are the peach, redbud, flowering crab, and tree wistaria, suggested as landscape items in front of the house. Plum tree branches, in a deep purple, and matching purple leaves in the fall, are effective. The same leaves are red in spring. They linger long after most trees have shed their leaves in the fall. Both the Hopa and Bechtel, in the flowering crab varieties, are handsome. Paul's Scarlet Hawthorn does well in the southern parts of our region. Flowering trees as a whole do well in our section. In a home we owned, a double flowering peach was planted at one side of our modified French Provincial doorway. When planted, it was waist high. When we left it, two years later, it was as high as the house itself. No one can ask for a faster growing tree.

Many newcomers from the eastern portions of the country where trees are plentiful, desire shade so badly they'll plant anything to get it. Our brilliant sunshine overcomes them, and they turn to hardy Siberian elms. Regret comes later, when the trees drop countless seeds to develop tough little seedlings everywhere, or when they "weep" on a car parked beneath them. This undesirable tree is often misnamed, for it commonly is called the "Chinese" elm.

New materials, such as the floribunda roses, are excellent for color and landscaping effects. Nearly every color is represented, with even a lavender shade now on the market. The glossy green leaves and bark are an additional attraction for winter seasons. The size ranges from 18 inches to 5 feet in height, giving much leeway for planting in specified areas.

Simple lines are the best for small homes. Spotty yards are not appealing. Patios and back yards should have some focal point or center of interest. Plants grow and stretch with the years, and their growth habits must be considered by the homeowner as he envisions his surroundings in the years to come.

Larger plants in the background of borders, with colors complementing one another, is the rule. A fool-proof color plan puts oranges, reds, and yellows on one side of the yard in the perennial border, while pastels take over on the other side. Blue and white seem to blend on both sides.

Here is your opportunity to indulge the color preferences of the family. My younger son likes purple and rose red flowers. Tulips, poppies, and zinnias are tucked into the border for him. My daughter wears pink well, and loved to go out with a nosegay of dainty roses in her hair. For her, then, I added Cecile Brunner roses, Pinocchio, and the Picture rose.

My beige suit won't take a small pink rose, or red poppies, but bronze and yellow chrysanthemums this fall will make a handsome accessory.

It is fun to try different color combinations. Place a clump of Colorado blue columbine with airy, lacy flowers dancing like butterflies about iris of tan lightly touched with blue. Or, yellow and pink columbine with yellow iris. Watermelon pink oriental poppies planted in front of blue delphinium will more than repay the effort of combining them.

Corners of a house can be softened by heavier planting or a bare wall may be made to appear smaller if well planted. Usually larger materials are used for corners and against walls. Low planting goes under windows.

Variation is necessary, in order to avoid monotony. Something higher on either side of a doorway suggests itself. The door is the entry to the home and should be a center of interest. It should go further; it should be an introduction to the personality of the family beyond that door. Should your entry be formal, plan a formal arrangement there. Climbing roses go well about the informal doorway. Outstanding plants are a must for the entry to the home.

A perennial border or a shrub can be brought right down to earth with a second transitional border of a lower variety. Most of the truly attractive perennial or annual gardens I have seen are bound to the adjoining lawn, walk, or patio floor with their borders.

Neatly clipped borders of santolina, fairly evergreen and with a light gray and blue-green foliage, are a delightful contrast to the green of floral foliage or the green of grass below it. Or possibly the dainty blue lobelia, in the light or dark blue or perhaps in the purple variety. Sweet alyssum is an old garden favorite, making a ribbon of white to bind the garden and the flower bed into one. I am partial to the variety called Little Gem for compact, neat growth.

A variety of others are available. Alyssum Royal Carpet is an attractive bordering plant. Ageratum Blue Mink is perfect for sunny spots. Nierembergia Purple Robe can be remembered here; also the perennial alyssum saxatile, which is a brilliant yellow. Pansies are beloved by gardeners and are good for the border, as are dwarf snapdragons, chrysanthemums, dwarfed petunias, and marigolds. Sometimes two or three borders can be planted to round out a year of growth and beauty. Try the pansy for early spring. Replace this with alyssum for warmer weather; and climax in the fall with dwarfed chrysanthemums. Most of these plants can be started in seed flats and transplanted. Alyssum can be planted between pansies. When the pansies become leggy or unsightly I remove them, and my chrysanthemum plants are ready to be slipped into place for the fall blooming. The new growth will not obscure the actual bloomer which has the spotlight for the season. Castorbeans, zinnias, cosmos, and tall marigolds are good to use in between shrubs while they are attaining size. They will tide the garden over from looking too bare that first year.

For a taller border, the Korean hybrid chrysanthemums are ideal. These are easily grown from seed. I pinch these back every month to keep them low. When a planting warrants, use the hedge shears to clip the plants down as though they were a hedge. This is discontinued in August, to allow the formation of buds.

In planning a new home and garden, the long list of things I wanted became almost discouraging. The price tags sometimes meant some cherished fancy must be sacrificed. The best advice to avoid these little heartbreaks is to plant the smallest size of all you wish for, instead of splurging for one-third to one-half grown trees and shrubs.

When these things are in, you may feel your grounds are bare and incomplete. The speed with which the smaller plants grow and develop will amaze you at the end of the first season. In two or three years, the landscaping will be more advanced and flourishing, with specimens better established than gardens started with plants of larger size.

The shock of transplanting larger specimens slows them up, particularly if the plants come from a distance. Maybe the shock will be such that not much progress will be made by the tree in its first year in the new home. In most cases a smaller tree, in a couple of years, will be just as beautiful and its life span will be longer. Important, too, you will have a hand in the actual shaping of the tree as it grows. Feature whatever tree, shrub, or flower that brings you the most pleasure. Make it a personal project, not just a garden-planting chore.

Remember the present trend, indoors and out, is much color. These cheery, strong tones may in future years be discarded for the dead white and cream of walls and woodwork indoors and all evergreens outside that we left behind us not too long ago. Take advantage of the color popularity and match it with much color in your garden.

Families that include small children should plan a play area. Plants that cannot take the rough tramping of little feet should not be considered here. This does not mean that the play area should be a barren spot apart from the beauties of the home and garden. Shrubs peeping over the fence can take the eye. Lilac bushes with their fragrant spikes of flowers are favorites for the purpose.

Be sure and put a fruit tree in the play yard, so that the children can enjoy the flowering beauty. Fruit trees by nature are constructed to accommodate climbers (in this case children, not roses). Branches hang low and are strong to carry fruit. They will carry the weight of a small boy or two with no strain. An apple tree on my grandfather's farm is an outstanding memory of childhood. It was my playhouse and I clambered over it and played about it to my heart's content.

Give your child a little garden plot if any interest is shown. You may be pleased and surprised at the results. I know my love for all growing things was encouraged by a plot in my grandfather's farm where we spent many summers long ago.

Have an area for your clothesline and for general utility purposes, such as to mix soils, manure pile, compost pit, fireplace wood, and garden materials in general. Don't forget the spot for the trash can. Hide it with a trellis that carries a rose, or hide it with shrubs. The camouflage should be hardy enough to take the rough brush of the garbage collector.

Driveways need careful planning. Ease of getting the car in and out of the garage with as little waste of planting area space as possible, is to be considered. Choice and tender plants have no place along the driveway, for all too often a misguided car will literally "mow them down." Violets will take as much abuse as any edging we might grow easily.

Sun-loving shrubs should be planted on the south and west of the garden wall. Those which can take the sun or leave it and will thrive in shade can be planted along the east side. Put the shade lovers on the north side.

My crapemyrtle grew with ease because it was placed in front of the south wall in a protected corner of the patio. Had I placed it in the north spot where cold winds could hit it, no doubt the plant would have curled up and refused to grow. Each plant should be located with consideration for its desires, if it is to prosper in your garden. A perennial or annual border should have much sun, as most flowers bask in sunlight. Rose gardens need sun, but if the garden is in a warm spot, the rose will appreciate a bit of shade in midafternoon.

Renewing a garden is a chore that many with long-established homes must face. Shrubs and trees almost dead from neglect and overgrowing present their problems. In many cases the wisest course is to remove them and replant. Often newer varieties are on the market that are much superior to plants of a decade before. The matter of the new versus the old may not hold so true of roses as of other plants. Even though new varieties come along, many of the old varieties of roses remain superior.

It is the wise prospective gardener who works out his plan on paper, and even keeps a file of notes and sketches of his future garden as he plans and prepares to build his new home.

Bring all the facts together when the actual planning is done. The type of home and the type of living the family expects to use it for are important, together with the pets and their needs. Remember the indoor color scheme should tie in with the outdoor planting. What service areas will be required, for the laundry, garden supplies, garage? Combine all these factors in your sketch. Consider the growth habits and eventual appearance of plant material to be used.

By all means don't discard your own likes and dislikes when working out your garden plans. A copied garden looks it, usually having no individual style to its credit.

By this time you are ready to order your supplies, arrange for professional services required, and outline your working schedule, season by season, until the plan becomes an actuality. All the while, of course, you will be making changes and adjustments as new ideas regarding color, variety, and location suggest themselves to you, since your garden is a growing, living thing and will demand such changes.

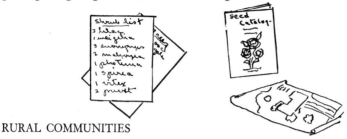

RURAL COMMUNITIES

Rural communities in the Southwest present serious gardening problems, with accent on lack of water and their position on windswept, barren stretches of desert and mesa land. Yet, tucked away in these small towns and villages are gardens of true beauty. Often members of a garden club, by working together, can transform an entire community by the encouragement introduced by programs and gardening contests.

State and county fairs often disclose the excellent gardening practices of small communities, with the prizes many times carried away by the farmer's wife or the young boy or girl in club work.

Group planning can make small towns outstanding. A row of trees around the town itself will add to beauty as well as grow into a protective windbreak. Thus the two-fold advantage of creating an atmosphere of unity, and protection of individual gardens is achieved.

My annoyance with the Siberian elm and its countless seeds is temporarily abated when I consider its value to the outlying communities where little or no water is available. Cemeteries bare with sand and stone can be ringed about with these elms. They can stand neglect under these circumstances and thrive on it.

Weeping willows are native to valley areas where underground water is available. Native conifers are easily secured from mountain areas. Street plantings of these trees would beautify, while, in areas where rainfall is a little more abundant, flowering and fruiting trees would be a delight to traveler and resident alike. Farmington, in New Mexico, suggests itself for the fruit tree decoration. Cottonwoods root easily in a small space and later can be transplanted when a little growth is attained to place them in spots where they can beautify the entire town. The Russian olive is an excellent tree that can be used as a windbreak.

Professional tree growers usually are willing to give reduced prices for community project planting. Each home owner could enter the joint plan for planting and an order could be prepared that would provide the variety and beauty desired.

Although the lack of water is the greatest drawback in rural areas, wasteful watering habits could be eliminated to save the precious fluid. Most families waste enough water day by day to water several trees.

We who live in the Southwest know what it is like to drive for many miles along a barren area to arrive at a charming valley or mountain community. Picture this spot, by nature endowed with beauty, if it were further enhanced with thoughtful planting of trees and shrubs. Annual seeds are inexpensive. Marigolds, zinnias, castorbeans, California poppies, and bachelor's-button are among the flowers that require little water and can grow with very little attention. Hollyhocks and cosmos can take the place of shrubs, and they harmonize with our western colorings. Perennial asters grow well and will multiply.

City garden clubs would be only too happy to share their more bountiful supplies of materials with rural areas. Thousands of iris, daisies, violets, daylilies, and a score of other easily grown varieties of plants could be distributed in a community-wide planting program.

Native plant materials can be used to great advantage in rural areas. Yucca is plentiful in some areas and grows easily. The astonishing total of 122 differing native plants was grown by one of our rural inhabitants who specialized in native plant culture. Her specialty made her widely popular as a speaker, who encouraged the continued planting of desert plants adaptable to home use.

Lack of money never need be an excuse for drabness or ugliness. A few dollars can buy many seeds (See "An Economy Garden" page 193). Compost made from leaves and garbage will provide food. Expensive insecticides may be eliminated by choosing the more pest-resistant plants, such as castorbeans, cosmos, marigolds, zinnias, and flowering trees.

Soils and Fertilizers

NEXT to the sun itself, the soil is of the greatest importance to human life. We who grow things must treat it with respect, aiming always to improve it, and gardeners, especially should feel it a duty to improve the soil in their own gardens. It has been a bad habit of man to take away from the soil, not putting back into it. As a result, erosion and dust storms have caused much destruction in our region.

I have noticed, time after time, that a garden is nearly always successful in the first year. The next year it still is all right but from then on it becomes poorer and poorer until I hear "I just can't make anything grow any more." Often the blame is placed on trees, which some gardeners say "just keep everything from growing." This need not be the case with proper ground fertilization. One of my best gardens was grown on a lot where there were far too many trees, with neighboring lots filled with them, also.

In this area it is almost impossible to over-fertilize, as food is leached from the soil by continuous irrigation. Since, aside from some mountainous areas, the soil generally lacks humus, water is not held naturally as in other parts of the country. This makes more frequent irrigation necessary. In many of our valley regions the soil is heavy adobe and does hold the moisture better, but needs humus to lighten and aerate it.

In our higher levels where much of the soil is sandy, humus again is necessary to help retain moisture. Most of the soil has the fertility to begin with, but needs adjustment in its chemical makeup. Nearly all the Southwest has an abundant quantity of alkali, which alone makes our soil treatment entirely different from eastern areas in our nation. It is from the eastern and coastal areas that most of our garden books, encyclopedias, and

magazines originate, and although their general broad instructions are excellent, they miss the needs of our region.

Caliche soils, with their alkaline reaction, are a great factor in the difference in treatment here. Heavy irrigation brings the lime content to the surface by leaching, with a cementing process resulting. Thus, where the underlying soil is of the caliche type, the gardener must constantly war against it by the addition of "acid" foods: compost, farmyard manure, and mixtures of sand, vermiculite, and peat moss. Ammonium sulphate is excellent to use for this purpose. It seems to be a help in breaking up the tough caliche surface.

Often the addition of lime is recommended, but more Southwestern gardens have been ruined by this one piece of advice than for any other reason. It seems no authority residing in areas outside our own Southwest has any idea of the high alkaline content of our soil. To add lime is to increase the alkalinity.

The lime content of the soil in our region sometimes is 50 times as much as is required for most plant life. Potash seems to be found in sufficient quantities, while the phosphates are low. Phosphate fertilizers have been proven to increase the yield of most crops in this area.

At the risk of becoming too technical, I will outline the basic soil needs which are important to the beginning gardener. The term devised by chemists for measuring acidity and alkalinity of the soil is based on the hydrogen ion concentration, or "pH" value, as it is called. The pH value 7 is considered neutral and most plants get along with this degree of "sweetness." Many plants have decided preferences in one direction or the other. A lower pH or more acid soil is preferred by roses. A pH of 5.5 to 6.5 is favorable to the rose, while a pH of 7.5 to 8.5 is detrimental. Azaleas like a very acid soil. Iris enjoy alkalinity.

More plants tolerate an acid soil than an alkaline one. In our locality, the pH usually reads 7.5 to 8.5 and higher. It's a wonder we can grow anything in the ground here in its so-called "natural state." We work continually to bring the pH down, not only because of our soil content but also because our water is alkaline. Kits are available from garden supply centers that will determine the pH content of your soil, and most communities now have firms that specialize in chemical soil analysis and give excellent service. They also supply the needed chemicals to add to the soil, often properly mixed for use.

State agricultural colleges are helpful with soil analysis. And don't forget your County Agricultural Agent. He is invaluable in giving you helpful advice regarding your immediate locality and its variabilities.

Three fundamentals are important to the growth of plant life. These are nitrogen, phosphate, and potash. It is these three, listed by percentage content, that we read on fertilizer sacks. Popular is the 4-12-4 proportional percentage, in the named order.

Nitrogen makes good green leaves and stems, with crisp growth. Its use makes a tender vegetable.

Phosphates (phosphoric acid) aid in bringing plants to maturity, particularly in the final development, help to ripen tissues, increase hardiness, and encourage flowering.

Potash is needed for the manufacture and movement of food in the plant. It helps color flowers and makes plants disease resistant. In our region there is more potash than other nutrients.

Trace elements are important and play a part in releasing foods to the plant. These include iron, magnesium, manganese, boron, lime, zinc, sulphur, plus others. They sometimes are added in commercial fertilizers. Recent products of trace elements are a splendid addition to our garden feeding.

Mixed commercial fertilizers are applied on the soil at the rate of three to four pounds per hundred square feet, with thorough irrigation following immediately. Ammonium sulphate, urea, tankage, dried blood, cottonseed meal, and foliar foods, are several products added to supply nitrogen to plants, the lack of which is detected by small pale-colored, sickly-looking foliage. Sulphate of ammonia used one-fourth cup for each two and one-half gallons water, urea, and foliar foods can be applied in liquid form. Sulphate of ammonia is strong and should be used carefully, as too much will kill earthworms. There are new products on the market which are valuable for supplying nitrogen gradually over a long period, but their high price has kept them from general use. Sewage sludge, in analysis, does not show a high nitrogen content, but in contact with the soil reacts to greatly increase nitrogen, giving much more than the percentage on the bag indicates. Tankage, or dried blood, is spread dry around each plant. A handful suffices. If dogs are around, they will dig for it.

Superphosphate or rock-phosphate adds the needed phosphate to the soil. Use this dry, about three pounds to the hundred square feet, or a tablespoon per plant. A small handful can be dropped around a shrub or large plant. Bonemeal adds nitrogen, phosphorus, and calcium, used dry at the rate of five pounds per hundred square feet, or around each plant. Its pH is around 10, so I avoid it, not wishing to make an already naturally high pH higher. Iris and tulips can take a little, however. Potash also may be supplied by using sulphate of potash or muriate of potash.

Wood ashes have an alkaline reaction, and are a source of potash and calcium, which are not needed. I do use wood ashes in the compost pile, however. Iron sulphate lowers the pH reading and supplies iron, which much of our soil lacks or which cannot be absorbed by our plants, due to alkalinity. Apply it in liquid form, one-fourth cup to two and a half gallons of water. I use ten pounds of iron sulphate to each 100 pounds of sewage sludge or with commercial fertilizers for the lawn. This use of iron is a must for Southwestern gardens. In fact, if only one element were allowed for my garden, I would specify iron. Iron chelates are being used but directions must be followed carefully to prevent burning.

Agricultural sulphur lowers the pH reaction, and is applied dry at the rate of one to three pounds per hundred square feet. Exceptional cases may require lime but this is seldom in our area.

Aluminum sulphate, used for lowering the pH, is toxic to lower life in the soil, so should be used only as a last resort. Cottonseed meal is excellent for lowering the pH, and for nitrogen. It is safe, and may be used dry five pounds per hundred square feet. It is one of my favorite fertilizers, especially for roses.

Sewage sludge is fine, and when properly produced by the manufacturer will contain all the elements necessary for balanced plant life. It is another of my favorites.

Organic fertilizers are my choice, rather than the chemical mixtures. Be safe rather than sorry, is my advice on the latter group. I would rather

use a very small amount often, being careful not to place it close to the plant. Avoid getting it on the leaves, as it will burn them.

A cool day is better than a hot one for fertilizing. If I use a dry fertilizer, I apply it when the soil is not too dry and irrigate thoroughly immediately after application. When the liquid form is used, I irrigate first. Fertilizer can be applied at any time, but too large a dose can injure a plant enough to destroy it. Again, let me stress care in application.

Foliar feeding (applying food directly to plant foliage) has been done in the past and apparently gave good results, but in recent years its benefits have been scientifically proven when radioactive tracers showed nutrient substances being absorbed by the plant immediately through the stomates, or breathing pores. I have used a foliar food (23-21-17) for a number of years and it appears to be one of the finest products for the gardener. Especially it is valuable at the time fertilizing is dangerous—during hot, dry weather in the Southwest, but also at a time plants make their greatest demand—especially of nitrogen. This is a safe method of feeding if used early mornings according to directions. It is odorless and clean, and attracts no flies. Avoid formulas with too high a nitrogen content, or lacking phosphates, or soft growth will result; a well-balanced formula is important. An applicator producing a fine mist when attached to a hose which has a good pressure works best. It can be used every two or three weeks from the time leaf buds swell until frost, strengthening plants to withstand cold weather. Seeds, bulbs, and roots soaked in a solution of this foliar food prior to planting do better. My new rose bushes are immersed in it and are more easily established. Seedling plants thus treated show little wilting.

In discussing fertilizers I have left the best for the last.

Animal manures are excellent and can be applied as mulch or in liquid form. The latter technique is to saturate manure in enough water to make a liquid the color of strong tea. Apply on irrigated soil.

Some animal manures are stronger than others, and all should be aged before applying. It should not be so old, however, that its beneficial elements

Compost heap

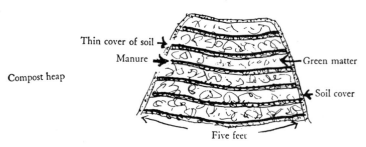

Thin cover of soil →

Manure →

← Green matter

← Soil cover

Five feet

are leached from it. Cow manure is safest and can be used an inch in depth at a time, building up to a four-inch depth over a period of several months. Weed seeds can be eliminated if the manure first is mixed in with the compost heap.

Cow, horse, goat, sheep, chicken, and guano all are fine manures. Chicken and guano are strongest, and must be handled carefully.

Probably the best way to use manure is to compost it with green material. Composting is nature's way of preparing fertilizer and a wise gardener realizes that nature's methods are best. We can hurry her, but we cannot fight her. Soil is not dead, inert material, as has sometimes been assumed. It is full of bacteria, working toward an end. Some are good, some harmful. Generally the good overcomes the bad. All work in continuing life cycles to improve the soil.

Organic gardening is nothing new. Our grandfathers didn't know commercial fertilizers, but kept their soil fine and productive by returning to it waste materials. The late Sir Albert Howard, of England, has done the most work in actual experimentation and his conclusion (and those who follow) are that food grown on composted land not only improves the life and health of humans, but of animals as well. Disease is less prevalent and harmful insects are not as numerous. Composting increases the lowly earthworm, which is one of man's best friends. These little creatures make a perfect soil after taking it through their bodies. Tests have proved that their casts contain all the needed elements in proper proportions. They are little fertilizer factories.

A good gardener does everything he can to make possible the existence of earthworms and to keep them contented, since they are the best garden workers obtainable. They not only improve the soil but aerate it with their little tunnels. The whole garden improves with them.

Many recipes are given for composting, and much advice as to what should go into the compost heap. No two composts may be the same, but the end result, improvement of the soil, is there, and that's what counts.

My description will be simple and brief. Cutting and grinding coarse materials speeds the composting process, but those of us who must conserve time, effort, and money find this step unnecessary. Use all green materials from the kitchen, also orange and grapefruit skins, melon rinds, coffee grounds, tea leaves, scrap bread, cigarette butts, and other waste material. Avoid greases and sugar.

Outdoor contributions are all grass clippings, leaves, weeds, and other garden discards. Make a mat of these five feet across and four to six inches deep. Over this put a couple of inches of manure, the greener (fresher) the better, and a thin layer of dirt. I do not use lime as recommended by some composters, as our water contains so much alkali that lime is unnecessary. Repeat the piling-up process until the whole is four or five feet high. Keep it damp, but not soggy. If at any time I want to add something from the kitchen, I just dig a little hole in the pile, slip the waste material into it, and cover with barnyard fertilizer or earth. I put whole plants and weeds in, and, although the coarse stems may not be entirely decomposed, they seem to aid in transmitting air into the center of the pile, thus keeping it from becoming too heavy. The pile will heat enough to kill many weed seeds and bugs. This is one important reason why processing manure in the compost heap is valuable.

I have found that sprinkling additional chemical fertilizers or sewage sludge over the heap aids quick decomposition. A product on the market, containing natural soil bacteria, activates the heap. Because iron improves

Compost box, five feet square is a good size

soil, I make several applications of iron sulphate to each heap. Ammonium sulphate also is valuable. To get a more acid humus which helps combat our alkaline soil, the addition of soil sulphur is good.

After the finished pile has stood five or six weeks, it may be turned. (Recently I have not bothered turning the heap and I find little difference in the time it takes to have finished compost.) Turning is difficult work and may be very haphazard, but the composting seems to be successful just the same. A second turning is recommended by some, but I don't do it. When I work and turn the heap myself, I don't insert crowbars for aeration, nor do I take its temperature. When making the compost, a box helps keep it trim and intact. Do not make a cement floor, or any floor for that matter. The contact with the earth helps start bacterial action and allows the earthworms to come through. Compost will ripen and decay almost as readily if placed right on top of the ground, although some recommend digging of pits. A husky gardener might enjoy this pit digging, but I avoid it. Should you want to acquire a regulation compost box, information is available for its construction, or you might be able to purchase one ready to set up for use.

In this dry climate it takes a little longer for the compost pile to ripen thoroughly because of low humidity and hot, dry winds. I have had good compost results in three months, and my last one, started in the fall, should be ready by early May. Some composters do not recommend starting them in the fall, but mine has proved satisfactory.

It is better to use a compost pile when it is ripe and ready than to let it stand for any length of time. If it must stand, keep it damp and cover the whole thing with a couple of inches of soil to seal in the goodness.

Compost water is prepared by mixing water and compost, allowing it to stand, then draining off the water with nutrients held in solution. Use two trowels of compost to one bucket of water. This special water treat revives backward plants and often has saved some valuable specimen that droops for no apparent reason.

Let me emphasize that it is better to have a compost pile, even though it is not perfection, than not to have one. The help any plant derives from this fertilizing aid never ceases to amaze me. A night-blooming cereus that had "stood still" for a year threw out new leaves in six weeks after I repotted the plant with compost and gave it a weekly drink of water in which compost had been dissolved. I had given it all sorts of fertilizers, but the compost literally brought it to life. Compost or humus is available for sale in some places for those unable to make it. Fertilizers should be used when needed with it.

Cold Frames

PLANT material in abundance can be obtained by the seed-flat method, using the cold frame or hot bed. Since our daytime temperatures are higher than in other sections of the country, with fewer cloudy and rainy days, the artificially heated seed bed, called the hot bed, generally is not necessary.

Practically every plant in my garden comes from seed grown in a small cold frame. One-by-twelve lumber five feet long was used for the rear board. The lumber was cut to an eight-inch height for the front piece. The side sections, three feet in length, were slanted from the twelve-inch backing to the eight-inch front board. (See illustration.) The covering was a frame made with one-by-two-inch wood, binding a plastic "glass" top. If the price for plastic or glass tops is prohibitive for you, tack on a piece of old sheet or plastic. Light, and easily moved, the frame top gives protection from inclement weather. Weight it down with bricks to prevent it from blowing off.

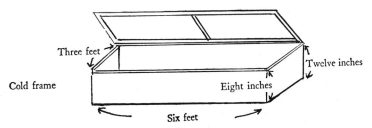

Three feet

Twelve inches

Cold frame

Eight inches

Six feet

The cold frame is located in a protected spot, preferably facing south. Dig the soil out to a depth of sixteen inches. Place twelve inches of manure, either cow or horse, with "green" or fresh cow manure preferred. Put a mixture of equal proportions of sand, compost and vermiculite or peat moss, rubbed through a wire screen, over the manure. Sterilize with boiling water or a commercial preparation to kill off unwanted bacteria.

Gardeners in the Southwest rarely have trouble with "damping off," because of our dry atmosphere. I protect myself in advance against this damage from fungus parasites with the sterilization process. Damping off can sweep through a seed flat and kill all its plants in a short time, and is

Cross section of cold
frame mixture

Four inches good
garden soil, compost,
peat moss, sand, or
vermiculite, all
screened   ↓

↑
Twelve inches
Fresh manure

generally the result of too high a moisture content of the soil, and lack of aeration.

Make a ruler from a half-inch board cut slightly less than the width of the flat. While the sand is moist, use the ruler for pressing depressions one-third inch deep as seeding rows. The rows should run the short way of the flat, about four inches apart. Have the labels ready at hand. I write labels for what I intend to plant soon after the seeds arrive.

When planting, avoid too large a quantity of any flower seed for the small garden. As many as three kinds of seed may be put into one row, maybe as many as fifty varieties in the frame.

Each seed must be treated according to its preference. The tiny petunia seed is left uncovered. Press the seed into the soil with the ruler you used for making seed rows. Larger seeds, such as the zinnia, are covered with just enough to hide them from view. Sprinkle a mixture of sifted sand and peat moss for the covering. Press into the soil with the ruler. The lighter the cover the better. Too deep seed coverage seems to create more failures than any other gardening misstep. Nature drops her seed right on the earth. Maybe that's a tip for us.

Irrigate lightly. Here is an idea I picked up that works quite well. I use my vegetable brush to sprinkle in order not to disturb the tiny seeds or wash soil over them too deep for their comfort. Dip the brush into the water bucket; sprinkle over the row with a shake.

Never allow the seed frame to dry out at any time. A newspaper or burlap sack anchored over the plastic top will keep the frame shaded while the seeds germinate. Three or four sprinklings a day when is it windy is suggested. When it is cool, one or two sprinklings a day will suffice. If your seed bed is allowed to become dry and dusty, very few plants will show up. As much as a six-hour period without water might spell the difference between success and failure.

Remember, too, not to water too late in the day, and do not over water. When I have to be away from town my seed bed always suffers from too much water. Whoever I leave to take care of my garden generally is so afraid of under watering that they often overdo as a result.

Wet foliage at night can bring about damping off. Always give the flats a little fresh air. On warm days I lift the cover a few inches, propped up with a board to let the fresh air in gently.

Fresh seed is important, and here we are at the mercy of the dealer. Experience has proven that sometimes a dealer carries over seed for a couple of seasons. Some seed can take it, others cannot. Should you suspect seed of being old, try this. Sprinkle water over them, then place them in the freezing compartment of the refrigerator for an hour. Often this will crack the hardened shell and allow the seed to germinate. When seeds are received, place them in the refrigerator for twelve hours before planting. This is particularly important for pansies and delphinium. In fact, a sprinkle and a freeze can be a standard procedure for delphinium.

Larger seeds with hard shells, castorbeans for example, often germinate more easily if soaked in warm water. Heavenly Blue morning glories will take a scratch.

Naturally, good seeds are the most economical in the long run, and this is true with grass seed as well as unusual flower specimens.

When the plant is established, with true leaves showing, and of a size easily handled, transplant into the open. Consult your local weatherman for frost schedules, and do not transplant outdoors until all danger of frost has passed. Harden the plants gradually while in the seed flat by exposing them to more and more air and sun each day. Leave the cover on during harsh days and lift it up on warm days. Finally, on mild nights, leave the cover off or partially open. Decrease the amount of water.

If the weather is not settled, no harm is done if plants grow three or four inches high in the frame before outdoor planting. By this time, however, the plants may be seeking more food. Give them a weak solution of liquid manure, but avoid sprinkling this on the leaves. Foliar food may be used every two weeks.

Suggested planting dates follow: first planting, about February 15 and extending to March 1, according to the locality and variability of the weather. March first is about as late as possible for any seed planting when considering the spring garden.

Fall flower planting can be from August through October, depending upon the heat of the sun, since the seasons vary. Seed packet recommendations for August planting sometimes should be ignored, for the heat is too intense then in the Southwest. Late September brings more success. Pansies, delphinium, campanula, shasta daisies, pyrethrum, nierembergia, and alyssum saxatile are best planted in the fall.

Thus, you see, seeds get an early start when tucked into cold frames for germinating and early growth. The heat from the manure base acts like an incubator. Easy access to the seed frame insures steady and careful sprinkling. Plants left in the frame also can reach for the food elements in the manure base which will be leached to the surface with heavier watering. Sometimes a sudden blizzard may hit in fall and young seedlings are endangered. Covering flats with blankets, old rugs, newspapers, or foil, is wise. Do not be alarmed if some plants such as delphinium freeze, because they generally will come up again from the root.

With the cold frame, the gardener controls each plant, knows where it is located, and plants it exactly where he wants it. Sowing in the garden itself is a simple process, but an unsatisfactory one. Plants come up in bunches, are washed across boundary lines, pop up where they are not wanted, or simply disappear from the indicated spot.

I am becoming quite partial to the small, indoor seed flat that can be carried from one place to another. The new metal ones are arranged for sub-irrigation. Soil for these starts with pure compost at the bottom, and a topping mixture of equal parts of sand, vermiculite, and peat moss. A newspaper or cardboard can cover the top until germination. Keep the crust of the soil mixture moist.

Clothes closets are a good place for these portable seed flats until their seeds germinate. Then move them out to a sunny window of the storeroom or garage. Slow growing seeds, such as geraniums, coleus, and lobelia, thrive on this special attention.

Seed flat
Be sure to label each
row

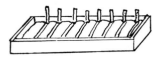

In the past year I have been planting seeds directly in the spots where the plants are to remain. I dig a generous hole and fill it with my "transplanting mix" (See chapter on Transplanting), or compost. Over this is spread one inch of the mixture used to top the cold frame bed. Four or five seeds are planted as directed. They are irrigated, and over the area is placed one of the types of cardboard cartons equipped with a plastic top (I call these my baby greenhouses). A few small holes punched in the sides with an ice pick will give ventilation. The soil should be kept damp, and when the plants are an inch high the weakest are pulled. The protection is removed when frost no longer threatens.

Rarely throughout the year is my cold frame empty, although sometimes it may be filled with cuttings that are becoming established. It is an excellent place for pots of bulbs planted to be forced. After placing them close together, I fill the spaces and tops with leaves. Some future activity for my garden is lodged in the seed flats all around the calendar of the gardening season.

Once a gardener learns to garden from a cold frame or from seed flats, he can hand himself a blue ribbon for achievement. It brings the greatest return for the investment of any gardening expense.

Transplanting

TRANSPLANTING is the one thing in my garden that I do myself. I am almost superstitious about letting anyone else handle plants that need to be moved. Each plant is a living thing and I transplant with the utmost care, being conscientious about every step along the way.

Each plant likes a certain type of soil, and it is natural that it will thrive if given access to its preferences at transplanting. Should I strike poor soil when digging a hole for transplanting, I make up its deficiencies by adding well-rotted manure, compost, peat moss, vermiculite, and perhaps a little chemical fertilizer. For this last item any well-balanced preparation will do.

Often I discard the subsoil, retaining the topsoil for tucking around the plant to finish it off. Much of the subsoil in this section is extremely poor, especially on higher lands. Lucky is the gardener with a vacant lot next door where he can toss the discarded dirt. Otherwise, the service yard must take it and soon starts building up its level. If the soil is heavy, the final mixture may need sand. Valley soils usually are heavy, with areas near rivers more apt to have heavy, clay-like soil.

Sponge rock is gaining in popularity to lighten soil. Mica derivatives, such as vermiculite, are valuable also for conserving moisture, since these little particles absorb their weight of water.

When doing a lot
of transplanting
mix pile of good
soil, compost, peat
moss and a
mica product
and use some
with each plant

Larger plants, such as trees, shrubs, and roses, will take a shovelful or more of manure dug into the bottom of the hole, to be covered with topsoil. The hole is then filled with the soil mixture.

When working with small plants, carry a bucketful of specially prepared soil along as you go. This will be topsoil, peat moss, manure, compost, and vermiculite in equal proportions. As holes are dug, topsoil is laid to one side, and the prepared mixture is placed in the bottom of the hole with the trowel or shovel. Topsoil that was laid aside is firmed about the plants. If the plant is tender, water should be trickled into the hole and the mixture well moistened before the plant is inserted. Be sure that the soil surrounds the plant firmly. After the planting process is completed, water again thoroughly.

Irrigation immediately after transplanting is essential, should be generous, and should be repeated daily for at least three days. Wetting the foliage is helpful.

By use of the soil mix when transplanting, the gardener not only gives the plant a proper start but he renews the garden bed. This continual addition of soil needs into the garden bed keeps it in proper condition, and the need for digging up an entire area in order to renew its soil is avoided.

Firming the plant into the soil is most important. It gives a good base, holds the plant upright, and puts the roots in close contact with the life-giving soil. Plants that are called hard to transplant can be helped with commercial hormone preparations, used according to directions.

I cover or shade newly transplanted plants. Roses can be mounded with earth for protection. Berry boxes may be used for small, delicate plants. Evergreens can use a burlap frame. Allow this extra protection to remain for several days, judging for yourself when the shock of transplanting has been absorbed and the plant is ready to go ahead. Large shrubs, usually dormant when planted, need no shade.

Trees and large shrubs should be planted with their stronger roots pointing toward the prevailing winds to give anchorage against those winds.

When plants have been properly transplanted and have passed their convalescent period, they look crisp and firm; their leaves are straight and generally have reverted to their erect position.

Growing things that are planted correctly will have much more of a chance for a long, healthy life than those handled improperly.

Good gardening means few losses over the years, if correct planting is practiced. Good transplanting principles top the list for "most important" tips in gardening.

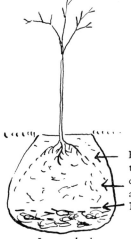

Fill in with
topsoil
compost, peat moss
and good soil
Manure

Large holes are important
when planting trees and each
hole should have good soil.

I never hesitate to transplant at any season. While building my new home, my nursery row was planted against a wall but I didn't realize that electric conduit would have to go underground at the site. One day, in the middle of July, with the temperature at 96 degrees, I was told that the new trench would have to be dug "right now." This meant I couldn't even wait until nightfall. Choice shrubs and perennials had to be moved. Big balls of earth were dug with them. Shrubs and plants were "heeled in" outside the border, well away from the path of the diggers. The plants drooped and looked unhappy for a few days, but within a month few passers-by would have guessed they had been moved.

Chrysanthemums can be moved any time, whenever they are in the way or needed elsewhere. My cutting area contains chrysanthemums that I use for "filling in" right after the bulbs and early annuals, such as larkspur and poppies, have completed their blooming.

Another point to remember when transplanting is to keep the roots of plant material covered while preparing the holes and soil. Wet burlap or newspapers saturated with water and placed over the roots is sufficient, with the whole kept in the shade.

Plant material, when received in a wilted or dried condition, can be aided by placing the roots in a bucket of thin mud, allowing it to stand in a cool, protected spot until the plants appear to revive.

Dormant roses that look dull often are "brought back" by heeling the plant in earth, tops and all, and keeping the mass moist for a few days. Wet sphagnum or peat moss covering the plants has the same effect and is not as messy to handle. Excellent results are obtained in bringing back poor plant material by using compost water, a shovel of compost to a bucket of water.

A large and expensive order of exhibition chrysanthemums once arrived far past their time for normal delivery. Only the tips of the leaves showed life, with the bottom leaves decayed, and the entire package permeated with the odor of decay. My first impulse was to throw them away, but previous good results with compost water encouraged me to try to revive these plants. They remained in the solution for a couple of days with astonishing results. Out of the order of 35 plants only three were lost. Since this episode I always try compost water or solution of foliar food to revive plants, with excellent results repaying my effort.

In recognizing the special needs of plants, remember acid-loving plants will take more peat moss and humus, with perhaps some acid fertilizer. Tuberous begonias, columbine, and lily bulbs come to mind offhand as in this class.

Pansies seem to gorge on rich food, so I toss them an extra trowel of manure in the bottom of the hole when transplanting. I cover it with topsoil so the tender roots don't immediately hit the manure. Chrysanthemums, too, are heavy feeders, and can take the extra manure.

Preferences and the best times for transplanting will be discussed in sections devoted to types of flowers and plants. Gardeners should learn to transplant easily, just as furniture is rearranged in a living room. It must be done properly, however, with a regard to color and form and with the utmost care in the actual transplanting. Most plants are lost because of careless treatment; and the gardener, unknowing, becomes more and more hesitant in moving plants about the garden and in individual beds.

Plant each seedling with same individual care given a rose, bush, or shrub. Use special soil mixture for mound in bottom of hole.

Irrigation

IRRIGATION is one of the most important phases of gardening in this area. It is a must, as in no spot in the Southwest is there sufficient rainfall to take care of our gardens, unless it might be in some high mountain locality. Even there, contrary to general opinion, moisture is not plentiful.

Since our sun is so hot, and the atmosphere dry, the ground quickly assumes a parched appearance, leading to frequent, but often not thorough, irrigation. Take a deep trowel of soil and examine it to make certain just how your irrigation is penetrating the soil and reaching the root systems of your plants.

When a plant needs water is easily recognized by experience. If the foliage is crisp with substance and is bright green, the amount of water is correct. If the leaves feel limp, the plant isn't receiving enough water. Too much water is detected by yellowing of foliage and too abundant growth. Too much water can "spoil" a garden, making its plants soft and dependent, lacking stamina and "backbone."

I irrigate roses each five to seven days in the spring and summer, and about every ten days in the fall. Many say "my roses can't go that long without water, the leaves and blooms will look all wilted if they do." If the season is started with a proper schedule, this firmness against water indulgence will work. Bushes accustomed to too generous watering cannot suddenly be deprived.

The perennial or annual border, if lowered to hold water, can go without irrigation for three or four days and as long as a week. Close planting and careful mulching are helpful.

Chrysanthemums like water every day, and wetting the foliage of these plants daily is good, since more transpiration of water takes place in the leaves of the chrysanthemum than in most plants. Tuberous begonias love having their leaves wet, too.

Most lawns do very well with water every third day during hot and windy weather. Every three or five days in normal weather is good policy. Blue grass and Bent grasses require more water than the Bermuda variety.

All through this region, trees suffer from the lack of water. No tree, unless the water table is quite high, can be at its best with water from the lawn sprinklings alone. My habit is to allow a hose to run slowly at the base of a tree for a full half day once a week for trees under three years of age. Older trees can wait two or three weeks between long drinks. Big trees, such as the full-grown cottonwoods, only need watering about three times a season. Newly planted trees must be irrigated every other day. A root feeder is a valuable tool for tree irrigation. For watering, just remove the fertilizer capsule.

Winter watering is essential. More evergreens are lost in the winter by lack of water than by the cold weather. This applies to shrubs as well. Pick warm days, when pipes are not dripping with ice. In the Southwest we have plenty of sunny days for this winter chore. Irrigate about noontime once or twice a month, but if a warm, dry spell comes along, water fortnightly.

Since drainage is not a problem in this country, too much water is not as harmful as in other sections. One danger of watering too deeply, however, is bringing to the surface the alkali that burns plants.

Conservation of water is important and proper care when planting can be helpful in keeping down water waste and water bills. Humus from the compost, addition of peat moss, and manure aid in retaining water. Mulches are fine. Close planting is an ideal water saver since it shades the ground about the plants.

Newly planted materials may need several irrigations a day until started. Small plants do better when shaded in some way until they are established. Berry boxes are excellent for this covering. I never throw away a carton from ice cream or berries, putting them aside for this use later.

Sprinkling systems are becoming more popular, but should you depend upon hosing, let it do its work by letting it run slowly, with a can, flower pot, or the commercial soil soaker at the end so as not to wash the ground away from around the plants. Water is always running somewhere in the garden when I am at work in it. In fact, the hose is trickling away all day long in the summer. It takes quite a while to get over the entire garden in the intense heat.

Very often I water the trees on days when I expect to be downtown shopping. The water seeps around the larger trees until my return. Let the water run slowly enough so that it seeps down and doesn't just run off and

down the street. An area of watering should cover the outer belt or leaf line. For new trees, deep water will cause roots to grow deeply into the earth and prevent the tap root from forming surface masses. Some trees have a tendency toward such rooting anyhow.

Morning is the ideal time to irrigate. Then plants have water to carry them through the heat of the day. Irrigation after four o'clock in the afternoon is not wise, since many fungus diseases and such troubles as root rot, mildew, and black spot can be started by too wet ground or foliage during the chillier night hours. Night temperatures vary from 30 to 40 degrees below the heat of the noon sun in the Southwestern regions. Do not be misled by the gardener who gets by, for a while, with night watering. Sooner or later trouble will arise.

Some gardeners may think that if they water early in the morning, by ten o'clock the surface soil has dried out. To these I would like to suggest that they dig down below the surface to check this "dried out" soil. When properly watered to a sufficient depth, the garden bed, on digging, will reveal a moist sub-surface to which the roots of the plants have access. Too, the plant already has had its drink and absorbed its moisture allotment.

Good sense dictates extra watering after a windstorm or an extremely dry day.

Where the watering system is automatic and the outlets planned to handle the garden area capably, a 20-minute period should be enough for the average irrigation. The hose follows through into planted areas hard to reach by the watering system or in spots here and there requiring just a little extra moisture.

Most experts hesitate to give actual instructions on watering. The gardener must study the needs of his own garden, the plants in it, and the type of soil. Recognition of the combination of needs will solve the day-to-day watering problem.

Conservation in the Southwest is a serious matter. Water shortages are always near at hand. To properly water a garden often means the conservation of water, since the sensible method grows strong plants able to withstand drouth periods.

Since the first edition of this book appeared, the Southwest has suffered severely from drought and many towns were rationing water. Denver was under strict rationing, and Albuquerque had shortages for two years. It was during this period I did much experimenting and discovered that we can go much longer without water than we believed; however, I leave sprinklers on for a longer period. My usual practice for several years had been to irrigate my lawn twice a week—my garden did not suffer nearly as much as those irrigated every day or two. In fact, when my lawn once went eight days without water, it looked wilted, but the first irrigation brought it back to normal. It all proved more than ever that my theory of deep irrigation with stretched-out applications, is good. Since rationing is over, I irrigate only when needed—always after mowing and every four to five days. Some of my areas are shady and some in full sun all day and those in full sun receive the same treatment. Areas around walks or drives dry out quickly as the sun heats them. I put the hose to these if needed and save much water by not irrigating the whole lawn area. Since I go longer without water, I have had less trouble with pests, diseases, and weeds. Worms are smart and they enjoy tender over-watered grass much more than the tougher grass with more substance, and crabgrass is far less a problem.

Many new homes are built on terraced areas and naturally the water runs off these more. It is better to irrigate for ten or fifteen minutes and turn off for a half hour—then repeat. Another help in saving water is shown in the drawings on page 68. In fact, after many years in my home, I am going to do this reshaping, even though my lawn was planted four inches below walk and drives. Denver badly needs to use this method—it may experience another drought and much water is wasted over high lawn edges—especially when so many lawns are terraced.

SPRINKLING SYSTEMS

Since irrigation is a necessity, preparing for it should be a part of every new garden plan. Watering lawns should be by the usual sprinkling system, there should be "bubblers" for the flower beds, and in addition every gardener will find himself using the ordinary garden hose for additional "spot" and deep-soaking areas.

Your house should have a water faucet located on two sides so that water can be obtained easily with a garden hose both front and back and along the sides. Hose has been improved now to the point where it is extremely light in weight, for easy carrying, and is attractive in color.

It is important to know what type of garden you will want in your new home, how much lawn, how much shrubbery, and how many trees right from the start when the house is being planned. For it is then that the water faucets and sprinkling system should be specified.

Designers of sprinkling systems now have a variety of sprinkler heads for the several jobs to be done. Too, these experts know what is needed, so the homeowner can rely on their judgment if the plan is submitted to them. Their services usually are supplied free by the installing firm.

Some sprinkler heads "pop" up and are fine for many sections. The water when turned on, forces the head up. They are handy, since the lawn mower moves right over them with no damage. However, since we have so much sand blowing in to build up our lawns, I do not use this kind, as the sand soon would swallow them up. In fact, when placing sprinklers I specify that they are to be built with the heads above the level of the area because of rapid building up of the soil.

The bubblers mentioned above are excellent for watering flower beds. They should be placed on a special "turn on" control, for beds do not need to be watered as often as the lawn. Beds should be made level and lower than the lawn area. These water heads release the water slowly, with a gently bubbling effect that allows water to cover the beds without washing the soil.

Proper preparations for watering your garden can make a great deal of difference in the eventual enjoyment of your home grounds. However, regardless how complete a system you install, there will always be a certain amount of hand watering with a watering can or hose.

Trees do not always have to develop with a single trunk to be beautiful. "Forked" trees are always valuable for artistic effect

Pruning

SELDOM does a tree grow perfectly in its natural outline, with the exception of forest evergreens, and from the time a tree or shrub is planted, pruning should be a regular part of its care. A young tree can be grown into a perfect tree if correct pruning is practiced from the start. Too often a gardener "lops off" superfluous parts of trees and shrubs and calls it pruning.

Perhaps the most unattractive sight is the whiskery shoots that grow up and down the trunk and branches, just like little bad habits beginning in a child. Soon these shoots become spreading branches that add nothing but droopy limbs in unsightly, straggly fashion. When at the base of a tree these shoots are called suckers. All such growth should be clipped off regularly.

No branch or growth should be allowed below a reasonable and attractive height. Be kind enough to the passer-by to remember his hat, or the top of his car if the trees grow at a curbing. Visualize the limbs of the young tree at its full growth. See the space it is to occupy with the picture of the tree within it. Then prune to fill that picture.

Sharp pruning shears or saws are used, making the cut in line with the trunk and as clean as possible. Early pruning leaves a wound small enough to heal in a smooth, clean surface, with less chance for disease to enter. I constantly prune, never allowing shoots or limbs to grow to the point where they need to be lopped off. Pruning shears go along with me when I enter the garden to cut a bouquet. The shears snip off shoots and branches from shrub or tree as I go by. When I snip, I do so on a slant, cutting just above a leaf or a shoot. This insures a graceful line, with no stubby branches at the end. (See illustration.)

Many growing things beside the trees and shrubs need pruning.

Chrysanthemums may be topped or pruned to make them branch. Many perennials are neater, making a more compact bush, if they are cut down to encourage shoots. Phlox and Michaelmas daisies may be cut back if too leggy.

Shrubs may be kept completely in shape and under control by proper pruning at the right time. Some shrubs do their best when cut right down to the ground. The buddleia or summer lilac is an example. It loves being cut back severely. Spirea and forsythia are more colorful under strong pruning.

On the other hand, the true lilac resents heavy pruning and so cutting off the bloom and suckers about the roots fulfills its needs. No set rule for pruning to the needs of each plant can be stated. Learn the ways of the plant and treat it according to your requirements from it. Any growth spoiling the symmetry of a tree or shrub, and also dead and diseased branches should be removed.

What a tragedy to see plantings in some old garden that has been neglected for years. In this case pruning must be severe and harsh. Plants never will look as well as when pruned through the years as they grow.

When pruning, should the wound be large, it is wise to follow through with a pruning paint or shellac. A little wet soil to make a clay pack can be used. Some frown on the pack method, but I have used it most of the time with no bad results. Perhaps our wonderful sunshine in the Southwest aids us in healing plant wounds. The dry air is helpful, stopping the bleeding of most pruning cuts in a short time.

Flowering trees should be pruned into artistic shapes. I don't like to see them cut too perfectly. They always seem more beautiful if some of the growth is removed from the center and several forks allowed to grow gracefully. These can be pruned to lacy patterns. A Japanese print of flowering shrubs might be studied for artistry in tree shaping. To shape by pruning and to prune for the future sometimes is beyond the scope of the average gardener. If you feel hesitant, hire an experienced gardener to do it. Some of our professional pruners have no artistic ability in the best sense of the word, so keep an eye on them. Some of my favorite pruning habits are frowned upon by professionals, too.

Do not allow formal evergreens to grow like this

Prune to shape and neatness which also makes for denser growth

Rub off tiny shoots from young trees to send strength to top

There is never an excuse to butcher a tree

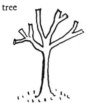

Prune off top to keep trees from dwarfing flat-roofed houses

Keep whiskery shoots off tree trunk

Prune where lines cross branches. Make cuts parallel with the branch, as close to branch as possible

Pruning roses is discussed in the chapter devoted to the rose. How to prune a rose is the subject of more varied opinions than any other type of pruning. One gardener finds a technique pleasing, while another would discard it. Gardeners have a way of changing their habits and ideas from time to time, resulting in confusion to a novice. At present the trend seems to be away from severe pruning.

When pruning, the entire garden must be considered. Should the garden be expansive, with space for vistas, landscaping could tolerate tall growth. Background and distance planting allows for larger plants. Restricting the growth of plants is desirable for smaller gardens compacted into limited space.

A good rule to remember is to prune after flowering. Much pruning can be done by cutting for indoor floral arrangements. Remember, cut each branch back to where a strong healthy shoot already is developing to insure continuation of the graceful line of the shrub. Spirea and forsythia particularly suffer from eager-beaver pruners who cut it straight across in the spring, before it blossoms. Vitex, which blooms on new wood in July, can be pruned in January. Crape myrtle also blooms on new wood, but I wait until March or April to prune it just before leaf buds appear. Holly and aucuba may be pruned in the spring. Conifers may be pruned very early and, contrary to popular opinion, pruning does them no harm.

Hybrid tea rose
before pruning

After pruning

Pests and Diseases

WHENEVER we in the Southwest complain about some of the less favorable aspects of gardening in our region, I like to point out that on the other side of the ledger are the comparatively few pests and diseases that attack our growing plants.

Many pests and diseases remain unknown to me in my own garden and I become more and more convinced that a garden which is well fed and properly irrigated will be healthy and can stand the few pests and diseases that may occur. There are seasonal cycles of pests and in rare years when we have more rainfall, they are more prevalent—although drought may bring such pests as red spider.

It is true that with the rapid increase of people and houses in some areas since the first edition of this book was printed, we are more plagued with pests and diseases. Mildew is more often a complaint but we still are fortunate, except in rare instances, to be free from black spot.

In Arizona and warmer parts of the region, nematodes are becoming a problem. The gardener should watch for indications of these, a general decline of health, or stunting, and a drop in production of a plant. Roots must be dug up to finally prove infection, and the gall-like formations (growths or knots) can be seen. Humus rich soils are seldom affected.

Many of the wonder killers of a few years ago are losing their effect as pests develop an immunity. Today, malathion and dieldrin have an important place in the battle against chewing and sucking pests. But I almost am afraid to mention them; next year it may be something different. Much work is being done with systemics (highly toxic as yet), a material taken into the plant by roots or foliage, thus repelling or killing pests and diseases.

Antibiotics show promise and there are preparations for agricultural use. Recently in experimenting, I had success using one with foliar food, spraying it into a bleeding crack in the bark of a cottonwood tree trunk. After three applications, spaced ten days apart, it was completely healed and dry. The use of antibiotics is believed by some to be generally beneficial to the health of plants, but two years of its use on roses does not convince me that there is any improved vigor. I have not used check plots nor have enough of one variety to test against each other, which is necessary for a conclusive result.

More work needs to be done in using natural enemies in fighting pests, such as using "milky spore disease" to wage a successful battle against Japanese beetles.

Friends

It is wise to study all the information available and to seek the aid of your County Agricultural Agent, reputable nurseries and garden supply dealers. Try new pesticides when proved.

Cold water sprayed on rose bushes and other garden plants will control aphis, red spider, thrips, and other insects. I repeat this treatment for several days until the tiny little pests literally wash away. Too, I use the thumb and forefinger to "wipe" them away. (See drawing in rose chapter.) Aphids have been controlled in my garden for years by this simple process. Don't pass a cutworm by when you catch a glimpse of it while doing other garden chores. Pick it up and end its trouble-making. The same goes for the grasshopper fattening on choice chrysanthemum buds or the sow bug that is burrowing itself down among your cold frame rows.

red, good

Never use a product harmful to plants, soil, or animals, including yourself in the last classification. Some of the preparations advertised are toxic to human beings and should be handled with care. Often such deadly products kill bacteria and insects that are of great value to your garden, such as the lady bug, which eats up hundreds of aphids. The praying mantis is a funny fellow to look at, but your true friend in the garden for he also eats harmful insects. Some wasps, dragonflies, and bees, all garden helpers, should be protected. Below the surface are the earthworms in little armies that work ceaselessly to give you a better garden.

Follow directions exactly when using sprays. Manufacturers spend many thousands of dollars experimenting with them. Few of us can improve on their findings. Don't follow the line of thought that if a little is good, a lot is better. This extra amount of spray can be just enough more to kill the helpful insects and bacteria in your garden and destroy the plants. Recent tests show dilution of sprays just as effective. Don't use a spray in severely hot weather, in the direct rays of the sun, or during a windstorm. In summer, spraying is best done in early morning (following irrigation) or late evening when there is no wind. If using sulphur or karathane for mildew in hot weather, it is best applied late in the day and washed off the following morning before the sun is hot.

Amateur gardeners sometimes think they can save some money by mixing their own sprays. Unless they have a knowledge of the chemicals and their effects on plant and animal life, I strongly object to this plan. Mixing two sprays together may destroy their effectiveness by untoward chemical reactions.

Sprays containing arsenic should not be used on fruit and vegetable crops soon to be harvested. Better lose a little of the crop than take a chance on injuring human life. Dieldrin should not be used on food crops.

Science always tries to make our tasks easier and our problems simpler. The good gardener should learn the basic principles of pest destruction that will serve him through the years.

Each insect and each disease has its own natural enemy. Destroying the pest by strong substances often destroys its enemy or predators as well, thus upsetting the garden balance to disadvantage.

The most important pest and disease control which I use is the dormant spray, also called the "cleanup spray." This is used every year in the early spring, just as buds begin to swell. The spray eliminates fungus spores and the eggs of pests and generally cleans up the garden from pests and diseases. I use lime, sulphur, and oil blended into a stable emulsion. Some years this dormant spray has been sufficient and I emphasize that if other spraying is eliminated, this "clean-up" is a must.

Foes

Each year it is becoming more necessary to protect the gardener. Never do I go into my garden to spray without being completely covered, even to gloves. I now cover from the waist up with a loose, plastic bag, which I have found very helpful. Use caution. Do not allow children or pets to play on treated lawns. Cover pets' dishes, pools, or bird-baths before spraying. Keep all pesticides high on shelves away from food or children, and pour left-over sprays down the drain and wash spray equipment. Empty containers should be washed and then wrapped in paper for disposal. I am convinced that organic gardening is helpful in maintaining a healthy garden, but the method has not completely eliminated problems. As much as I dislike using poisons, I do so when necessary.

green, bad

SUCKING INSECTS

Aphids—Tiny, soft-bodied bits, usually black or green in color, that cluster on stems and leaves, sometimes covering entire portions. Easily controlled with weekly or biweekly sprays of cold water in the heat of the day, repeating for three or four consecutive days. Also can be controlled by nicotine, pyrethrum, or malathion sprays.

Mealy Bugs—Whitish, cottony-looking little bugs that enjoy soft-stemmed plants and succulents. A spray of vegetable, mineral, and organic oils, combined with free nicotine will suffocate the mealy bug. These sel-

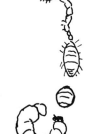

dom are found outdoors, but they do frequent house plants. I use a toothpick with a small cotton swab attached and dipped into alcohol. Touch the bug lightly with the swab.

THRIPS—Tiny insects about one-sixteenth of an inch long, and looking like a clipping of blond hair. They move quickly and are hard to detect. Blow into a balled rose bud that looks sickly and will not bloom, and you'll see the thrips scrambling about. They are hot weather insects, but I start the cold water treatment when leaves start to bud. Often they breed in iris and then turn their attention to the roses, so wash the iris with cold water sprays when the new leaves begin to grow. Use an insecticide or malathion; if severe, use a combination of malathion and dieldrin. They are the worst enemies of rose growers in this region. Gladioli bulbs sometimes will harbor thrips. When they are about to be planted, submerge the bulbs in a solution containing nicotine and cyanide to kill the insects. Also, when storing the bulbs, place a few moth balls in the bag or box, protecting bulbs from actual contact.

LEAF HOPPERS—These little insects hop about from leaf to leaf and from plant to plant. Although they are not numerous here they do appear and are best attacked with an insecticide or by hand picking. They can carry virus diseases about with them.

WHITE FLIES—Small and bothersome insects of several varieties, but not much in evidence in this area. An insecticide will suffice.

MITES—"Red spider" mites appear during hot, dry weather. At first the foliage has a dusty or "webby" appearance, and discoloration to a yellow, then brown, occurs, causing the foliage to drop if severely affected. Check these little insects with a good cleanup spray in the spring, using the lime sulphur emulsion. A cold water spray is effective on red spider mite later in the season. Wash the infected plants with plain cold water sprayed from a hose for four or five days in succession, my favorite treatment for many pests. Kelthane gives a good kill. Evergreens may be badly infested. Clover mites infest sections of our area and are hard to control. They resemble a sprinkle of red pepper. Use contact spray of malathion or manufacturer's combination of dieldrin and malathion. A dust containing piperonyl and a combination zinc, copper, and chromium formula with inert materials is effective when mites invade the house. Household ammonia wiped around windows is effective.

BORERS—These attack peach trees in particular. Use a non-oil ether emulsion about the base of the tree on a warm day in February or March. Moth balls may be used. Cover with soil. Use dieldrin on non-fruiting trees.

SCALE—Scale usually fix themselves to a branch or leaf and resemble a series of shells. San José scale has been a major problem on fruiting and flowering branches. Branches appear to be covered with a sprinkling of black pepper or dirt. When scraped with a twig they will exude insect substances. It appears very quickly. Immediate control is essential. An oil spray in a lime sulphur emulsion is recommended.

CHEWING INSECTS

Hard-shelled bugs, such as squash bugs and beetles, can be controlled by a contact and repellent spray. It may be of a pyrethrum product, combined with synthetic pryrethrins in the form of a cynergist. The mixture is non-poisonous to humans and animals, and is non-injurious to plant life. Malathion is good.

Worms such as the cabbage worm, leaf looper, miner, or bag worm, can be cleaned up with a contact spray. I see so little of them in my garden that I don't consider them a menace. Of course, the neglectful gardener watches them multiply and will find himself in trouble. The cabbage worm appears in my garden when I plant flowering kale for use in flower arrangements.

ARMY WORMS—This worm becomes a moth, but it is while in the worm stage that it eats the roots of lawn grasses, causing considerable damage. A bait mixture brings the worms to the surface for feeding and I have found it successful. Use a mixture not harmful to birds or dogs. Dieldrin or chlorodane may be used.

SOD WEB WORMS—Troublesome for lawns. When tan moths are seen flying around, usually the lawns thereabouts are infected. Moths lay their eggs at the base of the grass blade. Gives the lawns a truly "moth-eaten" appearance. Use a spray of metallic copper soluble in water combined with ether or dieldrin. Over-all treatments at the source of the trouble will eliminate it.

CUTWORMS—Moths when in the caterpillar stage often are the damaging cutworm type. They seem always to be starving and wreak havoc among the tender plant stalks and leaves. Sometimes they nip the stalk right in two at the ground level, leaving the plant dying. Gardeners sometimes protect plants by wrapping the stems with heavy paper partly inserted into the ground and extended an inch or two above. Poison bait or dieldrin are good for ridding the garden of cutworms.

SNAILS AND SLUGS—Becoming more of a problem particularly where ground covers are used. Cleanliness and refraining from over watering are important for control. A circle of coarse sand or wood ashes around such plants as delphinium or pyrethrum is helpful, or a poison bait formulated for snails or slugs.

Sow Bugs—Sometimes called pill bugs. Found in abundance around damp, rotting wood and in corners that are damp and decaying. They feed on roots. Poison baits will kill them.

Grasshoppers—Picking them off the plants while they are feeding is the best way to clean up a garden infested with grasshoppers. The neglected garden needs such measures as chlorodane. Try putting a poison bait mixture out on paper plates along the fences and walls in the flower beds so the grasshoppers can feed on this instead of on your tender garden materials. Don't let dogs or children reach the bait mixture. Best to pick up the plates through the day and put them out at night for the early morning feeding.

Ants—Ants themselves do not damage the garden, aside from making unsightly spots with their hills. Their greatest damage is due to their habit of "tending" aphids for the food they get from these tiny insects. Ants move aphids about, also their eggs. Aphids are dependent upon ants for transportation. This promotes my theory that when aphids are washed off the plant by cold streams of water they are unable to find their way back.

Where the more prevalent insect pests are apt to be found in the garden:

Aphid—Tulips, roses, chrysanthemums, iris, goldenglow, lettuce, cauliflower, apple, flowering crabapple, pansies, hawthorns.

Mealy Bug—African violets, coleus.

Thrip—Roses, gladioli, iris.

Leafhopper—Roses, chrysanthemums.

Red Spider—Roses, evergreens, phlox, hollyhocks.

Borer—Cottonwoods, peach, fruiting and ornamental cherries, locust, sycamore, willow.

Scale—Rose, Siberian elm, oleander, arborvitae, euonymus, juniper, lilac, flowering crabs, apple trees, and plums.

Squash Bug and Beetles of Various Sorts—Squash, cantaloupe, cucumber, beans, box elder, elm, cottonwoods, roses, chrysanthemums.

Cutworm—The young worms like tomatoes, zinnias.

Cabbage Worm—Cabbage, cauliflower, kale, chrysanthemums, and other flowers.

Tomato Worm—Tomatoes.

Army Worm—Grass and other plants are attacked by some types of army worm.

Caterpillar—Cottonwoods and others.

Grasshopper—Almost anything in the garden, with the chrysanthemums and iris considered very choice.

Sow Bug—Seedlings and plant roots.

Curlyleaf

FUNGUS DISEASES

Good housekeeping practices in the garden and proper early-morning irrigation methods will help eliminate these troubles.

MILDEW—Spores will be reduced greatly by a cleanup spray in the spring and by using agricultural sulphur in the soil. Wash the plants with water to dislodge mildew. For spraying, use fungicide, dusting sulphur, phaltan, or karathane. There is no perfect remedy. Acti-dione P M is the best spray I have used. It must be used regularly to keep it under control. Follow directions explicitly. It may be combined with foliar feeding.

RUST—Seldom found in this region. Use a cleanup spray and fungicide.

CURLY LEAF—Sometimes found on peach trees, which then should be given an extra feeding of iron sulphate. Use a cleanup spray and fungicide. Do not prune too early. Wait until the weather is moderate. This will help keep the tree from acquiring this disease.

BLIGHT—Treat as for rust.

WILT—Asters and tomatoes particularly are affected by wilt. Use a fungicide or dust. Be extremely careful in irrigating practices. Always get wilt resistant seed and practice crop rotation. Spray with sulphur to save a plant, if not too far gone.

BLACK SPOT—Roses are mostly affected by this disease. Leaves turn yellow and sometimes drop off in numbers. Although in some parts of the country this is our most serious of rose diseases, we find it mostly in the southern sections of this region. Faulty irrigation practices usually are to blame. Sometimes gardeners call and ask me to look at the black spot attacks in their gardens, but the damage usually turns out to be from the sand blasting in our severe windstorms. The leaves look burned and drop off. Sulphur dust, too, can burn rose leaves if the spraying is done in too hot weather. Burn fallen leaves and irrigate in the early mornings. Use a wettable sulphur or copper fungicide for spraying.

DOLLAR SPOT OR BROWN SPOT—Looks exactly as its name indicates. Use a fungicide containing copper, ether, and oil.

SHOT-HOLE FUNGUS—Attacks some peach trees and may be controlled with a copper spray.

Diseases attack as follows:

DOLLAR SPOT—Lawns.
BROWN SPOT—Lawns.
FUNGUS—Lawns.
RUST—Carnations, snapdragons, hollyhocks, roses.
YELLOWS—Asters.
WILT—Tomatoes, chrysanthemums.
MILDEW—Roses, delphinium, phlox, zinnias, euonymus.
MOSAIC—Lilies.
BLACKSPOT—Roses.
CURLY LEAF—Peaches.

WEEDS

Weeding is a task that the gardener can always count on at any time. It is more bothersome here than elsewhere, since we have so much uncultivated space that grows nothing but strong, vigorous weeds, and we have plenty of wind to carry their seeds about.

Control of weeds is not too difficult if they are pulled out or eliminated before they have a chance to settle down or to reseed themselves. Weeds are not used to a well-ordered life and very few will thrive if the garden is well fed and well watered. Weeds flourish where gardens are forced to shift for themselves. Take good care of your garden and the weeds will be less troublesome.

Even the hated crab or devil grass does not like rich soil and a well-fed lawn generally does not tolerate it. Dandelions like food a little more and can thrive in a well-ordered lawn. Even these, however, cannot get much of a foothold in a heavy, healthy lawn carpet.

Crab grass   Plantain   Dandelion   Crab grass

I believe in digging and pulling weeds to keep them under control. Weed killers must be used if they have gotten a good head start. When using killers be careful not to allow the mist to reach other plants. Never use the same spray container for roses or other plants. Too, clover dies along with the dandelions and crab grass when such a spray is used.

Crab grass is one of the worst offenders in the garden. Many new preparations are being marketed that are supposed to be good crab grass killers. Some do a fair job, but most seem to damage the lawn too much. Be very accurate in measurements when using any of them. Start early in the season when the crop is germinating and use several applications during the season. Most gardeners wait until the crab grass is pretty well developed before they start to do anything about it. Be very sure of the product used and note its contents to see if any harmful chemicals are included. Potassium cyanate used to direction is good. Excellent products have been introduced for pre emergence control keeping weed seed from germinating. Weeds will not be as much a problem in lawns if the grass is not cut short.

Chickweed, purslane, and spotted spurge, each a spreading weed, hug and smother out grass. Have been serious pests in recent years, but fortunately are not deep-rooted and often can be raked out. A dressing of sheep manure and spraying with iron sulphate discourage them. Avoid overwatering.

Dodder is a parasitic thread-like weed that twines itself tightly about the plants it envelops, literally "loving" them to death. It should be pulled out as soon as discovered, as it spreads quickly.

More troublesome than any weed in my garden is the Siberian elm seedling. When the seedling is hidden behind another plant and grows to a foot or two in height it becomes a real demon, rooted strongly and deeply in its position. There is no way to handle this problem except pulling or digging. The seeds can be swept from the lawn and scooped up from flower beds, thus eliminating the chances of many seedlings.

Siberian elm seedling   Dodder

Tools and Time Savers

TOOLS

Gardeners should realize when shopping for tools, fertilizers, plant materials, and other supplies that a wise selection is most important. Just as the housewife learns to shop for family needs at reputable firms that carry superior products, so does the gardener turn to supply houses and nursery catalogues that present items superior in quality for the cost involved.

Proper tools are most important to good gardening and every gardener should own a few implements in order to do his work more effectively. Lawn mowers and grass catchers should be purchased with an eye to service and durability. The mower should have regular attention in sharpening and care. One of the chores that the young boy garden helper neglects is wiping off the blades after mowing, to remove moisture. Some tools you will need:

Clippers are needed to trim the lawn. Hedge shears are valuable for clipping the hedges and shrubbery, and also for shearing perennials, such as chrysanthemums and hardy asters.

Pruning saw, if you plan to do your own bigger pruning jobs.

Spade for digging garden beds.

Shovel for moving dirt, manure, and other materials.

Fork for turning compost and garden refuse.

Pick for breaking up caliche and other hard soils.

Floral shovel or spade, smaller than the customary spade and a favorite with me, since I am small-size, too.

Small rake that can get between rows of plants. I rake lightly instead of cultivating.

Hand cultivator. There are many varieties of these, so pick the one best fitted to you.

Dandelion rake helps dislodge weeds and crab grass.

Broom rake for leaves.

Wheelbarrow or garden cart for carrying leaves, fertilizers, and similar jobs.

Buckets, baskets, and other containers for carrying fertilizers and soil mixtures, and for other chores.

Edger or sidewalk scraper for cutting back grass.

Trowels of several sizes, cultivator forks, and other small hand tools. These usually are "collected" by the gardener who is always on the lookout for helpful or new tools.

Labels, permanent type for long-lived outdoor material. Wooden labels for seed flats and annuals.

Stakes, preferably redwood or metal.

Watering hose of the best quality you can buy is a good investment. I prefer the lightweight types as they are easier to handle. Keep additional coupling and washers on hand. Learn to mend your hose.

Watering cans, useful for seed flats, young plants, and for liquid fertilizing mixtures.

Sprayers, according to types of sprays used. Might be a matter of preference but it pays to get one not too flimsy. Even the very best doesn't last too long.

Pruning shears, which probably will be among your most useful gardening tools. You will find that you pick them up for pruning roses, cutting flowers, nipping off dead blooms, shaping shrubs and small trees, and scores of other reasons.

Root feeders are coming into popularity since chemically filled capsules that fit into the end thrust into the ground will bring plant and tree food right to the roots where needed. These feeders are attached to the water hose and the water combines gradually with the chemicals to seep gently about the roots of the plants.

TIME SAVERS

How to find time to maintain a garden with so many different plants and flowers is a question often asked of me. Habits which save considerable time are suggested, with the practice of being on guard against weeds, insects, and pests among the most valuable.

This method of a stitch-in-time is all the more important with the increasing difficulty in securing good gardening help for the jobs that are a little too much for a woman. Raking the leaves, cutting the lawn, and the heavy digging for transplanting and preparing beds are among those chores. School boys and university students often are eager to earn extra money as garden help.

Sometimes I rob Peter to pay Paul, so to speak, for when I have good house help I make the most of it by catching up on garden work. Again, my love for gardening has led to neglect indoors at times. Neglect of a tiny plant needing water and attention leads to its loss, while the dust cloth always can pick up the extra accumulation inside. And as all good gardeners know, no matter how perfect the situation, we exhaust ourselves planning just a little bit more than we have the time or strength to do.

Never stand and hold your garden hose! That one item alone wastes more time than any other. Put the hose down and let it run slowly in the spot where water is needed. Go about your garden work, then come back and move the hose a bit. Lawn sprinklers now are being marketed in wide variety, so watering the lawn is no longer a problem in wasting time.

Keep your pruning shears near by! When making the rounds of the garden, don't pass a faded rose or daisy without snipping it off. Should a branch appear to need trimming, trim it. Pinch off the pansies that have bloomed out as you are kneeling down in the border at some other task. Don't set aside a certain time for these tasks. Do them continuously.

You've passed a plant that is calling for extra food. Next time you go by, take out the extra ration in a bucket with you, then dismiss the plant from your mind, for it will prosper.

You've gone out for the morning paper and you've noticed a few bright yellow dandelion heads. Pull them off right then and there, and remember to return later with your little digging tool to remove the plants themselves. Get all the roots.

Don't be irritated if your husband is fifteen minutes late for lunch. Spend that extra fifteen minutes disbudding the chrysanthemums. It is surprising how many buds you can pinch off, and more surprising how quickly your disposition will improve.

For the "big times" in your garden, the half and full days you can have to spend, don't be reckless and work aimlessly here and there. Do big jobs to match, such as the major task of pruning roses, fertilizing the lawn, or spraying.

Mulch instead of cultivating is another important time-saver. Here you accomplish two purposes. You conserve water as well as time, and you sometimes provide extra food in the mulching process, providing compost or a similar covering is used. By planting closely the soil is shaded and irrigation need not be so frequent.

During daily garden rounds any harmful insect that comes across my gaze usually is caught and eliminated. Grasshoppers are picked off and disposed of, so are sow bugs if I notice them as I lift the cover of the cold frame in the morning. Cutworms are just tossed off on the hot sidewalk or street pavement.

Clumps of iris that are infested by aphids get their cold shower bath spray. If a newly formed rose bud is host to an aphid or two, I gently rub the bud with my fingers, smoothing aphids out of the way. No one practice saves so much time eventually in the gardening season as this one of eliminating insects on sight.

By combining all these habits into general gardening routine, the extra time saved allows for the good garden practices that result in a well-planned, colorful, season-by-season beauty spot.

Holding the hose is a time waster. Lay it down and allow water to run gently into the flower bed to flood it. Many good flooding and sprinkling devices are on the market

Lawns

A FEW SIMPLE RULES help in making and maintaining a good lawn.

The most important point is to make a good bed, remembering that it must last a long time. Good preparation of the soil saves trouble in the years to follow. The bed should be at least eight to ten inches deep, and more is desirable. If the expense of proper soil preparation is prohibitive, I advise planting straight clover for several years—it is attractive and improves soil for the future. Strawberry clover is good also. Add superphosphate and soil sulphur, three to five pounds per hundred square feet.

All building debris, in the case of new homes, should be removed.

Builders often cover up chunks of cement and plaster with basement excavation soil. The unsuspecting homeowner then builds his lawn on top of all this rubbish and wonders why his lawn misbehaves. Excavated soil is undesirable. Topsoil should be hauled in only in the case of necessary fills to level or contour the grounds. Otherwise, it is much cheaper to condition the existing topsoil with manure and peat moss.

Soil that is heavy and clay-like may be lightened with sand, pea-size pumice, or a mica product. Some lawns where pumice has been used have not done well and this probably is due to its chemical make-up. The product should be analyzed to find if it is free from toxic substances and has nearly neutral pH.

Lawns need additional products since most of our soil is highly alkaline, agricultural sulphur or cottonseed meal may be used at the rate of three to five pounds per hundred square feet. Superphosphate is added in the same amount, since it, too, is lacking in most of our soils. Should new soil be brought in to level or fill in a lot the same treatment should be followed. Many lawn makers will not use barnyard manure because of its weed seed content, preferring chemical fertilizers. Weeds are bound to appear, and since barnyard manure has so many desirable qualities, I recommend it. Organic fertilizer is a necessity for lawns over a period of years since our soil has so little of organic material naturally.

Manures are applied at the rate of two yards to a thousand square feet. If I were planting a new lawn and could possibly afford it, I would use twice this amount of manure. I know of several excellent lawns where this was done. Peat moss is good to use also.

The cost of a lawn is very much lower if organic materials are used. This is important to most of us. Soil preparation should start as soon as the lawn is contemplated. If planting does not start immediately, at least the soil may be readied. A practice too seldom followed in this area is the planting of a cover crop, such as rye grass, that will be dug into the soil before the lawn is attempted. New home owners generally are too eager for a lawn to mark time with a cover crop. Compost is excellent for the new lawn, but seldom is available in sufficient quantity, so the average lawn maker uses manure and peat moss. Fresh manure, mixed with straw, is good if planting will not be immediate. Leaves and grass clippings may be mixed into the soil, too, and allowed to decompose. Keeping the bed wet will hasten decomposition. Aged sawdust is excellent. I was able to get only fresh sawdust for my lawn. This was spread over the ground, exposed to the sun for several months, and wet down periodically. Nitrogen should be used with sawdust, and my young lawn showed its lack by pale color, but a feeding of ammonium sulphate did wonders. Since my soil is heavy adobe, the sawdust has been invaluable for it.

A lawn may be planted at any time, even in July, provided the soil is never allowed to dry out. It is better to take a chance on its coming through than to live in a house without lawn or cover crop. New rugs and floors can be ruined by tracking in sand and gravel from an unplanted area. Fall is the ideal time for planting a lawn, however. From early September through early October are the most popular dates. Fall planting is less tedious, since lawns do not tend to dry out as quickly as in the spring, when warm days and hot winds create rapid evaporation.

Roots become established more deeply in the fall, and weed seeds germinate and are killed by the frost before they have a chance to reseed. Should seeding take place in the spring, wait until the weather is settled.

When the bed has been readied for seeding, it should be irrigated thoroughly and allowed to stand for several days. Then rake again carefully, levelling uneven spots. Rake a thin cover of peat moss into the surface. Should the planting be in the fall, half of this cover may be pulverized manure. Rake this in, then plant the seed. Do this on a day free from wind, preferably in the early morning. A spreader may be used, starting in one direction and then crossing for even distribution. I use a circular arm motion when seeding by hand. If clover is used in the seed mixture spread it separately or agitate the mixture frequently, since clover is the heavier seed and tends to settle toward the bottom. After seeding, rake the entire area lightly. Irrigate gently. Few lawns sprout evenly, but the bare areas may be reseeded later. Rake the thin spots, apply seed and rerake.

Selection of good seed is important. Many weeds are brought in sometimes with the grass seed itself. For this reason purchase of quality seed is stressed. The few extra pennies spent for seed will save greater amounts spent later in removal of weeds. My preference is bluegrass, though it does suffer from hot, dry, and windy summers. Clover mixed with it improves soil conditions and protects bluegrass while it develops. It is particularly valuable to the young grass, since clover germinates quickly and protects it in big brother fashion. Clover turns green early in the spring and remains so until late fall. I use a little more clover than usually recommended for a mixture. My proportion is one-fourth pound of clover seed to one pound of the bluegrass.

There are other grasses, such as redtop, Chewings fescue, and creeping fescue, but I have found no particular merit for these mixtures in this area. In southern sections of the Southwest, Bermuda or St. Augustine grass is used, but these are not free from faults. Keeping them from creeping into flower beds is a constant chore. In colder areas they brown early in the fall and turn green late in spring. Bent grass is used on golf greens to make a fine carpet. It requires frequent mowing, constant care in keeping the pH low (since it prefers a more acid soil), needs more water, and demands more food. Dichondra will grow in warm areas, and in sheltered patios in more severe areas. It is a lush green and makes a nice carpet that seldom requires mowing. Several plantings I have watched have stood lower temperatures than thought possible.

The perfect grass, free from troubles, is yet to be found. It is hoped some of the new grasses will be as good as they are claimed to be. My experience has been, from my own lawns and from watching others, that a bluegrass and clover mixture is the most beautiful and suitable for our area.

There is a constant cry for new and better grasses. These are not needed as much as better lawn management, which includes soil preparation and week-to-week care.

Zoysia, one of the newer grasses, is performing well in Arizona and warm sections, but in altitudes of 5,000 feet results have been disappointing in the length of time it takes for coverage. Since it is planted by roots instead of seed, it is slower than most people want to wait for, or have an unsightly or unfinished lawn. It is subject to chlorosis. There are several good lawns in this area but they do turn brown with the first light frost.

I have been very pleased with Merion bluegrass. Some of the finest lawns I have seen are Merion even though three years should elapse before it is judged. As it is difficult to get started in established lawns, growing a little plot and sodding small pieces at intervals is the best thing to do. Worms and fungus attack it but the tuberous-like roots run under the sod to fill in the spots. The seed still is expensive, but it is small and covers almost twice the area that bluegrass does, thus it is well worth the additional price. A small amount of clover and even some bluegrass can be planted with it for a nurse crop as the germination of Merion is slow—from eighteen to twenty days, usually. It needs the same fertilization as bluegrass and the fall feeding is most important. It is a cool weather grass but will come through extreme heat better than expected, with good management. It turns green about three weeks before bluegrass and stays green until severe frosts arrive. It will do well in warm areas and there are fine Merion lawns in Roswell and Amarillo. Newport bluegrass, like Merion, will make a fine turf and would be my choice for a new lawn. It will not tolerate overwatering.

The African Bermudas are not without troubles and in some areas have developed rust and insect damage. U3 and Tifgreen are showing more promise. These are warm weather grasses and in higher altitudes really good lawns of this type are scarce. If they are good, I find the owner giving them the same care as bluegrass. They must be cut shorter than bluegrass and do not require as much water. Often it is advisable in the fall or early spring to burn off the thatch. Children and dogs may be allergic to them.

Bermudas should not be planted in a bluegrass area except in walled gardens (if you wish to keep your neighbors' love) as the color and texture do not correspond. They do not stand shade as well as the bluegrasses, and are best planted by stolons.

Strawberry clover lawns are attractive and require a minimum of care. If expense is a problem in preventing proper soil preparation, straight clover makes a good and attractive cover and improves the soil as it grows. It can be dug in later if another cover is wanted. It makes an excellent seed bed and seeding over it later with bluegrass often is sufficient.

Next in importance is irrigation. After the lawn is planted, irrigate lightly. From then until germination is complete, the lawn never must be allowed to dry out. In windy weather this means constant attention, even though the extra irrigations are light. After the lawn is up, follow the same procedure but increase the amount of water. Twice daily watering may be necessary for several weeks, and once daily thereafter for a month, or until well established. Skip a day, watering the lawn more deeply progressively. Later, water every three to five days, depending on the type of soil and amount of wind and heat. Areas with higher humidity require less water.

Deep irrigation encourages the roots to strike deeply into the soil and make a stronger, healthier sod. My observation and experience is that the average gardener waters entirely too much. This weakens the lawn, making it more subject to pests and disease. Decrease the amount of water in the fall. Some irrigation during the winter is necessary, since we have little snow and rainfall then. Pick a warm day, around noon.

During the growing season, irrigate in the early morning or around four o'clock in the afternoon. Our cool nights encourage fungus in wet lawns and mildew on wet garden plants susceptible to the disease. Notable exceptions against night sprinklings are where the lawn is open, as in the country, open parkways and on golf courses, where enough air circulates to dry off the grass before damage sets in.

A healthy, well-fed lawn, like any other growing thing, is not apt to be bothered with weeds, pests, and diseases. Feeding is important when a lawn is well established. With us, where irrigation is so constant, nutrient substances are carried down into the subsoil, past the root area, and must be replenished. In an established lawn, sewage sludge or commercial fertilizer is preferable to manure, since weed seeds are prevalent in the latter. Every three to four years manure should be used, however, to renew the organic content of the lawn. Compost is ideal, but manure is a good substitute. Ten pounds of iron sulphate to one hundred pounds of fertilizer is a good feeding combination. Use it once a month in the growing season unless the weather is very warm, when it should be skipped for the time being. Do not use plant food too early in the spring. Wait until the lawn is turning green. It should be discontinued when the growing season ends. Early morning or evening is the best time to fertilize, never in the heat of the day or on a hot day. The lawn must be dry, then irrigated immediately following application of the fertilizer. Foliar feeding is best for hot weather.

Compost is a fine food and may be applied straight from the compost heap, raking well to eliminate coarser materials. Spread it a little more heavily in the space about trees and shrubs. Commercial fertilizers should be used lightly, three to four pounds per hundred square feet. In the Southwest, alkali from the subsoil may rise to the surface with heavy irrigation, and a yellowed lawn results. It is a constant task to keep the pH lowered to neutral. Agricultural sulphur, applied in the spring and fall as directed in the chapter on soils and fertilizers, is helpful to counteract the alkali. A small feeding, two pounds to one hundred square feet, of ammonium sulphate is excellent to produce nitrogen, which will turn the grass into brilliant green. Clover and earthworms will object, so use sparingly. Iron sulphate is also good for lawns tending to become yellow. Apply this in liquid form with a sprinkling can, one-fourth cup dissolved in two and a half gallons of water. Brown stains will be left on any surface such as cement, stucco, and painted wood, so be careful in handling the solution. Irrigate immediately upon application.

Proper mowing of the lawn is most important. Avoid setting the blade of the mower too close to the ground during the full heat of summer. The grass then should be between an inch and a half and two inches high when cut, high enough for the remaining grass to shade its roots and soil. Although a closely clipped lawn gives a fine appearance, hot weather can destroy the shorter grass. A newly planted lawn should not be cut too soon. Wait until the grass is three inches high. Leave the first clippings on the lawn for added protection. Subsequent clippings should go to the compost heap. To allow clippings to remain on the lawn is not advisable, even though they may be finely ground. Our dry climate prevents their ready decomposition. Then, the combination of the hot sun with the moisture from watering creates a hot little blanket that smothers the grass. Too, the appearance is against such practice. Why work toward an attractive lawn, then cover it with dead clippings?

Weeds should be dug from the lawn as they appear. If overwhelming, and weed killers must be used, be very careful not to get the substance on other plants, and follow directions explicitly. Many of the products used for this purpose also kill the clover, and often the grass. Crab grass is the worst offender, since it quickly smothers surrounding grass. It generally appears in full sun. Dandelions are another lawn nuisance. Just plucking the heads of the blooms, to prevent reseeding, is a good precaution if the gardener finds himself too busy to dig these weeds regularly. If dandelions are dug out, care should be taken to get all of the root or new growth will spring up. Fungus, brown spot, and alkali burns may be controlled by proper irrigation habits.

Pattern to follow for mowing and fertilizing

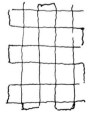

Do not clip too short and expose root to hot sun

No matter how capable a gardener may be in handling a lawn, there always are some spots that need redoing. They may result from lawn diseases or pests, from removing too big a stand of weeds, or from a path that has become packed and worn. These spots may be restored with sod removed from about the flower bed or by reseeding. When using sod, dig out plenty of space so that the sod itself will fit into its new location. Sprinkle a trowel of compost or mixture of peat moss and manure into the bottom of the hole. When the sod is in place, fill in cracks with another sprinkle. Smooth with back of the rake, step on sod lightly to firm it into the earth, irrigate. If reseeding is the method, rake thoroughly, unless packed very hard. In that case, loosen the soil with a cultivator. Use a thin layer of compost or manure over the area. Rake well, then seed. Now spread another layer over the seed, and rake once more. Irrigate carefully.

When the lawn has risen too far above the surrounding sidewalk or driveway, lower the grass level itself in a border about the edge. This is better than digging a debris-catching trench next to the walk. Lower the grass level by digging out the sod, then removing soil underneath to the needed depth. Do this in a gradual slope toward the sidewalk. The strip can be from twelve to twenty-four inches in width. Replace the sod, which will now be the desired depth (usually three inches) below the level of the walk.

Renovating old lawns sometimes means re-establishing the entire plot. Sometimes an old lawn can be redeemed by a vigorous raking, reseeding, and fertilizing. In fact, most lawns need a little reseeding every fall. Often

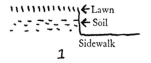

←Lawn
←Soil

Sidewalk

1

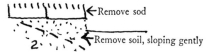

←Remove sod

←Remove soil, sloping gently

2

To lower the edge of a lawn

Replace sod → Walk

3

a hard-packed lawn can be improved with a fork, spade, or other implement that digs into the soil just enough for aeration.

For lawns that cannot be redeemed and must be dug up, a good, but troublesome, method is to take up the sod in squares, remove soil underneath four or five inches, then return the sod upside down so the roots show on the surface. Add new soil, mixed as directed earlier in this chapter. The old sod will become an excellent compost to encourage the new grass plot and serve as drainage for the new soil. Proceed as in planting a new lawn.

Good lawns are the result of well-prepared soil, careful feeding, and proper irrigation. To neglect of any one of these three basic factors will lead into a troublesome lawn, tempting gardeners to resort to poisons and strange mixtures. The poisons might eliminate pests and worms, but also will upset the bacteria and friendly elements sheltered by your lawn.

Edges of redwood or brick laid level with lawn eliminates some clipping

When traveling through the East and South, gardeners note lawns gasping for water that nature has neglected to send. These lawn owners, depending upon nature alone, have made no provision for auxiliary irrigation, allowing grass to wither when prolonged dry spells come along. Since, in the Southwest, we are dependent upon regular irrigation, due to our limited rainfall, better lawns often are the result.

Many timely tips for the continued care of grass are picked up by neighborly chats over the back fence, in the garden specialty store, and at garden club meetings. Advice thus picked up can be advantageous, since garden experts vary in methods. A dangerous practice, however, is to rush home and put into action lightly given advice that is not applicable to specific problems. Months of labor and much time and money can be wasted by even one ruinous direction.

Many persons pamper their lawns far too much. All enjoyment of owning a lawn is lost by the over-frequent hosings, the sprinklings, the coaxing with special feedings. Often these pampered lawns become weakened enough to allow disease to enter freely.

My advice is—plenty of food, not too much water, not mowing too closely, and good soil preparation in the initial process.

Trees

TREES provide a background for the house, shelter the building from the direct rays of the hot Southwestern sun, and, with their airy branches and leaves, form a protective blanket of coolness. No tree fails to add to the general landscaping appearance of a garden, and many, by their symmetry, coloring, and beauty in flowering, enhance the scene considerably.

Wooded areas preserve moisture, and rainfall generally is higher where trees abound. However, in our garden plots, trees sometimes suffer for lack of water since the amount used in ordinary irrigation of lawns and flowers is insufficient for a tree.

Trees beloved "back home" cannot always be grown successfully here, since they will not tolerate our alkaline soil, the heat, or the dry atmosphere. Some sections of the Southwest will accept species which do not grow well in other sections.

Among the trees ordinarily not successful in this area are the oaks, sugar maples, magnolias, dogwoods, eucalyptus, citrus, and avocados.

More trees and more varieties could be grown if gardeners realized the wide range available. There seem to be a few favorites and they are chosen by succeeding gardeners who seem unsure about introducing new varieties. Too, often a gardener hesitates to plant trees since he is impatient and will not wait for his trees to mature.

Differing conditions are met by trees imported for planting throughout the area. Hard, rocklike soil is encountered, adding to the hazard of transplanting shock. In El Paso, instances have been known where near-cement qualities have been encountered in gardens when digging a hole to accommodate an imported tree.

A tree needs more attention than just the planting. It must be fed and irrigated. A small tree requires additional attention for vigorous growth, while older trees too often suffer from lack of feeding and watering. Deep irrigation once or twice during the growing season is recommended. The hose can be allowed to gently seep water into the ground for several hours at a time while the gardener is busy with other duties.

My own trees have proved the importance of feeding—their growth and health have been double the average. After seven years I still have wells around them to keep bark from being scraped by lawn mowers and to add compost and other foods. The irrigations and feedings with a root feeder have been helpful. Pruning is an ever-present chore and a part of my yearly garden expense. I inwardly weep at the neglect of trees. Only one place in a hundred shows proper care of them.

Pruning often is neglected while the tree is young, when it should be shaped for future growth. Twigs that could become awkward branches must be snipped continuously. When severe storms break off larger branches, the wound remaining should be trimmed and treated without delay.

Shade frequently becomes a problem when too many trees are planted near new homes to overcome the bare look and to give quick shade. Some persons, like myself, have a passion for trees, wanting every new one available. Shade problems can be overcome by pruning out trees rather severely, removing secondary branches along the larger one, and lightly pruning the ends to relieve terminal weight. Silhouette and shade patterns from trees pruned in this manner are attractive and interesting, allowing more sun underneath. My cottonwoods are pruned in this manner every year, and general health and beauty have improved. This task should be done by a trained tree surgeon—I shudder over much of the work done in our area by the inexperienced.

Flowering varieties of trees usually are small enough to fit comfortably into the average-size garden. Evergreens provide good foundation planting and boundary borders. Trees emphasize by mass and height, and can provide shade and still be decorative. Their pictorial effect in combination with the horizon and the sky gives artistic satisfaction.

Flowering fruit trees cannot be surpassed for beauty. It is recommended that the non-bearing varieties be planted, since the labor of picking and the attraction of insects and small boys are among the detractions of the fruit bearing varieties. For line effects, the flowering trees are perfection.

Evergreens often are planted for winter color, but they too often become tired, dirty trees with dusty, brown, and generally unhappy foliage. To me the red branches of a flowering plum tree against the wintry sky are far superior to any evergreen colors, from the aesthetic point of view.

Remember to water evergreens during the winter months, since we have dry winters as well as the other dry seasons. Many evergreens are lost through the winter due to lack of moisture. They also appreciate a good shower bath several times during the winter. In summer, a cool spray of cold water will help control the red spider. Proper feeding and watering, too often neglected where evergreens are considered, will restore these trees to beauty.

Never plant trees with spreading roots, such as the poplar and the cottonwood, closer than fifteen feet from a house foundation or wall. These roots eventually become powerful levers that will produce cracks and other damage. Trees with fast-growing roots often clog sewer lines where they can gain access at joints.

Fruit or flowering trees and evergreens have more central or tap root growth and roots will not spread enough to cause damage.

Probably the wisest course in selecting trees is to visit a local grower or nursery where selection of trees already in stock can be made.

EVERGREENS

Coniferous evergreens need special care in transplanting, with only balled and burlapped stock acceptable. Humus or peat moss should be used generously in the planting, and the ground should not be allowed to dry out until the tree is well established. Burlap frames may protect the newly planted evergreen in windy sections.

Small plants recover more quickly from the shock of transplanting and in the long run might be better than the larger tree that will "stand still" for a long time before regaining the urge to grow. Those available in the home area are preferable.

Contrary to a popular conception, evergreens do like extra food. Compost or organic fertilizers are the most desirable. Frequent washing of the foliage with the water hose is welcomed, as well as watering through the dry winter months.

This list includes the most popular, easily grown evergreens:

Arborvitae

As a rule the arborvitae would make a much better appearance if gardeners gave them the careful cultivation showered on the rest of the garden. *Thuja*, botanically speaking, is a valuable evergreen with rather flat sprays of lacy branches that is extremely popular. It is handsome when

well pruned, but too often its pyramidal shape is allowed to grow off in all directions.

BAKER.

BERCKMANNS—Dwarf, compact, with yellow accents.

BONITA—Golden-edged.

BREWERS HYBRID.

DWARF HOVEY.

EXCELSA.

FLAT TOP.

PYRAMIDAL—Good as a slender column to emphasize height.

ROSEDALE BLUE.

Junipers and Cedars

These are a large group of popular evergreens of the pine family.

PFITZER'S JUNIPER—Has a spreading habit, with a gray cast to the foliage. Will stand shade.

RED CEDAR—Compact, slender growth, with reddish cast to foliage. Attractive gray-purple berries. One of my favorites. Prune this at Christmas time to have material for wreaths and decorations. Keeps its color in winter.

EASTERN RED CEDAR—Another fine tree.

SPINY GREEK JUNIPER—One of the most attractive types of lacy blue gray that prunes well. Does not get tall. Watch it for red spider.

SABINA—Spreading branches of dark-green foliage and very popular.

SILVER JUNIPER—Excellent in this area. Good color.

DUNDEE—Slight lavender cast.

Spruce

COLORADO BLUE SPRUCE—One of our most beautiful trees. Grows well in most areas but is better in the higher and cooler regions. Use this tree only where there is plenty of space. Many fail to realize this is a large tree when fully grown. Will take pruning and can be well shaped.

ENGELMANN SPRUCE—Ideal for parks. Makes a good specimen if given rich soil.

Other Varieties

ARIZONA CYPRESS—This is a large, fast-growing tree of lovely color, silver gray. May be pruned to perfect proportions. Dependable and hardy. Roots do not sink in deeply enough for anchorage during severe windstorms and sometimes is uprooted.

AUSTRIAN PINE—Valuable since it tolerates our weather conditions.

DOUGLAS FIR—Slow growing, narrow, and of symmetrical growth habit. Responds to pruning. Rather tall for average home grounds.

ITALIAN CYPRESS—Tall, slender, and handsome, but not hardy in colder sections. Prune to keep in good shape.

PIÑON—Very popular for typical Southwestern landscaping.

FLOWERING VARIETIES

ALBIZZIA JULIBRISSIN—Erroneously called a mimosa. Grows a flat top thirty-five feet in height. Extremely open head. Light green leafage and summer masses of pink flowers. It is a hardy deciduous tree. Charming with its airy, feathery, light foliage. Seed pods a nuisance.

APRICOT—Select a late-blooming variety if you live in a region where late frosts are usual, for the apricot is one of the earliest to bloom in the spring. Dawn is a mid-season variety, with double, very fragrant flowers. Rosemary Clark is a new pure-white flowering variety.

CHERRY—Many varieties to choose from, with Kanzan or Kwanzan one of the loveliest. It is a little difficult to get started, and, if available, fall planting is advised. This tree must be sprayed and treated for borers just as the peach.

CHINABERRY TREE, *melia azedarach*—Also called bead tree, is very neat, round-headed and symmetrical. It has rich green leaves.

CRAB—Truly one of our loveliest and most popular. No other tree equals the flowering crab for its profuse bloom. The graceful growth and fine foliage make it a favorite, even when not in bloom. It is among the last to lose its leaves in fall. The Hopa and Bechtel are among the most popular varieties. Both are pink. A pink "weeper" makes a fine lawn specimen. Crimson Brilliant is a variety with vivid color. Others are Eley, Almey, *Baccata mandsdaurica, Hillieri,* Red Jade, and Strathmore.

FLOWERING DOGWOOD—Twenty to thirty feet tall, very ornamental, with blossoms appearing before leafing. The buds are formed in the fall, thus giving an attractive winter appearance. After the flowering, the fruit appears, small and berry-like. Flowers of the Redflowering variety are pink, four-petalled, and four inches in diameter. White Cloud is a new white variety of promise. Leaves are oval shaped, with pointed ends, about five

Fruit blossom

inches long, thick and attractive. Transplant in early spring, using well-prepared soil and plenty of peat moss with compost. Takes a sheltered spot. Afternoon shade and protection from wind are requirements. Sulphate of ammonia and soil sulphur added to the soil several times a year helps keep the soil on the acid side, necessary for this tree. Only the most ardent gardener should attempt to grow the dogwood, but it is well worth the effort in warmer areas. Likes a daily sprinkle as well as the regular deep irrigation. Is the last tree to lose its leaves, which are colorful.

GOLDEN CHAIN, *Laburnum vossi*—Ornamental, with long chains of golden, pea-like flowers similar to wistaria. The leaf resembles clover. I planted a clump of Happy Days yellow iris beneath mine and it creates a pictorial effect. Needs well-drained soil and can take city conditions. Where winters are more severe and in higher areas the tree may not be as hardy and should be protected from too much wind. Erroneously called a yellow wistaria. Will produce blooms the first year after planting. Yellowish-green bark is attractive in winter.

GOLDENRAIN TREE, *koelreuteria*—How could I forget this charming dependable tree that I had in my garden about twenty years ago! This ornamental tree has airy, yellow flower clusters that appear in July when few flowering trees are in bloom. Its lacy, alternate, compound leaflets arranged feather fashion are decorative. In fall its attractive, balloon-like pods are fine for flower arrangements. In Colorado Springs they have more of a pink tinge than ours, and seeing them there reminded me to plant one again. Ordinary culture suffices.

HAWTHORN—The English hawthorn is slow in starting but requires only the regular culture. The fruit is scarlet, making a desirable fall item. An occasional spray of cold water is helpful against the green aphids that seem to enjoy the tender leaf of the new growth. Paul's Scarlet is a popular variety.

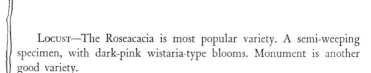

Locust—The Roseacacia is most popular variety. A semi-weeping specimen, with dark-pink wistaria-type blooms. Monument is another good variety.

Magnolia—Can be grown in the warmer sections and requires an acid soil. *Magnolia soulangeana* is tender but *Grandiflora* (evergreen) is to be recommended as far north as Albuquerque.

Maple—Red or purple leaf maple, while not thought of as a flowering tree, is very ornamental in spring and fall, mostly due to its colorful leaves. A fine contrast to other spring-blooming trees. I feel it is worth the effort, due to its beauty. Very slow growing and slow to become acclimated.

Peach—The Cardinal variety is truly glorious in bloom, with rich rose double flowers. This brilliance makes it a showy tree. One that I planted at the left of a white, colonial style front doorway caused many admiring comments from passers-by. The flowering peach is not a long-lived tree, and I cannot stress enough that good cultivation is required and that this tree should be treated yearly for borers. Altair is a fine variety, beautiful, and bears good fruit as well. Iceberg is one of the best varieties for white blossoms. The Helen Borchers has a large, shell-pink bloom and is profuse. The weeping types are appealing. The peach should be pruned yearly for a healthy, well-shaped tree. Pink Charming has double pink blossoms.

Plum—This tree is rewarding in the Southwest when it is glimpsed against the brilliant blue of our skies. The *pissardi rosea,* with deep purple foliage and branches of the same deep tones, is another breath-taking combination against our daytime heaven. Its flowers are pale pink. There are several other fine varieties, such as Veitchi, Cistena (common, but lovely), Blireana, and Triloba, a small, very showy lawn specimen.

Redbud, Judas Tree—Showy, grows well, with good foliage. Its leaf is glossy, and heart-shaped. Eastern redbud has been known to withstand zero weather. Often the grower becomes discouraged because it takes a couple of years for a redbud to take hold. Spring sandstorms pit the leaves of the young trees. An acid fertilizer and compost encourage growth.

SMOKE TREE—Handsome tree that grows twelve to fifteen feet in height. Takes zero weather (even 11 degrees below, one winter in my garden). Slow growing in our locality. Has feathery panicles with lavender tint which suggest the name "smoke." A season of growing the redleaf smoke tree gave me much pleasure because of its colorful foliage. *Rhus Cotinus Foliis purpureis Notcutt* is worth a trial.

WISTARIA—The tree wistaria makes a striking lawn specimen. Very successful in this region. The blue tree wistaria is the most popular. Ordinary good culture meets its requirements. It is one of the most artistic of all trees. The leaves have a tendency to become yellow and can be corrected with occasional applications of iron sulphate.

SHADE AND BACKGROUND TREES

AILANTHUS—See Tree of Heaven.

ASH, ARIZONA—Requires little water and likes an alkaline soil, so should be planted more often in this locality. Clean, bright foliage makes it desirable. Grows to thirty feet in height and can take zero weather. Grows fast. Modesta also good.

ASPEN—The quaking aspen is native to our mountain areas. Some varieties are planted outside their habitat, but not often. Dislikes low altitudes and warm weather.

ASH, MOUNTAIN—Not used enough in this area. Most of the species are grown easily, even in dry soil. Attains fifty feet and more in height.

BOX ELDER—Thrives in semi-arid regions and is useful as a windbreak. Three to five leaves arranged in feather fashion. Hardy. Must be sprayed for beetles.

CATALPA, OR UMBRELLA CATALPA—Nice, ornamental specimen with clusters of gray-white flowers; cigar-shaped, long seed pod.

COTTONWOOD, MOUNTAIN VARIETY—The type seen most commonly in our area apparently is a natural hybrid produced by the plains or valley cottonwood, with which we are so familiar, and the true native mountain cottonwood. The true species has narrow leaves in comparison to the wide, heart-shaped leaf of its valley cousin. The bark of the hybrid tree retains the smooth, whitish surface of the true mountain variety, but sends out leaves resembling those of the valley tree. With age, the bark of the hybrid roughens and turns gray. The tree is not desirable in this area due to its infestations by tree borers. Also, it is short-lived. On the credit side, the mountain cottonwood does not bear the obnoxious cotton pods.

COTTONWOOD, RIO GRANDE—A stout tree, with shining, somewhat heart-shaped leaves and a rough bark that is firmly entrenched in the Rio Grande Valley area. The tree is native to the area and grows fast, sometimes as high as 100 feet and with tremendous girth. In the fall the turning of its leaves to golden yellow is a vision long anticipated. The tree takes much from the soil and likes plenty of water. It requires more space than the average grounds provide. The female of the species is a nuisance because of its grape-like clusters of pods that open and scatter soft cottonlike down. To assure non-bearing trees are being planted, make cuttings from trees known not to bear the pods. Subject to disease and borers.

Mistletoe has attacked many cottonwood trees in the lower Rio Grande Valley with fatal results. Should you find an infestation, prune the infected spots severely. The wind does break off branches of these trees and they are subject to several diseases, but seem to survive all of them for many, many years even under unfavorable circumstances. They particularly lend themselves to shelter the popular ranch type of house. Prune every year if possible.

DESERTWILLOW—Small, twenty to thirty feet high, with narrow leaves. Cultured for ornament. Needs a warm climate and will grow with little water, though it appreciates more. Sometimes called the "mimbre" in New Mexico and Mexico. The flowers are short, trumpet-like with terminal clusters. The pods are long and the seeds numerous. Can take to five degrees below zero.

ELM—Three elm trees are listed. The name "Chinese" often erroneously is assigned to the Siberian elm, which has very undesirable root and seed habits.

1. American Elm—Slow growing, but excellent. Subject to scale and disease. Upright, with good habits. A good elm tree will grow to 120 feet in height. Leaves are long and oval, smooth on top and hairy under-

neath, three to seven inches long. Flowers are small. The tree likes lots of water.

2. Chinese Elm—Upright and more compact than the Siberian elm. Blossoms in small clusters in August and September. Quick growing and hardy and remains green, with leaves lost for only a short period in cold areas. Smaller in size than the Siberian elm, but desirable for shade. Preferred to a true Siberian elm.

3. Siberian Elm—Grows fifty to sixty feet in height. Takes zero temperatures. Upright and trim in appearance. Grows rapidly. Subject to disease and its worst habit is throwing off countless seeds that take deep root as seedlings where they are not wanted. Gardeners must pull them out by the hundreds each year. Sticky substance is exuded in spring to become a nuisance to cars parked underneath. Leaves are shiny topped, hairy underneath, about two and a half inches long, color is retained until frost, so no fall coloring is added to the landscape. Trees along the west coast and warmer areas do not produce seeds, thus eliminating what I consider the worst nuisance. Its roots penetrate sewer pipes and clog them, as well as snatching food away from all other plants in its area. The greatest value of this tree is its ability to thrive under the most unfavorable conditions, bringing green and shade to places where they are most needed. Elm beetles are moving into the Southwest and are killing this tree, which for many years was thought to be immune to both the leaf and bark beetles.

HACKBERRY—Valuable shade tree with rapid spreading growth. Should be used more. Easy culture. Sometimes called nettle tree. Stands alkali and thus should be desirable. Fine in Denver.

AMERICAN LINDEN—Handsome tree of good habits, and comparatively rapid growth. More of these should be used. Excellent shade. Suffers in dry spells.

BLACK LOCUST, OR ACACIA—Feathery leafage, with white, pea-shaped blossoms in sprays. Suckers are numerous and should be clipped away for neatness. Produces borers. One of the latest trees to leaf. Straight trunk and attains seventy to eighty feet in height. Branches appear scraggly in winter. Seed pods pea-like and a nuisance.

HONEY LOCUST—Thorny, with flowers in clusters. Sturdy, rapid grower. Likes moist soil. Will take heavy pruning. Tall, handsome; not comparable, however, to other locusts. Not particular about soil. Is included in this list as desirable. In the list of flowering trees a locust commonly named the Roseacacia was included for its attractive blossoms.

Locust, New Mexico—Also called the thorny locust.

Locust, Moraine—Hardwood tree, thornless and seedless; grows in most soils, and its shade is not so dense that it ruins flowers and grass. Fast growing. Friesia has golden yellow foliage, and Rubylace, red foliage.

Magnolia—Deciduous variety. Will grow eight to ten feet tall. Prefers rich, moist, and well-drained soil. Difficult to transplant; care must be taken to prevent air from reaching the roots. Needs protected area except in extreme southern section. Should have a windbreak, and plenty of water.

Norway Maple—Should be tried more often. Mine has grown slowly but is as colorful in spring as a flowering tree. No pests in its sixteen years. Fine purple leaves in spring and fall.

Maple, Silver or Soft Variety—Does well and should be used more. Grows thirty to sixty feet high; will withstand temperatures to twenty degrees below zero. The leaves are deeply lobed, with green top and silvery under surface. The leaves turn yellow in the fall. The tree is hardy, needs a good soil mixture, and does better than other varieties. Nurserymen seem to shy away from it, probably confusing it with the sugar maple, which is difficult to grow. Water generously.

Mulberry, Fruitless Kingan—Handsome tree that should be planted more for shade since it grows to forty feet and withstands 20 degrees below zero. Grows rapidly. Resists wind. Suitable for desert regions.

Mulberry, Weeping Variety, *morus alba*—Non-bearing preferred. Fine for shade with attractive lobed leaves. Takes wind, tolerant of soil conditions, hardy, and takes temperatures twenty degrees below zero. Fast growing. Compares with Chinese elms in vigor. The Red, Pinkfruit, and Black are popular fruiting species. However, the muss of berries suggests the Fruitless Kingan as the most desirable.

Pecan—Can be grown as far north as Albuquerque and grows extremely well in southern section. The Texas Prolific and the Burkett grow well locally. Good leaves, and the trees make excellent shade producers without too much care. Roots cover a large area, with a deep tap root so care must be taken in transplanting. Should not be closer than eighty feet apart. Your County Agent can tell which varieties are suitable to your area and how to cope with its diseases.

Poplar, Lombardy—Short-lived, hard on garden due to absorption from soil. Roots will shoot out 25 feet to steal food from your rose beds. Subject to disease. Good for landscape effect if properly placed. Best used in groups of three and five rather than rows. Nice for suburban property and windbreaks. Only a large lot in the city suitable for them.

POPLAR, SILVER LEAF—Better than Lombardy. Not quite so susceptible to disease.

RUSSIAN OLIVE—Alternate, short stock with silvery scales that give the entire tree a silvery appearance. The flowers are small, greenish yellow, not showy but extremely fragrant. Hardy, wind resistant, and of landscape value. A good windbreak and attractive for color. Fast growing, thorny. Can be used as a ragged hedge or trimmed and shaped as individual trees. Birds love its berries which are sweet when ripe, bitter when green, and resemble tiny olives in clusters. Called a "dirty" tree, but I don't consider it so if well watered and cultivated.

AMERICAN SYCAMORE—Smooth bark, almost white as the tree ages. Must be sprayed regularly for blight that makes leaves look rusted and causes them to drop early. Likes a neutral soil.

SWEET GUM—A favorite in my garden and since planted it has gone through several seasons of variable weather changes. Its maple-like leaves and furrowed bark make it a pretty tree. It grows in a pyramidal shape which should allow planting in a small lot. It does not have the brilliant reds that are found in fall in damper climates, but does have good color and its corky winged branches are valued in flower arrangements. West Coast hybridists have developed trees with more red coloring such as Palo Alto.

TREE OF HEAVEN (Ailanthus)—Does very well, with numerous seed pods that give the tree a reputation for being untidy. Really attractive when the sprays of pods turn brilliant red and yellow as fall approaches. Grows quickly, undaunted by neglect or lack of water. Little forests spring up about the parent tree. Only the female should be grown, for pollen from the male has a disagreeable odor.

WEEPING WILLOW—Forty feet in height, takes zero weather. Picturesque with its long, pendulous branches of slender whips covered with narrow leaves. One of the first trees to leaf in spring. Grows rapidly and does best in the valleys rather than on the mesas. Requires plenty of water. Lack of water kills many of them. Vitellina species is yellow-barked and lovely, but needs lots of water to grow well. Humilus and rostrata species can take arid conditions. Easily propagated by cuttings and any soil suits them. Subject to pests and diseases.

Shrubs

SHRUBS, like trees, are important garden background. Varieties can be selected to present a blooming schedule through the seasons and they add more to the garden with less effort than most plant material. Variety can be introduced, and most gardens look unfinished without a few well-placed shrubs. Evergreens are popular, but others lend an all-year-round beauty with handsome bark and twig color in winter. Not only the browns and greens, but red and purple tones are part of the shrub's attraction. By clipping off branches of early-flowering varieties for forcing indoors, impatient gardeners can produce blooms as early as January. The pussywillow, jasmine, and forsythia are among these.

Winter bouquet arrangements that I have used include artistically formed branches, with leaves from such house plants as coleus, philodendron, and geraniums. Summer bouquets often are improved when height is provided with shrub sprays. Evergreen leaves of the photinia and mahonia are useful, with the latter particularly desirable in winter, due to its purple-bronze, holly-like leaves.

Shrubs do not require as much water as most plants. Their pruning needs are not as constant, nor do they require as much fertilizer. As with all gardening, good care makes for better specimens.

Tried and true shrubs are included in the following list. Their descriptions, and the addition of their likes and dislikes allow the gardening novice to select those varieties he may have noted in gardens which he admired before he acquired one of his own.

Many fine shrub varieties are not found in present-day nurseries and catalogues. If the reader does find others available that appeal to him, let him keep in mind that most any variety will do well if given the proper soil and growing conditions.

ABELIA—Member of the honeysuckle family. Small, but with pretty, bell-shaped flowers that form clusters. This hardy shrub prefers rich, well-drained soil and plenty of sunshine.

1. *Chinensis*—Low and spreading, about five feet tall.
2. *Grandiflora*—Most popular variety, with almost evergreen foliage in warmer sections. Corolla of blossom flushed with pink.
3. Edward Goucher—New, with bronze-tinted leaves in spring, and covered with pink flowers.

AZALEA—Not hardy in most of this area. Does not tolerate alkaline soil or dry climate. Can be grown in protected patio or north side of the garden if the soil is made acid and kept that way. Sprinkling every day with a fine spray helps provide the moisture needed. Should be heavily mulched with peat moss, and for this reason should not be planted too deep.

1. Kurume—Can stand a low temperature to ten degrees above zero.
2. Rutherfordiana—Takes zero temperatures, but flowering buds may be lost at twenty-five degrees above.
3. Mollis—More hardy and supposedly tolerates lime, but not thoroughly tried in this area.

BARBERRY—

1. *Berberis mentorenis*—Drouth resistant, dark evergreen foliage with fine fall coloring which makes it a favorite for decorative uses. Clean, upright growth.
2. *Darwini*—Fine for native architecture. Not formal in shape, and evergreen in appearance.
3. *Pruinosa*—Popular variety.
4. Crimson Pigmy.

BEAUTYBUSH—From the honeysuckle family, growing four to six feet in height. Hardy, and may be forced into early bloom by bringing cuttings indoors. A fountain of bell-shaped, light-pink flowers. Stands poor soil.

BRIDAL WREATH—(See Spirea).

BUDDLEIA—Also called summer lilac or butterfly bush. Easily grown and desired for its variety of colors. Flower spikes are six to eight inches long. After blooming or during winter should be pruned nearly to the ground. Hardy in most all regions. A white variety is called Peace. Popular also are Purple Prince, Flaming Violet, and Fascinating.

CORYLUS, *Avellana Contorta*—Purple-leaved filbert, referred to as Harry Lauder's walking stick bush, is doing well for me in partial shade and a rich, humus soil. It was placed in a position where it would cast winter shadows on a wall to show off its corkscrew-like branches. I am look-ing forward to the time when it is large enough to use for flower arrange-ments. Its leaves are increasing in size as the plant slowly grows, and they are a rich green. The minute flowers are insignificant.

COTONEASTER—Thrives most anywhere. Clusters of berries make this shrub attractive, for the flowers are inconspicuous.

1. *Multiflora*—Makes a fine hedge, growing five to eight feet tall. Branches excellent for arrangement.
2. Rock variety is low, and has deep-red leaves in fall which add to its beauty. One of the most hardy.
3. Spreading—Rich-colored leaves in autumn. Grows five to six feet high.
4. Parnay's Red Cluster Berry—Popular, but doesn't stand cold weather.

CRAPEMYRTLE—Crinkled crepe flowers which are showy and continue through an unusually long blooming season. Watermelon-red blossoms striking, but most varieties produce magenta, pink, and white. Will not take cold weather, usually lost at temperatures under twelve degrees. With its location in my garden each year I worry for fear it won't come through because it begins leafing out so late, even though planted near the south wall of the patio. Should be pruned after flowering, but I usually wait until after leaves appear the next spring. It likes rich soil. Grows well in the south.

DAPHNE—Grown in this area, but with difficulty. Should be grown in a protected spot in good soil.

DEUTZIA—Small bush, one to two feet high, with clusters of white flowers. *Gracilis* and *Crenata suspensa* are good varieties, with the latter superior.

DOGWOOD—Tatarian Dogwood. Showy shrub noted for its bright-red branches. Fine large leaves are valuable for flower arrangements. Adds much to winter landscape and its branches add to winter bouquets. Grows ten feet tall. The flowers, in clusters of white, are not showy. The shrub is very hardy, stands any soil, and will do well in the shade or in the sun.

Dogwood

EUONYMUS—A deciduous shrub that is always evergreen. Can be shaped and grown to fit any situation, sometimes flat against a house wall or fence or pruned into formal pillars. Am partial to this shrub which I feel is valuable for landscaping. Will take zero temperatures. Its flowers are inconspicuous although its berries sometimes are attractive. The leaves are lush, glossy, and bright green. Valuable for pueblo-type architecture. Scale has attacked this shrub in recent years and many have given up growing it. Failure to fertilize it, I believe, weakens it. Feed with compost and cottonseed meal.

1. Evergreen—Most popular, quite hardy.
2. *Patens*—Orange berries. Can take shade.
3. Silver variegated.
4. Puchellus.
5. Goldspot.
6. Alatus compactus. Red fall foliage.

FLOWERING ALMOND—Not a true almond, but a showy shrub not over four or five feet high. Flowers in numerous clusters along stems which make fine sprays for arrangements. *Glandulosa rosea* has pink blossoms.

FLOWERING QUINCE—An early bloomer, with brilliant wax-like blooms in clusters which may vary from pink through red. Many fine varieties, which grow from two to six feet in height. Among them are Stanford Red, Coral Sea, and Juliet, with fine new ones being developed.

FORSYTHIA or GOLDEN BELL.—Popular shrub with profusion of yellow flower sprays that bloom before the appearance of leaves. One of the earliest blooming and can be cut for easy indoor forcing. Grows in any soil, but appreciates attention. Wise to prune right after blooming, for it can grow out of bounds up to heights of twelve feet. Excellent against massive building foundations. Often vine-trained. Should be represented in every garden. Nicely combined with daffodils and other spring flowers. My favorite—Lynwood Gold.

FUCHSIA—Can be grown in warm sections of this area, but in protected places on the north side of the garden. Will not winter through excepting in the southerly portions of the Southwest. Can't stand temperatures below twenty degrees. Likes rich, moist soil.

GOLD-DUST PLANT, *aucuba japonica varigata*—How delighted I was to have this lovely plant be so successful after several years' trial, as there are so few broad-leaved evergreens that we can use in this section. This is as far north as it would be hardy. Often the leaves will hang limp after a very cold night, but when the sun shines they will raise up as before. It is on a protected, north side, and was planted with a rich compost, peat moss, and soil mixture. I foliar feed it often during the summer and give it lots of compost and acid foods. In very warm weather I spray its foliage with water frequently. The leaves, a brilliant green flecked with gold spots, shine beautifully. It will not tolerate summer sun.

HIBISCUS—Rose of Sharon or Althea. An erect-growing shrub of formal shape with blooms from July until frost.

1. Coelestis—Three-inch blossoms of rich blue. Does well with ordinary culture.

2. Snowdrift—Giant white flowers, four inches across.
3. Rubis—Rose pink.

HOLLY, CHINESE, *cornuta* Burford's, *cornuta F. burfordi*—Being tried with some success but have not been proved hardy north to Colorado.

HOLLY, WILSON'S *(illex altaclarensis wilsoni)*—I admire this large, glossy-leafed holly which I was told would never grow here but, since it is claimed to be hardy to five degrees above zero, I have had no trouble with it. About eight inches tall when planted, it is four feet high after three years. Lots of humus and peat moss were used in planting, and it receives foliar food, compost, and acid food—it especially loves cottonseed meal. With frequent hosings its leaves are kept clean and bright.

HYDRANGEA—Can be grown in protected places and in warmer regions of our area. Foliage glossy and regular, with leaves rather large and oval in shape. Requires acid soil.

1. *Paniculata grandiflora*—Common variety with white blooms and hardy. Doesn't make the showing in the Southwest that it does in other sections of the country.
2. *Macrophylla*—An old favorite. Domotoi is a double pink variety which has done well for me. Use a rich, acid soil and keep damp. Plant on the north or east side of the house or wall.

JASMINE—Poets sometimes call this the Jasminum or Jessamine. Often found listed under vines because of its rambling and spreading habit. Likes a warm, sunny place and blooms early in the spring. Yellow or white flowers, with yellow the most popular here. Easily rooted and generally passed along from friend to friend. Have never heard of anyone buying a jasmine plant for his garden. Excellent for early forcing.

LILAC—This old-fashioned favorite is very much at home in this area. Many fine varieties are found in catalogues, while the new hybrids are numerous. The bushes will grow high here, almost above a one-story house. Any good culture will suffice. Use cow manure about the plant each year. Iron improves color and they should have superphosphate annually following bloom. I prefer planting the lilac on the north or in cold areas so that it doesn't become frost-bitten by too early blooming. Cut shoots away from around the bottom of the plant and cut off blooms just after they have finished blossoming. A few prunings of dead wood or unwanted branches are all it needs. Color range from white into blues, pinks, lavenders, and purples, with varieties in doubles and singles. Santa Fe has accomplished wonders with some of the new varieties. Old favorites are seldom found in catalogues.

MAHONIA—Oregongrape. Ideal for landscaping effects and color. Used in formal or informal planting. Holly-like leaves turn from bright green to reddish purple in the fall. Clusters of yellow flowers appear in early spring, followed by grape-like, purple fruit. Range from two to six feet. Prefers shade, although my bush has done well on a hot west front. This little shrub is one of my favorites and gives color to the informal type of home in winter, and yields excellent leaves for arrangements. Recent attacks of a tiny unidentified worm have defoliated many to the extent that some are lost. Sprays or systemics have not helped.

MOCKORANGE—An erect shrub that is sometimes called the syringa. Its flowers are white, blooming late in the spring. They are showy and fragrant, with a waxy texture. Plant grows four to eight feet high. Does better in this area if given an occasional dose of iron sulphate.

1. Atlas—Large new single variety.
2. Belle Etoíle—Petals more pointed, with purplish blush at base. Delightful fragrance. One of the finest shrubs but not much used in this area.
3. Virginal—An old favorite. (*P. virginalis.*)

Mockorange

NANDINA—Handsome, low-growing shrub with small, dainty leaves, rather pointed in shape. Leaves turn vivid red in fall and remain on plant during winter. White flowers are inconspicuous, but are followed by clusters of bright red berries, brighter than the leaves. Grows from six to eight feet tall. Not very hardy and should be planted in a protected spot. Grows particularly well near a warm south wall. A heavy mulch is helpful. The nandina needs protection from cold even as far south as Dallas.

OLEANDER—Grows up to eight feet in height. Not hardy in the central area of this region, but around El Paso grows outdoors beautifully. Will take cold down to twelve degrees. Brilliant showy blossoms of terminal clusters and sometimes fragrant. Narrow leaves are thick and leathery. Grown as tub plants where colder and kept in the house during winter. Doesn't require much care and when brought indoors for the cold season should be watered sparingly. Caution children against handling the plant, since its juice is poisonous. Oleanders like sun and sandy soil, but do better with an occasional dressing of manure. Is subject to scale.

PHOTINIA—Often grows to fifteen feet. Shiny, thick, elongated leaves six to eight inches in length which are fine for arrangements. Early spring leaves turn quite red before being dropped for new growth, thus adding unusual coloring for the early season. Since it is informal can be used with Pueblo or Spanish Colonial homes. Flowers are white clusters, followed by red berries which sometimes give the plant the name of Chinese Holly. Grows with ease in any location, but needs good soil.

POINCIANA—Also called Bird of Paradise for its showy yellow flowers with long, brilliant red stamens. A native of the desert area, although it appears tropical. At one time it was scattered liberally in this area, but appears to be dying out, perhaps because of cold weather. When a child I used to see it growing along the mesa. Easily grown from seeds, which literally "pop" noisily from their pods when dry, but difficult to transplant. Seed should be soaked before planting. Tolerates dry sandy soil. Usually grows as a shrub but can be pruned and trained into a small well-shaped tree. This is such an unusual, handsome plant I wonder why it is not used more in landscaping about our native-type homes.

PRIVET—Valuable for hedging, with glossy, dark-green leaves. Fast growing. Blooms with clusters of little white flowers.

1. California—One of the hardiest types.
2. European—Most widely used. Stands almost any unfavorable weather conditions. The Lodense variety is the most popular.

PUSSYWILLOW or WILLOW—The French pussywillow is excellent. Grows easily. Fine for indoor forcing as early as January. Blooms from a cunning gray velvety bud, hence the name "pussy" willow. Should be pruned severely after blooming.

Firethorn

PYRACANTHA (Firethorn)—Fine shrub, much desired for its heavy sprays of brilliant orange or red berries. Bears attractive clusters of white flowers late in spring. Takes dry soil and can be trained to cover a wall, lean against a house, or in hedges and bushes. Can be grown almost to top a one-story house in a great flare of color when berries are mature. Small plants should be selected for it is difficult to transplant. Iron sulphate helpful as leaves sometimes become pale. Needs room. Should be out of way of traffic because of thorns.

1. *Coccinea lalandi*—Orange-scarlet berries.
2. Graber's—Fine red variety.

REDBUD—Can be grown as a tree as well by shaping and pruning.

ROCKROSE, *cistus purpureus*—Also supposed not to grow here, is doing well against a hot, south wall as it is not hardy below ten degrees. It is four feet high and has old-rose, single flowers about three inches in diameter. The foliage is a gray-green color and would be good for dusty areas as the dust would not show on it.

SNOWBALL—Old-fashioned shrub that grows just about anywhere and reaches eight to ten feet in height with ordinary culture. Several good varieties.

SPANISH BROOM or WEAVERSBROOM—Finely branched, compact shrub covered in early spring with bright-yellow, pea-like flowers. Almost devoid of leaves. Excellent in southern part of area, particularly around El Paso. Likes dry, warm location and can take the hot side of a house with reflected heat from cement driveway. Will stand a low temperature of ten degrees. Sweet-scented flowers which are fine for arrangements with strong lines.

Pussywillow

SPIREA—Botanical spelling is *Spiraea*. Popularly called Bridal Wreath. One of the most popular shrubs. Easily grown and makes a big spring show with branches growing in cascades covered with masses of tiny blossoms in sprays. Nice for border accents and boundaries. Not particular about soil and location. If in too warm a spot it is likely to be nipped by frost. Perhaps the greatest sin against the spirea is in pruning in the early spring, just before its curving branches have a chance to bloom. Thus its sprays of buds are cut off. Prune by cutting off dead flower sprays and removing straggly or dead growths within the plant or at its base. Next year's flowers are being formed just behind those that bloomed, so remember that when reaching for the pruning shears.

1. Vanhouttei—Most common and most favored.
2. Anthony Waterer—from *bumalda* species, with rosy red flowers, and many other varieties.
3. Caryopteris—Hardy. Not a true spirea, but known to nursery trade as blue spirea, or Blue Mist. A low-growing plant valuable for flower arrangements due to its flower form. Seed pods attractive for winter bouquets. Covered from August to frost with dainty, lacy clusters. Heavenly Blue: new rich color.
4. *Bumalda crispa* is a low-growing plant with crimson red flowers.

Tamarisk (*Tamarix*). Also called Salt Cedar—Feathered, slender plants of semi-desert country. Grows wild in much of our area. Valuable for hedging and for trimming into tall, heavily trunked trees. The pink blossoms resemble the heather family. Foliage and branches blend into a pinkish haze. Mistakenly called Tamarack, which is a larch. *Tamarix parviflora* grows easily and I wonder why it isn't used more with our native architecture since it is so graceful and appropriate.

Vitex—Blue chaste tree. Slender spikes of lilac-blue flowers in July and August, while the plant itself has slender, graceful lines. Remains dormant very late and needs care in transplanting. Prune in January.

Weigela—Funnel shaped flowers an inch to an inch and a half long, with long noticeable stamens. Plant grows six to seven feet high, preferring moist soil, needing sunshine and plenty of space.

1. Bristol Ruby—Does better in this locale than some older varieties. New varieties described in seed catalogues sound wonderful, but I have not tried them. It seems in this case different growers have different names for plants which appear to be similar.

Forsythia

Perennials

PLANTS that live year after year, appearing and reappearing in the garden for long terms, are called perennials. They are the mainstay of the garden, in that, like shrubs and trees, they need comparatively less attention than other types of plant material.

True gardeners mark the advent of spring with the first reawakening of our beloved perennials. Deep inside us comes an answering response to the delicate and fragile green of a new delphinium shoot or the red nose of the peony's clump as it thrusts its way out of the ground. Each perennial has its own thrilling way of returning to the surface of the earth after its winter nap and each has its particular charm.

Perennials make garden work much easier, since all that is needed after their yearly arrival is food, water, and a little staking. Their constant multiplication makes it necessary to divide clumps every few years for better culture, but even this has a dividend since those divisions enlarge the garden or are given to friends or new gardeners. Garden clubs often have season exchanges when members can add to their list of varieties.

Remember when planting perennials that a much better effect is obtained more quickly by planting in groups of three, five, and seven, depending on the space allotted, than stringing out single plants here and there. They will multiply in time when alone, but achieve a more attractive pictorial effect and grow better when in association with their own kind.

In the Southwest the dry atmosphere soon dispels the exquisite scent of most garden flowers. Since we have so little humidity, there is nothing to hold the flower essence in the garden. Ardent gardeners who waken early to go forth and labor have discovered that the very finest fragrance is offered at the extreme hour of four o'clock in the morning.

ALYSSUM—Rock madwort or gold-dust are other names. The daintiness of these blossoms and their brilliance among the spring bulbs makes them outstanding. *A. saxatile compactum* or Basket of Gold, with dense, brilliant-yellow flowers, is so profuse in flower that that the plant is hidden. Pansies and tulips are enhanced by the adornment of the alyssum.

ANCHUSA, ALKANET—This flower resembles the forgetmenot when in blossom and makes an airy accent in the perennial border. A distinct dwarf

Alyssum

species is called the myosotidiflora. Anchusa flowers in April and May. It is good in borders and rock gardens. Italica Dropmore grows as high as four feet. The culture is easy, but the plant dislikes crowding.

ASTER, or MICHAELMAS DAISY—Hardy, invaluable in the perennial border, due to their undemanding culture and their color range from white through pinks, deep reds, lavender, and purple. Pinching back the plant in early spring and summer occasionally makes it round and bushy. One reason this flower should be grown in every garden is that it can give a big splash of color in late August and September when not many other flowers are in bloom. Our arid section seems to be favored by the aster. It requires very little water. Can be used as cut flowers but its greatest beauty is in the border. Violetta is a deep violet and a handsome specimen. Redrover is a deep rose, and Beechwood Challenger is another fine red. Mount Everest is a white favorite. Gayborder Blue and Bluegown are blue-lavender in color. Survivor is a pink shade, and a variety that should be encouraged for its mass effect and adaptability to our region. Do not allow to reseed.

AUBRIETA—Purple rock cress. *Deltoidea leichtlini* is a good choice.

BABYSBREATH—Known for its daintiness, with great airiness to its stems and flowers. Bristol Fairy is the most dependable. Rosy Veil is lovely, though not as hardy. It needs room and sun. Pink Star is new.

BACHELOR'S-BUTTON—Culture is simple, and trim flowers in blue, pink, or white grow on erect plants up to two feet in height.

BEGONIA—See chapter on bulbs.

BELLFLOWER—Many types and varieties of this flower give the gardener much pleasure. Campanula *carpatica* is the most popular, and the Cullimore is a hybrid that deserves to be tried more often. I find these plants resent crowding.

BERGAMOT or BEE BALM—An attractive plant that grows in any soil, but must be confined, as it multiplies rapidly. Colors are lavender, pink, magenta, white, and scarlet. Foliage is aromatic, and for this reason I like to put bunches of it in my linen closet. Attracts bees and humming birds to its spot in the garden.

BETONICA—A border flower that is fine also for cutting. Santa Fe gardeners grow it beautifully. Advisable to grow from plants since seeds are difficult to handle.

BLANKETFLOWER, GAILLARDIA—Very brightly colored daisy-like flowers, blooming in profusion. A good cut flower, thrives in full sun and does not like too much water. Any variety is attractive. Grows wild in this area where there is sufficient warmth.

BLEEDING HEART—An old garden favorite perfectly named in description of the flower. Grows well in shade and needs protection in colder areas. Hybrid Bountiful, according to growers, is a new variety much superior to the older types.

BLUEBELLS or VIRGINIA COWSLIP—Likes shade and will grow in ordinary soil. Loses its foliage in the summer months, so mark the spot to prevent digging out its fleshy roots while dormant. Clear blue flowers which, when in bud, are touched with lavender pink.

CAMOMILE—This is a yellow, daisy-type flower, which produces blooms from July until frost. Winters well. Remove the bloomed-out flower heads, since they become a nuisance through reseeding.

CARNATIONS—Many types of hardy carnations do well in the garden. Their soft colors and fragrance, also their value for cutting, makes them popular. Riviera Giant has a nice mixture with a wide color range. The Chabaud Giant Improved is clove scented, deeply fringed, two inches and more across. It can be brought to flower from seed within five to six months. Likes rich, well-drained soil, and should do well in our alkaline soil since it likes lime so well. It dislikes crowding.

COLUMBINE—Spurred flowers shaped somewhat like a cup. The blue columbine which is native to our mountains is a special favorite. Many new hybrids range in the gamut of color. A combination of red and yellow is attractive in the garden. Another variety combines an old-rose calyx with a pure white double corolla at the base of which the rose red shows through. The Elliot hybrids are desirable. Do not allow your garden to reseed its columbines, for the seedlings will revert to the old yellow types with shorter spurs. The seed is a little difficult to germinate but this be hastened by placing them in the refrigerator, even freezing them a little. Columbines do well in the shade and are valuable for this reason.

CONEFLOWER (Rudbeckia)—Large flower on the order of a daisy, with pastel, garnet, or purple blooms with cone-like centers. Orange-yellow with brown cone is attractive, but I have never cared for the dullness of the purple varieties.

Daylily

DAYLILY—There has been great improvement in this flower in the past few years. Color range is improved and new hybrids range from yellow to bronze. The old types are greatly favored, however. Cultural requirements are simple, and varieties are very numerous. Grows on a single stalk to four feet, with spear-like leaves and lily-type flowers that bloom for a day and are replaced the next day with another on the same stalk.

DELPHINIUM—Great favorites in any garden, and even the beginner usually lists these among his first flowers. Some friends prefer the Belladonna and chinense types, since they do not require much attention and are better for the ordinary home bouquet. Once you have grown the Pacific hybrids you will never again be satisfied with the old favorites, however. Their color, structure, and general texture are so lovely and their range is so broad that selection becomes an adventure. In the past few years my plants have grown so tall that staking them against our severe winds has been the problem. Delphiniums require rich, well-drained soil. Contrary to popular advice, I have used a manure mulch with success, and plenty of compost. Care must be taken in the winter that the crowns are not covered with too many leaves for these, when they become wet, leave the plant a prey to crown rot. The finest and most perfect plants may die after a spectacular blooming. I plant new seed every year just to replace those I have lost. The seed often is hard to germinate and should not be planted until the weather is cool. Fresh seed is advised for good germination and once more let me caution against cheap seed. Staking is an absolute necessity, allowing some play of the plant against the wind, with a loose loop. Otherwise, the plant's head may snap with the wind. Big stalks are harder to keep fresh when in arrangements, so often I use the side shoots instead. Delphinium does not grow well in the warmer sections but sometimes can be handled if planted in the shade or on the north side of a building.

My favorites are the Round Table, Galahad, King Arthur, Summer Skies series, and Connecticut Yankee, a three-foot bushy plant.

DIANTHUS—Hardy garden pinks. These small, brilliantly colored blooms are perfect for rock gardens, edging, and cutting. The Crimson Bedder is a glowing single and semi-double fringed flower. Allwoodi mixed varieties are double and semi-double in a wide color range. Roysii is a neat dwarf plant in shades of rose and pink, very fragrant and nice for borders. Many other fine varieties.

ENGLISH DAISY—Splendid dwarf plant, early flowering. Does not always live through the winter in our northern sections. Prefers a moist but well-drained soil and will grow in shade. The plant is about six inches high.

FALSE INDIGO, or WILD INDIGO—*Australis* is a variety growing up to 40 inches in height. Flowers grow in clusters, pea-like. Rich, deep indigo blue. Closely spaced plants make a satisfactory herbaceous hedge, also used as a cut flower or as a border.

Flax—Light blue flowers which bloom in profusion from spring to summer. Easily grown, and likes a sunny location. Resents crowding since its light and airy branches seem to float out from the roots. There also is an annual variety.

Forgetmenot—Several varieties. Prefer good soil and shade.

Funkia—For use in shaded area. Its leaves excellent for flower arrangements. Several good varieties.

Geranium—Not used nearly enough in the Southwest, although our natives grow it handsomely in their windows. Easily grown from seeds or cuttings. Effective in pots for patio gardens and as house plants. Will not winter over.

Forgetmenot

Hibiscus—Dainty white, rose, pink, and crimson blooms, bell-shaped. The plant is shrub shaped, with enormous flowers in August and September. It needs protection from cold and winds, and does well in moist or dry locations. Will come up again in the spring even though it dies down in the winter. Flowers are glamorous for cutting, but close at night.

Hollyhock—Tall plants which grow straight up in single stalks into an artistic arrangement of leaves and ballerina skirted blossoms which provide contrast with our vivid blue skies and our native architectural walls and patios. The new double carnation varieties are exceptional. To keep them doubled do not let them reseed since they revert. Florettes floated in a glass bowl make a dainty luncheon centerpiece. To me hollyhocks are practically natives, since they harmonize so well with our native type homes. They make a lovely background and are valuable to use in the garden while small shrubs are attaining their size. Sometimes a little difficult to transplant, since they have a long, heavy root that must not be cut off.

Lilies—Grown easily from seed, which few gardeners realize. Will last for years once established. Blooms sometimes eight months after planting. See the chapter on bulbs.

Lupine—Not generally successful in the warmer areas, but can be grown in some sections where it is cooler and where the soil is more acid. The flowers need moisture. I have wanted to try them in the north spots of my garden to see if they will grow well.

Lythrum—Tall, showy plant which grows to about four feet in height with ease; is hardy. Gives a long period of bloom and adds bright pink to the perennial border. Morden's Pink bears phlox-like pink blooms.

Oriental Poppies—These gorgeous perennials should be put into their permanent beds in August or September. Each plant has one heavy root, so care should be taken when transplanting to get the entire root. To increase the plant, cuttings may be made right off the main root. During summer the plants die down so their resting place must be avoided when digging. New green growth appears in August, then they seem to remain inactive until the following April, when they rush up with a rapid, lush growth. April and May bring huge paper-thin flowers which remind us of crinkled crepe flowers. Their dark centers accent the petal colors. They like plenty of sunshine and good soil, without too much water. Once the gardener has glimpsed these, he is not satisfied without a representation in his garden.

Poppy

Barr's White is a good variety with purplish black spots in a white flower. Beauty of Livermore is the finest in dark crimson. Its petals can be sunburned so I generally place this variety where it may get a little shade. Helen Elizabeth is a fine pink variety, with a 34-inch stem, May Sadler is salmon, with black marking. Mrs. Perry is orange apricot. Watermelon produces a huge flower and is well named as to color. It seems unreal, with flowers seven and eight inches in size. Wunderkind, cerise, with sturdy growth. Wurtenbergia is glowing rose red of great size and substance. Common orange varieties are showy but more trying in the bed because of their color. The double ones are effective. Clumps do well year after year in one spot, increasing in size and beauty. The Iceland poppy is charming, providing an ideal cut flower when picked in bud. The plants are neat, compact tufts of bright-green foliage from which the graceful flowers rise. Do not always winter over in this area and may have to be treated as an annual in colder sections.

PAINTED DAISY (Pyrethrum)—Quickly and easily grown from seed, to bloom in late spring. Plants, when cut back, often will send blooms out late in the fall. Colors range from white through pinks and reds. Crested or double types very attractive. Valuable for cutting. Grows in shade. Chrysanthemum family. Protect from slugs and snails.

PEONIES—An old-fashioned garden favorite not grown extensively in this area. Do especially well in Santa Fe and Taos. Seem to prefer mountains and valleys to the plains section. I select peonies as to their ratings as well as to their color. Among those grown well in my garden are Festiva Maxima, Frances Willard, Lecygne, Longfellow, Mons. Jules Elie, Philippe Rivoire, Solange, and Therese.

PHLOX—Another "must" for every perennial gardener. They need room and they need good soil. Do well in this area where we irrigate. If the plants are set a little high in the border they will prosper. Do not allow them to reseed. A second blooming will appear if the plants are cut back after the first blooms die out, although they will not be as lush as the first. Nurserymen carry many fine varieties, so your choice will be only as to color preferences. Moss or Mountain Pinks are desirable for rocky spots and for edgings.

ROCKET (Sweet rocket)—Tall growing, biennial in colder areas. Very showy in the border. Appearance very much like phlox.

SALVIA (Ramona)—Long-spiked, bright-blue flowers which bloom through August and September. Unusual seed pods add to the attractiveness of the plant after the flower is gone. The stems have considerable blue coloring. Plants need winter protection. Patens is a species in deep rich-blue color. Farinacea Blue Bedder is showy.

SANTOLINA (Lavender-cotton)—Gray-green aromatic plant suitable for low borders. Its contrast of color with the green lawn is effective. Small, mustard-like flowers. Not hardy in northern sections of this area. May winterkill in Albuquerque, but comes back from the roots. Easily rooted from cuttings. I use a little sand in the soil mixture if it is heavy.

SCABIOSA—Fairly rich soil and sunny location for this flower. Color ranges through shades of lavenders and pinks. May be grown as annual.

SEDUM (Stonecrop)—Not too hardy, with the exception of the Purple Showy, with gray-green leaves and rosy, lacy flowers growing like powder puffs on the top of erect stems. A fine perennial for autumn bloom. More varieties hardy in warmer areas. Some low, trailing varieties are hardy.

SHASTA DAISY—A favorite with nearly everyone. Plants are hardy and like the sun. They multiply rapidly and provide masses of white flowers that are splendid for cutting. Alaska is a large white variety. Giant Double is lovely, likes a rich soil with an average amount of water. Edgebrook Giant is not as hardy nor does it increase as rapidly as Alaska. Mount Shasta is a popular double variety and an improvement over some other doubles. Readily grown from seed.

Shasta daisy

SNOW-IN-SUMMER—Creeping, mat-like plant with silvery white foliage and masses of tiny, star-like, white flowers. Likes well-drained soil and a sunny spot. Good for the rock garden or front of a border.

STATICE—Small lilac blooms on much-branched stems. Very dainty and lacy in effect. Wideleaf is a species with larger and deeper colored individual flowers with the same general effect. Likes plenty of room and good soil. Useful for cutting as a bouquet filler.

STOCK—Large fragrant spikes of flowers in a wide color range. Better as an annual.

SWEETWILLIAM—Showy flower heads with numerous individual blooms ranging from pink to deep red. Where the winters are severe a new planting should be made yearly. Newport Pink is a watermelon pink and one of my favorites because of its soft color which blends with so many things in the garden. Mass in one spot for best effect. Gives an old-fashioned color effect to the late spring garden. Often will not live through winter in colder section and, thus, better as annual or biennial.

TOADFLAX (*Linaria*)—Small, lilac-blue flowers on trailing stems suitable for rock gardens. Like a shady, moist situation.

TRITOMA or REDHOT POKER—Tall spikes topped with narrow tubular flowers ranging from orange to salmons and a new yellow called Primrose Beauty. Grass-like spiked foliage in clumps. Fine for border before blooming. Foliage desirable for flower arrangements. Springtime is a good variety.

VALERIANA or GARDEN HELIOTROPE—Smooth, with light gray-green color. Flower heads of very fine flowers in pink, rose, white, and lavender colors. Easily grown.

VERONICA—Speedwell has neat spikes of bluish lavender and purple flowers that are clean-cut in design. Neat and pleasing stalk. Excellent for line arrangements in bouquets. *V. longifolia* is a light lavender with dark blue tints, blooming in July and August. By keeping the dead spikes cut off, the blooming period can be prolonged. Easy culture.

VIOLET—Surprising that in a dry climate with comparatively poor soil the violet thrives well, multiplying happily. Not so fragrant, due to our lack of humidity. Native habitat is the woods and along the edges of streams, but in our gardens it provides borders and carpets of early blooms. Stems can grow up to eight and ten inches in length and the blossoms grow in white, pale lavender, pink, and purple shades. They like a rich soil, with lots of water.

WALLFLOWER—Old-fashioned English flower, producing abundant fragrant rich blooms, ranging from yellow to deep maroon. Petals velvety. One of earliest to bloom. Plant this at the base of yellow tulips for effect.

YARROW—Succeeds in any soil that is not too rich. Produces a round-headed, small, white flower which is a good filler in bouquets. A border plant used also in rock gardens. Sneezewort, the Pearl, is a good species.

Virginia bluebells

Columbine

Annuals

ANNUAL is the name ascribed to the flowers that complete their cycle within the year. They are planted from seed, grow to maturity, bloom, and die in the span of one gardening year. Thus the annuals can give a different look to the garden each year, for they can be selected on a seasonal basis. Annuals are satisfactory in that they grow easily and most annual seeds germinate quickly.

Perennials, when planted into a border or bed, remain for several years. It takes a couple of years for them really to achieve a showing, and they remain lovely for a long time. Peonies are a classic example. Grandmother's garden will reveal many a clump still beautiful, although untouched for years.

But with annuals, colors and ideas may be changed about. I love to tuck them into places near perennials to make their showing when the latter have fulfilled their blooms and faded away. My cutting garden always contains a few extra plants of marigolds, zinnias, asters, and other  annuals to dig up and slip into bare spots left by early spring bulbs. These have been transplanted as late as August with success. Often a half-dozen seeds are thrust into a bare spot, with a stick or garden label alongside as a marker. Frequently all six seeds germinate. This means pulling out all but the healthiest specimen. Annuals do not like to be planted until the ground really is warm, and this may be one of the reasons they pop up so well.

Annuals fill every need as to size, color, and shape, from the dainty sweet alyssum to the big, showy zinnias and the marigold collections. Newly planted gardens depend on annuals for landscaping effects that  cover up the barren spots until permanent but slower-growing plants mature. Cosmos grow to eight or ten feet tall now and are wonders as screens for unsightly objects. They screened my service yard in one garden. You may have a clothesline, a compost pile or a garage wall to hide. The castorbean is in this bracket. Its striking foliage, beautiful and glossy leaves, and colorful seed pods provide an excellent background plant in a season. The dustymiller with its woolly silver-white leaves is used here, and also yields leaves for attractive floral arrangements.

A cutting garden of annuals protects the main garden by providing blooms for indoor decoration and eliminates the necessity of destroying any artistic current seasonal blossoming of an "outdoor living room." At the same time, the cutting garden can be just as attractive as the "set garden" and is really an extension of your show place.

New varieties add excitement in the garden and we who play with these new plants wait eagerly to see what will develop. New specimens provide a large part of the joy of gardening. Nearly all varieties of annuals are good in arrangements, and all provide splashes of color well worth the effort of planting and cultivation.

Annuals sometimes winter over, in mild climates particularly, and can be enjoyed for several seasons. Annuals reseed themselves generously in many instances, making replanting unnecessary. Larkspur, bachelor's-button, and poppies are in this group. Double varieties sometimes do revert to the single type blooms when they reseed themselves.

Older and unusual annuals can be found by diligent searching through seed catalogues. More successful, as a rule, is a hint dropped to friends with old, established gardens which may result in gifts of plants or surplus seed. Seedsmen seem to be dropping a lot of old favorites, probably to make room for newer varieties that will be sold in greater quantity.

The annuals listed here are from my garden diaries of the past fifteen years in which I recorded successes and special attention. They are selected as known to thrive in this region. Descriptions include modifications for their proper care. Many varieties not listed here will grow in the Southwest. It would take an entire book to list and describe them and their culture. This list provides a good working basis for the beginning gardener.

ABRONIA, or SAND VERBENA—Indigenous to the Southwest, and one of the most attractive plants I know, but I have had little success with it in my well-prepared garden as it likes its sandy, arid habitat. Its seeds are slow to germinate and need warm weather to start their growth. Another love of arrangers.

AGERATUM—Grows in blues and lavenders from four to nine inches in height. Invaluable as a border plant, growing easily. Do not try to plant seed before weather is quite warm since this is truly a warm weather plant. Loves sunshine and takes ordinary culture. Blue Ball and Midget Blue are the most uniform dwarf types, and Blue Mink is the newest addition.

ALYSSUM—Often called sweet alyssum. A border plant of great merit. Its lacy spikes often start to bloom when the plant has not grown as much as two inches and it continues blooming until fall. Clipping back the plant restores its neatness. Plant very early in the cold frame and transplant or sow in its permanent place when the weather has settled. Violet Queen, Carpet of Snow, and Little Gem are good varieties. Royal Carpet—new and superior. Pink Heather—1959 All-America Selection.

ARCTOTIS—Sometimes called African daisy. Satiny flowers of fine texture. These close at night, so remember that when making bouquets. Grandis is a white variety. Hybrid varieties come in several colors. Do not plant in rich soil.

Hardy aster

ASTERS—Should be planted in every garden. Subject to wilt or "yellows" and for this reason buy only the wilt resistant seed and practice crop rotation. The improved Ostrich Feather type, American Beauty, American Branching, and California Giants are all excellent. The California Giants with single rows of petals and crested centers are to be considered, as well as the single varieties. I am partial to the imbricated pompon type, a small ball that keeps a long time and is fine for flower arrangements.

BABYBLUE-EYES *(Nemophila)*—Dwarf plant, about six inches in height. Sky blue blossom, grows quickly and blooms early. Ideal for borders and fine for edging and rock gardens. Dislikes being crowded in perennial borders. Reseeds itself.

BACHELOR'S-BUTTON or CORNFLOWER—Grows from a dwarf, compact, bushy plant about a foot high to plants several feet in height. All varieties do well, but a favorite is Jubilee Gem, a dark blue variety.

BELLS OF IRELAND—Wonderful for line in arrangements. Easily grown if planted in light soil in a sunny spot. My best plants come from seed broadcast in the fall.

CALADIUM—A glamorous-looking foliage plant that may be treated as an annual. It can be used in patios and does especially well in shade. Its variegated colors of green and white, with reds, also are excellent for flower arrangements. They require a rich, well-drained soil. They are hardy in warmer sections. Used with colors they can make a beautiful bed.

CALENDULA or POTMARIGOLD—Bright spot in any garden, but often creates a color clash if the bright orange variety is planted. Try softer colors in yellows. Easily grown and when planted in seed flats in the fall give exceptionally early bloom. Ordinary garden soil successful. Great size can be achieved by generous feeding.

CANDYTUFT—This charming little dwarf annual comes in white, shades of pink, and tones of lavender to deep rose. Ideal border plant. Easy culture. I prefer starting mine in seed flats rather than in open ground.

CAPEMARIGOLD—Mistakenly called African daisy. Similar in appearance to the Arctotis.

CASTORBEAN—Foliage plant from six to eight feet tall. In some warmer areas where it lives through the winter may become tree-like. Leaves from bright green to reddish bronze. Put seeds in the ground when weather has turned quite warm, planting about an inch deep. Germination sometimes hastened by scratching seed with a sharp instrument. Seeds are poisonous, so keep them from children. Crimson Spire is a beautiful red variety.

CHINESE FORGETMENOT—Blue flowers similar to popular forgetmenot. Grows easily, reseeds itself, and usually comes through in same color. Is eighteen to twenty-four inches in height.

COCKSCOMB—Adds spots of brilliant color to bare section of garden. Easily grown. Many curious forms which intrigue gardeners. Crested varieties plush-like. Giant plumed types in softer colors, particularly yellows, which are valuable for unusual flower arrangements. Many new hybrids.

COSMOS—Very easily grown. At one time this was one of the few flowers that grew easily in this area. Was introduced from Mexico. Once limited in size and color but now developed to unusual height and beauty. Grown in white, yellow, orange, and pink, among other colors. Ideal for backgrounds. Can become weed-like with their over-generous reseeding which provides countless tiny plants in the spring. New varieties are introduced each year. Sunset, All-America Gold Medal winner.

CHRYSANTHEMUM—Summer varieties. Easy culture, preferring heavy soil. Plants are reliable and bloom profusely.

COLEUS—Ornamental foliage plants generally used in the house, but should be used more outdoors in this area. Only a year ago I found how easily they can be grown from seed.

CUPFLOWER (*Nierembergia*)—Pronounce this with a soft or a harsh "g," but learn to say it, because you will love it and garden visitors will require you to repeat its name over and over. The dwarf plant has harsh, fernlike stems and leaves, six to eight inches in height and when in full sun the plant is covered with a mass of cup-shaped flowers in pale and deep lavender. Dwarf or Hippomanica is lavender blue, while Purple Robe is a deeper shade. Sometimes will winter over, but it's best to plant nearly every year to be sure.

Cosmos

DAHLIA—May be treated as an annual and grown from seed in both dwarf and tall varieties. Germinates easily. Comes in many varieties such as pompon, single, cactus, and decorative types. Needs rich soil.

DUSTYMILLER (*Centaurea*)—More valuable for the leaf effect than for flowers, which are small, lavender blossoms. Leaves very light, almost white gray, and delightful contrast to deep greens and colorings of flowers in a border. Leaves finely divided, with fine form for arrangements. Last long in water, so that new flowers may be added, thus leaves carry over into several bouquets. *Centaurea candidissima* fine for border. Has almost white leaves. Seeds for this are difficult to find. The plant grown by nurseries as *Centaurea gymnocarpa* or *C. cineraria* is usually *Senecio leucostachys*.

FEVERFEW—This chrysanthemum-like flower, tiny and crisp, is always a "must" in my garden. Grows prim and erect, with inch-size blossoms in clusters. Golden Ball is a variety with tall, graceful stalks with bright golden clusters much more attractive than the white variety. Long-lasting and ideal for corsages if you don't mind the wild and slightly medicinal fragrance. Easily grown and will reseed.

FLAX—Dainty red flower, about an inch across. Lasts only a day, but another blossom takes its place the succeeding day. Bush and flower present a picture of airy daintiness.

FLOWERING TOBACCO—Long, tube-shaped, petunia-like flower with petals forming a star. Very fragrant, especially after sundown. Self-sowing. Valuable as a cut flower, with tobacco-like leaf.

FOUR-O'CLOCKS or MARVEL OF PERU—Old-fashioned plant that opens in late afternoon, hence the name. Available in a number of colors. Often used as a hedge for large plots. Spreads quickly by heavy, bulbous roots which are difficult to eliminate.

FOXGLOVE—Has been a biennial, but Foxy, 1967 All-America winner, blooms from seed the first year.

GLORIOSA DAISY—A fine annual, showy and easy to grow, its diameter is seven inches. Its stems give it balance to make it excellent for large arrangements. It is a tetraploid rudbeckia.

HELIOTROPE—Fragrant, dainty clusters of tiny flowers above rich green leaves make this plant desirable. Succeeds in good soil and sun. Ranges from pure white to violet blue. Plants about two feet high.

LADYSLIPPER or BALSAM—Charming old-fashioned annual of lovely form, which blooms throughout early summer. Likes sunshine, and does well in poor soil. Reseeds and may revert to old magenta shades instead of handsome pink double variety which you ordered. A double camellia flowered type yields florets that are exquisite.

LARKSPUR—Found in most gardens and gives a big splash of color after the bulbs and iris have bloomed and before other annuals start. Scatter plant seeds in fall. If planted in cold frames, should be transplanted before warm weather arrives. Spring-planted seed germinates poorly unless refrigerated.

LOBELIA—Edging plant which should be started by seed in pots or seed flats early in season. Some gardeners have difficulty with this plant and must hunt around in their gardens for the right location. Can't take the hot sun. One year I put lobelia in front of the rose bed in the center of the garden, where it thrived. Ranges from white to deepest blue. The deep-blue flowers have plants with rich, dark foliage. Plants are compact and make a neat border. Favored varieties are the Cambridge Blue or Mrs. Clibran, an improved dark blue with a white eye. Crystal Palace is a deep, rich blue with dark foliage. Much more effective if not used as a mixture but of one variety in a border. Likes rich soil.

MARIGOLD—One of the best annuals, comes in almost any size from the tiny Signet to giant Climax F1 hybrids. No flower is being improved so rapidly. Yellow and Gold Nugget are triploids. These and the 1967 Bronze winner Golden Jubilee make a showy border with larger flowers for cutting. It will thrive in any soil, but the large types will grow to enormous size with extra care. The tall African near-white is the latest in color.

Morning Glory

MORNING GLORY—Valuable to shade a window until a properly placed tree will give the protection, or to hide a wall, climb a wire fence, or enhance a service area. All varieties like ordinary soil, not too rich, but full sun. Do not start really growing until the weather becomes quite warm. The Heavenly Blue is a handsome variety. Pearly Gates, a white flowered variety, is also attractive.

NASTURTIUM—Valuable for cutting. Does not demand much attention. Fills spots nearly everywhere. Longer stems developed in spots which are shaded during the day. Double type has almost replaced the old-fashioned single variety. Throat and veining of the single type are attractive and should be grown more. Tall double giants or Gleam types have a wide color range. I prefer the pale yellows and deep mahoganies rather than the brilliant orange. Dwarf double types are in many colors, and do not spread, thus are not apt to get out of bounds.

PAINTED TONGUE or *Salpiglossis*—Maroon to purple flowers, veined with gold and yellow, crimson and purple. Velvety and unusual blossoms which somewhat resemble petunias. Some have extremely good luck with this flower, others seem unable to grow it. My most successful stand, planted at the rear of the chrysanthemum bed, to be bloomed out and gone by the time the fall chrysanthemums became higher, was weeded out by a helpful maid while I was on a trip to California. She proudly informed me "your chrysanthemum bed was so full of weeds I just cleaned it all up for you." Does not transplant well.

PANSIES—Deserve a section to themselves for the pansy has made itself a favorite with everyone. One of the first blossoms to greet us in the spring, sometimes before even the tulip shows its pretty head. Vivid and fine colors give your garden personality. Fine strains are available. Long stems and good substance can be produced with a little extra care. The best seed available is my advice for pansies. Results compared with price are cheap when nearly every seed germinates with ease to produce a handsome, long-bearing plant. Oregon growers have worked wonders in hybridizing. Nothing will surpass the strains achieved by Mrs. Merton Ellis of Oregon. Ullswater Blue will take hot weather and gives good color and substance. Swiss Giant, and other improved Giants are recommended.

On arrival, my pansy seeds are placed in the refrigerator, where they are left until planting time. Order in August and plant in September. Start in flats outdoors in the fall, or indoors in the spring, using flats, boxes, or flower pots. The pansy seeds resent deep planting, so I barely cover them with soil. Deep planting can cause more failures in germination than any other factor. I cover the container or flat with paper or cardboard to keep the soil dark until after germination. See that the soil never dries, but use care in not over-watering, for then damping-off might result. A light feeding of liquid manure can be applied after several pairs of true leaves have formed. This will insure a good root system. I prefer leaving the plants in the flats over winter and transplanting in the spring. In southerly areas they can be put out about December into permanent beds for the winter. Straw used as a mulch will protect the plants should the weather become severe. Warm corners need no protection. When summer arrives, the pansy plant in the same warm spot begins to become uneasy. I usually do tuck a few into the warm spots just to assure blooms very early. The rest I plant in cooler spots for prolonged blooming. Don't feel too badly if you can't coax your pansies to bloom through the summer, for no plant gives of itself as generously in the spring as does this flower. I would rather count on a display in the spring and later concentrate on other annuals. Usually pansy plants become leggy as the season progresses. I find that planting on the north side doesn't produce plants as fine as locations where some sun reaches them.

Rich soil is needed when pansies are transplanted. I use a mixture consisting of manure, compost, and soil. My best blooms usually had a trowel of manure under each plant. Drop some soil over the manure so that the roots are not in direct contact until the plant is well established. Moist soil is a requisite. Blooms should be picked off frequently, with seed pods not allowed to form. Strains deteriorate if you allow pansies to reseed. Pansy plants are available at reasonable prices from nursery men, so it isn't necessary to grow your own plants. Many of us get a thrill out of producing our own. Pansies are good for borders and for individual beds. They make a nice carpet for spring bulbs. Root rot sometimes bothers them, when plants will turn yellow and sick looking. Dig up the plant that is affected and discard it. A cold water spray will remove any aphids discovered on pansies.

Ruffled Petunia   Pansy

Peat moss and compost mulches are ideal to use for a couple of months after planting. Slugs and snails love them.

PETUNIAS—One of the most satisfactory of all annuals. Can be used for many purposes. Lovely in flower boxes, borders, or large, showy beds. Range from dwarf plants with small, single blooms and brilliant colors to giant fringed types with beautiful veining and glamorous colors. All double petunias are showy but lack the striking beauty of the giant fringed types. Petunias are easily grown. Their seeds are among the smallest, smaller than a grain of sand, and are among the most expensive. Handle them carefully, setting them out in open ground when danger of loss from wind is passed.

Don't wash them out in irrigation. Start seeds in flower pots or the cold frame. The top of the soil should be sifted quite fine. Sprinkle lightly, then press the seed into it gently. Water by dipping a kitchen vegetable brush into water, then shaking it over the flat or frame. Don't plant on a windy day. Warm atmosphere is needed for germination, and stormy weather retards progress. Petunias like lots of sunshine and will reward the gardener with very large blooms if given good soil and careful feeding. Spare the water. Should a petunia appear that you would like to keep, dig it up for an indoor flower pot. Use a sunny window for the pot and it will provide many bright blooms. Self seedlings usually revert to single types. Many new varieties. Do not plant in same place over three years.

PHLOX—Easily grown and produces plants that are showy, ten to fifteen inches high. Excellent color range. Dislike being crowded among other plants, so do well in a bed by themselves. I like mass plantings for effect.

PIMPERNEL (Anagallis)—A dainty border plant, easily grown from seed. The vivid blue variety is attractive.

PINKS—Dianthus variety makes a nice edging, with plants growing eight to twelve inches high. Culture is simple, with ordinary garden soil required. Sweet Wivelsfield is a distinct race in itself, with large flowers in shades of pink, rose, and crimson. Nice for cutting, valuable in borders and the rock garden. Bravo, All-America winner.

POPPIES—California variety, most common, usually yellow or sunset shades. Flanders poppy is a vivid scarlet with black markings that has been familiarized nationally by Poppy Day sales. The opium variety has the most beautiful plant and flower, but sale of its seed is prohibited by law.

SALVIA—Colorful and charming for adding a brilliant spot in the garden. Blue shades excellent for arrangements. Splendens is a glowing scarlet. Is called a half-hardy perennial. Patens has extra large flowers of clear indigo blue. Likes sunshine. Free flowering and often lives through the winter.

SCABIOSA—A pincushion of a flower, also sometimes called "Mourning Bride." A good cutting flower of easy culture in white, rose, red, and lavender to deep maroon. Some varieties perennial or biennial.

SNAPDRAGON—Spikes of flowers that can be grown in several heights and many color varieties which make them useful for landscaping and for cutting. Best started in the seed flat, as the seeds are so small they may be lost if planted in the borders. If planted in warmer locations they can live from year to year, but new plantings give best blooms. Too many varieties to list. Select rust resistant kinds. Floral Carpet is a new border plant.

SNOW-ON-THE-MOUNTAIN—Green leaves, broadly veined and margined in white, with top leaves shading to near white and ending with florets in white and green tracery. Colorful as a foliage plant but its milky white juices irritate some persons allergic to it. Reseeds itself to the point of becoming a garden pest.

STOCK—Fragrant, erect plants in nice colors and greatly improved strains. Shades from white through pink, rose, lavender, and deep maroon. Dwarf, ten-week stock for quick blooms. Often winters through. Poor perennial plant.

STRAWFLOWER—Called Everlasting, and thus popular in winter bouquets. Colorful and trim.

Snapdragon

SUNFLOWER—Chrysanthemum variety, valuable as a screen. Seeds if left to grow after frost, which is nice for visiting birds. Many tall varieties with large heads filled with seeds.

SWEET PEAS—Rapid transition of winter into summer an obstacle to fine flowers. Fall plantings sometimes can solve this problem, yet an unusually wet winter can rot the seed in the ground. Santa Fe and other mountainous localities grow exquisite sweet peas. For warmer areas the north side of a fence is recommended for a cooler bed. Deep soil preparation necessary. Seed should be innoculated with a special preparation to enable the plants to utilize nitrogen from the air. Blossoms should be cut as they appear for continuing bloom. Sweet peas to me mean a quick splurge of beauty for a fortnight. Many are disappointed at the short blooming period. Judge for yourself if it's worth it. Cuthbertson varieties stand hot weather better. 1967 All-America San Francisco grows knee high.

SWEET SULTAN—Giant variety desirable for cutting. Blooms freely. Likes rich, well-drained soil in sections where the summer is hot.

SWEETWILLIAM—Old-fashioned flower with compact heads in mottled colors like a crazy quilt. Often lives through and lasts for years. Stems erect, leaves narrow, clean, and straight. My favorite is Newport Pink. Also listed as perennial. Vivid Red Monarch was a recent All-America winner.

TITHONIA, or MEXICAN SUNFLOWER—Tall, with dahlia type blooms three to four inches across. Good cutting and background plant. Blooms late in fall so should be avoided in early frost regions. Torch is a good new variety.

VERBENA—Needs little attention, but seeds can be slow and irregular in germinating. Once started will grow easily and well. Striking colors in beds. Scarlet or red for brilliant masses. A bed of pink verbenas edged with bright-blue lobelia is a vision. Amethyst was a recent winner.

VIOLA—Pansy-type flower but much smaller and daintier. In mixed colors or solid one-color varieties. Sutton's Apricot is my favorite. Yellow Perfection is deep yellow. Avalanche is snow white, while Admiration is a deep violet blue. Useful for borders and mass effects.

ZINNIA—The zinnia is intense in color, and varied in size, height, and form. Its variety makes it one of the important annuals. The plant will grow in almost any soil, with a minimum amount of water. Plenty of sunshine is advisable. Seeds germinate poorly in cold soil. When planted as late as May and June, germination often occurs in two days. Keep in mind, when selecting seeds, that plantings are more effective in one color rather than a mixture. The Cupid and Lilliput varieties are the small, pompon types, short-stemmed. On the opposite end of the list are the Giants: David Burpee, Giants of California, Luther Burbank, and the Dahlia type. In between are the Scabiosa flowered, Mexican, and Fantasy varieties. New F1 hybrids are enormous.

Sweet Pea

Zinnia

BULBS herald the coming of spring, for most of us think of those that do bloom in the early spring rather than the other varieties. Nor do we commonly think of the tubers, corms, and other bulbous root formations.

No flower seems to be appreciated more than the spring blooming bulb. First, a little nose of green appears, then the plant shoots up, and suddenly there are the bright spots of color so long and eagerly awaited. Gardeners wander about in their gardens as early as January to catch a glimpse of their little favorites pushing through the ground. Each day we measure and watch their growth, exulting in their buds, which seem to be the symbol of the excitement of spring's approach. The color of the blooms is so rich and bright they seem more beautiful than many other flowers, after the dullness of winter. Often their blooms begin in late January and early February. The scilla or squill is the first to force its way out of the earth.

Since true bulbs have their future flowers right in the bulb itself, we are almost assured of bloom from a new bulb. The bloom is not so positive after the first year. Bulbs need to store up food to nourish the flower for its next blooming. Neglect after blooming is often responsible for the lack of flowers the second year. Fertilize with high phosphorous food after bloom.

Since leaves manufacture food for bulbs, it is essential the plant be well cared for until it dies down naturally. Snip off the head of the bloom as soon as it is gone, leaving the stem full-length. Do not allow seed pods to form. One writer suggests snipping off the head before the petals fall because withering petals may harbor disease.

Tulips need their stems and leaves for healthy bulb growth toward the next season's blooming, so when cutting flowers for bouquets do not cut more of the plant than necessary for your purpose. Bloomed-out tulip plants need some food and water, although not too much. Most failures are caused from poor drainage of bulbs than for any other reason. This is a special point in growing good bulbs. Even in our region where we water by irrigation and the soil is dry by comparison, poor drainage causes damage. If the soil is clay or heavy, it can be made more friable and coarse by putting in a little sand and peat moss.

If the soil underneath is heavy and poor, this addition will do but little good. Thus, with bulbs, as for all general garden planting, proper and deep preparation of the soil pays dividends. Growers advise against using compost and manure for bulbs but I have for many years. Two to five pounds of superphosphate and cottonseed meal are used for each hundred square feet. Sand is put directly under and over the bulb so no fertilizer touches it.

Daffodils, narcissi, and jonquils can remain in their garden spot for a long period, but they will fail to bloom without sufficient food. Tulips and hyacinths do better when taken up every few years. It is wise to plant bulbs where there is no heavy shade. They will flower, since the trees and shrubs nearby are not yet in leaf and the sun can come through. Should dense shade develop after the bulbs have bloomed, their remaining plants will not get enough sun to aid in storing up strength for their next season's flowering. A few varieties don't mind shade. Some of my best tulips were in complete shade on the north side of the house. The Double Symphonia was as large as a peony, nor have I ever seen the Louis XIV so large and colorful.

Ideal bulb culture is to rotate crops and take them up each year. The average gardener doesn't always have the time or the space to do this.

Most of us with small homes put bulbs in the perennial borders. It is difficult to keep a good crop of them in such a bed, but we find it the best plan. The position in the perennial border is where we will enjoy the blooms most, and the border is greatly enhanced by their addition. The outlines of the border would be a dull display without their brilliance.

Dormant bulbs when in a perennial bed continue to receive food and water all summer with other materials in the bed requiring that attention. This is not relished by them and for that reason we cannot expect perfection in our bulb growing. It is thus we sometimes lose our favorites. The joy of that first spring burst of beauty is well worth it, and no garden should be without its scattering of them.

Planting in drifts of five to twelve in one color is much more effective in a perennial border. If you buy mixed collections, which are always good, at quite a saving in cost, use these in your cutting garden for bouquets and arrangements. Drifts can be enjoyed for landscape effects.

So much objection to the unsightliness of dying foliage of spring-blooming bulbs is held by the average gardener, that often such foliage is cut away in impatience, thereby injuring the chances of the delicate bulbs in their next season. More thought should be given to the original planting. Withering foliage would be unnoticed if the tulip had been planted behind a clump of oriental poppies, delphinium, iris, peonies, or one of the many perennials that rise up quickly to make a late spring display. Even if bulbs are planted in front of the border, good planning can present so much color to the eye that it will not immediately rest on ragged patches.

Daffodil foliage can be braided and pinned to the ground or tied upright in a sheaf. Experts frown on this.

Another of my practices is to plant annuals among tulips. These will surpass the browning tulip plant and cover it from sight. First the tulip plant shelters these tiny annuals until they are well started, and in turn the annual later will shelter the dying tulip plant. Close planting means everything must have more food.

Wait until the foliage is yellow or brown before taking up bulbs. The plant should be almost dead in appearance. As the clumps are dug up, place them on newspapers properly identified on the margins as to variety and color. When the bulbs are placed in an airy outdoor spot to dry, newspapers should be spread under them in their boxes to preserve their identification. An open garage is a good drying place. After a few days, the foliage and roots will be completely dry and can be removed. Do not remove the tissue-thin brown skin. The bulbs now are ready for storage in a cool, dark place. Net potato or orange bags are excellent to use for bulb storage. Be sure to include the names to keep colors separate. Store in a cool closet or basement. They need no attention and may remain in storage until a couple weeks prior to planting. I have found that refrigerating, which has been recommended for warmer areas, has merit.

Fall is the time to plant true bulbs. Although there are specified times for setting bulbs in the ground, I never hesitate to lift a bulb just past its blooming season to transplant it. Often (too often) bulbs become misnamed and a color combination is upset. Instead of waiting for it to wither, I just take up the odd one and move it to its proper color location, transplanting just as I would any other plant. Bulbs that I force for house use are handled this way. They have a better chance to store up food for the following year. Bulbs once forced seldom are good forcing material again. I always buy new bulbs for the purpose.

Forcing bulbs

Good soil
mixture

Charcoal and pieces
of broken flower pots

The best rule in each locality is to be guided by the season rather than by geographical location or the month of the year. Plant just after the first light frost, when the leaves have started to fall, and before they have turned brown from severe frost. By placing the bulb order in July, a gardener can avail himself of the special price offers made by growers and distributors. Late delivery sometimes delays the planting schedule. Many times my shipments have arrived a month after the best planting time. Those who order early seem to get preferred service and quality. Although I have planted as late as January and obtained blooms, the root system does not have enough time to develop large flowers.

Most new bulb growers are concerned about the depth of planting. Set rules cannot be made, although all growers provide charts indicating depth. Sandy mesa soils indicate greater depth for planting bulbs, while heavier soils, found in valleys, will allow more shallow holes. Articles have been written about deep planting to prevent bulb multiplication, thereby eliminating much lifting and dividing. I have not found any merit in this system although I have tried it in several areas. Why this is so I cannot tell, nor can gardening friends who have tried it without success. Should this method be attempted, keep in mind the soil must be cultivated to a greater

Plant in Fall

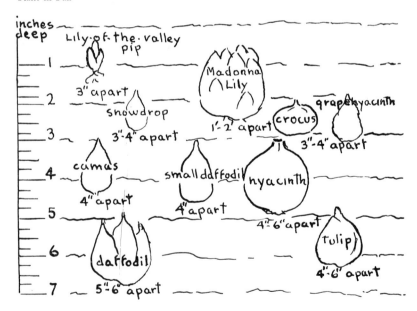

depth. Frankly, I plant bulbs in slightly more shallow holes than directed. This seems to give me better results.

Southern portions of the Southwest do not find bulb growing too successful. Gardeners in these areas must treat them as annuals. A good practice is to refrigerate them for a few days before planting. Later planting also is desirable. I would suggest they be planted in part shade, on the north side of the house, or in the coolest spots in the garden. It would be better, too, to plant the bulbs a little deeper.

Fortunately, not many diseases or enemies attack the bulbs in Southwestern gardens. Our dry atmosphere is protective against many ills. Should gardeners discover indications of trouble, much well-written material is available on the subject. With proper drainage, bulbs should grow easily and well.

Moles are troublesome in some regions, but I have never seen one. Mice and rabbits may be bothersome. Squirrels, another enemy to bulbs, are not common in our area.

Diseases such as botrytis or mosaic seldom are found. The former is more prevalent in lilies. The latter causes "broken" tulips. They become striped or a mixture of colors. Many growers like them that way and allow

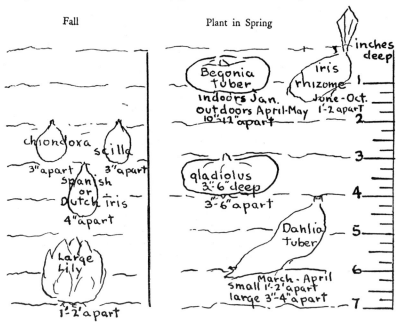

them to continue growing. Professional growers disagree as to whether the plant should be destroyed or allowed to grow. These two are virus diseases and are carried by aphids. Should you find aphids on your plants, give them the cold water spray treatment described earlier. I always discard a plant that is inferior. Never plant bulbs with soft spots in them.

Tulips, daffodils, and hyacinths are valuable for forcing for indoor bloom. Use large, shallow pots and arrange for drainage. Use a good potting mixture of compost, garden soil, and sand. Fill the pot about half way, then place the bulbs on this, so that the tops are a half to three-quarters of an inch below the lip of the pot. The bulbs may be close together, even touching, and can entirely cover the surface. Now cover the bulbs with the soil mixture. The pots can be left outdoors under a covering of leaves. I often put them in a corner of the compost heap, covering them with a few leaves. A cold porch or garage are good locations for them, with the pots placed in fruit boxes. Leaves, peat moss, or a vermiculite product may be used for covering. Keep the soil moist.

Hyacinth

When roots are thrusting through the drainage holes in the bottom and the tips of the bulbs are peeping through the tops, it is time to bring them indoors to a warmer, darker spot. I find my clothes closet just the place for them, remembering to spread newspapers on the floor for protection against water seepage. An inch-high growth indicates bulbs are ready for additional gradual light until they are finally transferred to a sunny window. At this stage they require more water for good growth. They thrive better if house temperatures are not too high. Some bulbs force well, while others won't make a special effort. Most growers mention varieties that will do well in indoor potting.

Listed are varieties of early-blooming bulbs too often not considered by the average gardener. They are colorful, easy to cultivate, and give rich rewards for the money and effort expended. Daffodils and tulips have been treated in a separated section following the list, since they are extremely popular in American gardens and there are many varieties.

Crocus

Crocus—Can be planted right in the grass itself, on the edge of borders or in corners. Their brilliant color will be the first in spring to catch the eye, blooming often through the snow. They grow easily and multiply rapidly. Tops should be two inches underground when planted, and can be set six inches apart. Divide every few years. There are many varieties and the new giants are most satisfactory. Colors range from white through yellows, lavenders, purples, and blues. Should they be planted in the lawn, their foliage should not be mowed off until they have had a chance to mature and recover for their next flowering season. Expect these bright patches to appear in late January or in February, to bloom for a month. Yellow crocus usually appears first. Purples are the last to bloom. Mammoth Yellow, Queen of the Blues, and Golden Goblet are fine varieties.

CHIONODOXA, or GLORY OF THE SNOW—Six-petaled flowers, very dainty and attractive, which bloom about the same time as the crocus. Plant two inches deep. Some are pink, but the *luciliae,* a lovely blue, is my favorite.

CAMASSIA—Blooms with long, graceful spikes that resemble veronica. Effective if planted in groups to a depth of three or four inches. The plants often grow four feet in height, and do well in any soil. Flowers are blue or white, and give added height to a bouquet. Leichtlini is a popular variety.

SNOWDROP—Among the best loved of the spring bulbs. They require little attention and like to be planted under shrubs or trees where the soil is moist and cool. Early to bloom. Should be planted three inches deep. Common or *nivalis* is the most popular variety.

HYACINTH—Loved for its fragrance and the waxy texture of its upright spikes of floret clusters. A wide range of colors that can be used for outdoor planting and indoor forcing. Double and triple rows in borders can be effective, but their expense always limits me to the usual single bordering row. Although recommendations are for planting four inches under the soil, I have been more successful with planting to a three-inch depth. My favorite varieties are: City of Haarlem (yellow), L'Innocence (white), La Victoire (deep rosy red), Princess Margaret (pink), Queen of Blues (light blue), and King of Blues (purple blue).

LILYOFTHEVALLEY—Grows from a pip, so is not a true bulb. Does well in the shade. Place where it can multiply, since it does so rapidly.

GRAPEHYACINTH—Tiny plants that look like bunches of little grapes with grass-like foliage that make appealing borders and are easy to grow. Their foliage comes up in the fall and by spring, when the flowers appear, looks pretty ragged. Although it is poor cultural practice, I sometimes just have to trim their foliage a little.

Muscari or grapehyacinth

SQUILL (Scilla)—One of the earliest to flower. More dainty in appearance than the hyacinth. Plants outdo themselves for two or three weeks. Flower is star-shaped, and hardy. Require little care and multiply rapidly. Mine grow about six inches high, although most catalogues describe them as growing three inches in height.

WOOD HYACINTH or SCOTCH BLUEBELLS—Each flower resembles the individual floret of the hyacinth. Come in white, pinks, and blues. Make a nice border for tulips and are good as cut flowers.

Scilla

DAFFODILS should be a part of every garden. Their varieties are so numerous and their forms and colors so varied that every taste can be satisfied. Nothing can take the place of the favorite King Alfred for mass effect, although it does have its rivals. Jonquilla Simplex grows in great masses in the south and can be used in many ways. New hybrids have brought pink into their cups. If you are as enthusiastic over daffodils as I am, you'll hardly know when to stop when making selections. Since I can never fit all the bulbs I want into my budget, I used to resort to collections, but now I have planted fine introductions, many from a hybridizer from our own Northwest, and growing daffodils has become my spring hobby.

Perhaps the most frequent complaint regarding daffodils is their failure to bloom. They'll grow good foliage, but stop at that. Failure to feed after the blooming period, crowded conditions, and insufficient sun to develop the buds are some of the reasons for this. Some clumps in my garden have not been divided for sixteen years and have produced sixty or seventy blooms. This is due to careful planting and feeding.

Space does not permit including divisions and classes of a few of my favorite daffodils. They are: Abalone, Angeline, Aranquez, Ardour, Beersheba, Binkie, Bithynia, Blarney's Daughter, Bonneville, Broughshane, Bushtit, Cantatrice, Ceylon, Chinese White, Duke of Windsor, Flicker, Foggy Dew, Galway, Geranium, Glendalough, Golden Crown, Honey ·Bells, Honeybird, Hunter's Moon, Jenny, jonquilla simplex, King Alfred, Kingscourt, Liberty Bells, Lord Nelson, Luna Moth, Lunar Sea, Mabel Taylor, Mrs. R. O. Backhouse, Mt. Hood, Nampa, Paracutin, Peeping Tom, Preamble, Redbird, Romaine, Shot Silk, Snowball, Snowdream, Spellbinder, Statue, Thalia, Tresamble, Trevithian, Trousseau, White Tartar, Zero.

Other bulbs are available that are seldom grown in this area and when grown do not seem satisfactory. Among them are the Mariposa, Anemone, Fritillaria, Fawnlily, Ixiolirion, and the Snowflake.

Daffodil

Narcissus
(jonquilla simplex)

TULIPS

Spring definitely is acknowledged with the advent of tulips in blossom. Beloved for their trim look and their color notes as well as for their early appearance, the tulip gives full promise to the richness and abundance of the approaching garden seasons.

Great variety in the color of the tulip leads to many combinations in the early spring garden plan. Too, the many variations of the tulip itself are endearing, although the modern Breeders and Darwins are the most stately of them all. Parrot tulips are being produced with greater color range than before until they are becoming the most showy and fantastic. These are the tulips with jagged and fringed edges, splashy with color. The double or peony types also are offered in a wide color range.

Old-fashioned, "cottage" type tulips carry the blooming season into May. Lily-flowered types are among the most graceful, while numbers of "species" types are almost unreal in their bizarre makeup.

Consider when planting that the tulip mixtures found in catalogue advertising are less expensive and are excellent for the cutting garden. But, remember, too, when planting drifts of tulips that they are most effective when scattered in patches of single color. Wise gardeners, those who need to consider the cost of anything for their flower hobby, buy good collections which they identify by color and name on their spring-blooming appearance. By replanting them for several years according to color and type production they soon have their color patterns lined up. By and large, tulips do not clash with one another even though their colors differ, and can be used in mixture more than most flowers.

Tulips are not as dependable year after year as other spring bulbs. They seem to lose their sturdiness and their flare after a season or two, sort of dwindling into rather ordinary performance. Therefore, greater care is required in the preparation of the tulip bed. By planting tulip bulbs among zinnias and petunias, which require less water, the danger of over-watering the bloomed-out bulb might be eliminated. Sometimes the back of the flower bed is a little higher than the front, thus allowing the water to run off the bulbs to the bordering plants below. In recent years I dig up the tulips each year, really treating them like annuals. By feeding them just after bloom is gone they multiply and produce excellent bulbs. This cuts down replacing them and money can be spent to try new cultivars.

Tulips listed here all have done well in my garden. There are many more, I know, that are available, such as the cluster of tulips blooming on one stem, called the multi-flowered variety, and the Chinese Lantern with its globe-shaped blossoms of iridescent hue. Species not often found here usually require special attention in location and other cultural requirements. They bloom earlier and in other ways simply are not as reliable.

Breeder, Darwin, and Ideal Darwin

Caroline Testout (pink), Charles Needham (red), City of Haarlem (cardinal red), Clara Butt (pink), Golden Age (yellow), Humming Bird (violet), Insurpassable (lilac), Indian Chief (copper brown, one of the best), Louis XIV (blue violet), Margaux (wine red), Mrs. Grullemans (white), Niphetos (yellow), Pride of Haarlem (brilliant rose), Pride of Zwanenburg (rose), Princess Elizabeth (rose pink), Queen of the Night (nearly black), Sunkist (yellow), The Bishop (purple), The Peach (salmon, with cream white base), White Giant (perfect white), Glacier (white), William Tell (raspberry red with lighter edged center and black anthers), Bacchus (violet blue), Chinese Bandit (orange bronze).

Cottage

Advance (red), Belle Jaune (yellow), Golden Harvest (yellow), G. W. Leak (orange red), Mongolia (yellow), Mrs. John T. Scheepers (yellow), Queen of Spain (yellow with pink edges), Rosabella (pink), Scarlet Glory (vermilion), Artist (terra cotta and green).

Lily Flowered

Fascinating (pale yellow), Golden Duchess (yellow), Yankee Girl (rose salmon), Mrs. Moon (yellow), White Cross (snow white), China Pink, Firefly (red), Maytime (purple).

Early Single

Generally shorter stemmed, DeWet (orange), Rising Sun (yellow), Keizerskroon (yellow, edged with red).

Early Double

Marechal Niel (orange yellow), Mrs. Van der Hoef (primrose yellow), Murillo (rose pink), Scarlet Cardinal.

Fosteriana

Red Emperor (vermilion red), actual flower one of the largest of all tulips. This one clashes with other tulip colors.

Tulipa Grullemanni

Inga Hume (golden yellow, touched with rosy red).

TUBEROUS BEGONIAS

Tuberous begonia

Tuberous begonias are one of the most glamorous of flowers that can be grown in much of this region. They prefer moist areas, but can be grown in warm portions of our Southwest in shaded spots or on the north side of a house or wall. They do not tolerate the western sun at all.

The tubers must be started indoors in January. They are planted outdoors in April or May. If the gardener doesn't want the bother of starting his own tubers, plants can be purchased from nurseries. Part of the fun of growing tuberous begonias would be lost to me if I didn't have the thrill of watching their little pink noses push out of the tubers.

Soil for begonias should be light, with plenty of humus. My mixture consists of one-half peat moss to one-quarter of sand and one-quarter of compost, adding a handful of cottonseed meal to each bucket. This is spread in a flat or shallow fruit box. The tubers are placed about six inches apart, with the concave sides up. Sometimes it is difficult to tell which is the top. By close examination you will discover on which side last year's root formations had grown. I press the tuber into the soil, but do not cover it until the plant actually begins growing. The soil mixture is kept damp, but not wet for too much water may cause the tuber to rot. Do not allow water to collect in the hollow section of the tuber when watering. As plants grow in size they can take more water, and their leaves will appreciate a sprinkle. No sun is required until the plant is growing. Then they will like a little sun from a window daily. Don't keep the flats in a room that is too warm.

Tuberous begonias
need to be pressed
lightly into the soil

Beds for the begonias should be prepared ahead of time with peat moss, manure, or compost. The mixture should be richer and lighter than for most varieties of flowers. When transplanting, take as much of the original soil up with each plant as possible. They should not be put into earth any deeper than they were in the flat, but the tuber can be covered with soil or peat moss.

Growers sometimes use flower pots instead of flats for starting tubers, bringing them, pot and all, into the garden bed. In that case, good drainage is important and over-irrigation must be avoided. During the growing season I sprinkle cottonseed meal, compost, or well-rotted manure about the plants. Fish fertilizer is ideal but is not generally available in stores in this locality.

Foliage of the begonia plants should be sprinkled daily in extremely hot weather. Soil around the plants should be kept damp. Do not over-irrigate, however, for since they are in a shady spot, the begonias will not dry out rapidly. Always sprinkle in the early morning.

Stems of this plant are extremely brittle, so staking is a necessity since the begonia grows a foot high and more. I use wire coat hangers for they are not so noticeable and can be bent into desired shapes.

Tuberous begonias have been developed into handsome forms and colors. Frilled begonias are available, also the carnation type that are specially crisp and effective. Single varieties are interesting, some with a crested ruffled center. Some can scarcely be distinguished from camellias, while others have the form of a rose. Colors range through white, rose, pink, yellow, salmon, and reds. Picotees are varieties with edges darker than the rest of the flower.

Although its rich beauty belies it, the tuberous begonia needs little care. Cultivating is not necessary. Pests almost never attack it. Disbudding is not necessary, and results are so rewarding. A begonia corsage always brings comment. When handling the bloom be careful not to break it. Use floral wire, forcing it through the center from the bottom of the bloom. Double the wire back and force it again through the center, this time from the top. Thus a loop is formed by the wire holding the flower erect and safe. Twist the two wire ends together to provide a firm support that can be worked into the rest of the corsage. Leaves from the euonymus shrub combine well with begonias.

Flat containers should be used when arranging begonias for the home, since their stems are not long. Soak them all night in the refrigerator or a cool place before arranging. Leaves of this plant are attractive and can be used with the flowers.

With the first frost, lift the plants carefully out of their bed and allow them to dry out in a protected place. Remove the dried stalks carefully, leaving none on the tuber. Clean the tuber, wash it well, dry it and store in a box filled with vermiculite. I sprinkle the vermiculite very lightly once or twice to keep the tubers from drying out in our desert atmosphere.

Tuberous begonias may be grown from seed, but only the experienced grower should try it, since they are difficult to grow in our dry country.

LILIES

Regal members of the flower world are the lilies, loved by everyone and attracting admiration by their sheer beauty of form. The lily's history goes into antiquity and its popularity has endured through the ages.

Lilies can be grown successfully in this region, culminating in perfection. Santa Fe has produced lilies that should satisfy the most particular grower, and I have had neighbors who grew the blooms with handsome results. I am looking forward to the day when I can try many more varieties than those which already have been represented in my garden.

Deep soil preparation is necessary for the lily bed. A well-known grower says to give the bed the same attention given to a rose planting. Lilies generally prefer a more acid soil so the addition of peat moss is necessary, while compost is an added help. Should the soil be somewhat heavy, use half sand, and to each bucket of soil add a small handful of cottonseed meal. Again, toss manure deep into the hole where the bulb will be planted.

Lilies are not planted as deep as was once taught. Some lilies root at the base of the stem and other sprout roots from the base of the bulb. For this reason, those with the former habit should be planted more deeply. The latter type, such as the Madonna lily, should be barely covered with soil. A general rule is to plant the bulb about the same depth in the soil as the thickness of the bulb itself. In heavy clay soil do not plant quite as deep.

Good drainage is important, as with other bulbs. Plenty of room should be allowed between bulbs, so as not to crowd the growing plant. Staking is a necessity. Most growers advise planting in the sun and in an open space, but with our almost too powerful sun and our strong winds, a spot where lacy shade patterns of a nearby tree can touch them is preferable.

One of the finest lilies I have planted was in complete shade, on the north of the house, and this is the desirable spot for this plant in hot sections where the sun is strong. Treat the faded flowers and stalks as other bulb plants. Long stems should not be cut if the bulb is to attain full vigor for the following season.

The development of lilies into more and more beautiful flowers is constant. Fine bulbs are grown in the Pacific Northwest. Be careful when purchasing to select the best, discarding bruised and damaged bulbs. Many growers dip bulbs in a chemical preparation designed to prevent disease. I find this unnecessary in our area.

Lilium shuksan

The most common diseases are the botrytis blight and mosaic, both a virus and sometimes introduced into the garden with the bulb itself. Proper drainage prevents much of it. They are not common here.

Compost and leaf mold are the best foods for lilies. A sprinkling of farmyard manure improves them. Well-aged cow manure is the best. Wood ashes are recommended highly for some areas, but are not beneficial in the Southwest.

Probably one of the most handsome combinations in the garden, utilizing the lily, is a planting of Regal or Madonna lilies in front of sky blue delphinium, both placed near a clump of pink oriental poppies.

Recommended as lilies that will tolerate an alkaline soil are: Auratum hybrids, Aurelian hybrids, Bellingham hybrids, Madonna, croceum, Davidi, elegans, Formosa, Giant, Hansoni, Henryi, Martagon, Olympic (Imperial strain), Philippine, Regal, Shuksan, Speciosum, Tenuifolium, Nankeen, Tiger, and Western Sunset.

GLADIOLI

Everyone loves gladioli, and no flower is lovelier for arrangements or easier to work with. Gladioli are simple to grow. Digging up their corms and storing them away until the next season is the only troublesome thing about them.

Corms of the gladioli seem more easily kept than those of the dahlias or tuberous begonias. They can be put in paper sacks, along with a few moth balls kept from actual contact which are a protection against the pest thrips. Store them in a cool place. Some growers soak the corms just before planting in a chemical guaranteed to protect them further against disease.

Planting may be started in March, with successions following each month so that the gladioli will continue blooming well into the fall season. As with other bulbs and tubers, good soil preparation pays dividends.

Almost any color fancy can be satisfied with gladioli. Groups in several colors in the perennial border can give attractive spikes, but they must be planted with sufficient room so other perennials will not be injured when the gladioli corm is removed for the winter.

Gladioli should be planted close together for effect. They need plenty of sun and should not be over-fed or over-irrigated.

Plant the corms four to six inches deep, depending upon the texture of the soil. If it is a heavy soil, four inches is deep enough. A six-inch space between corms gives enough room to each plant for development and at the same time they are close enough to support one another, eliminating the need for stakes.

No gladioli list is included here since this flower comes in so many colors and varieties that choice becomes a matter of personal taste and expenditure. Their culture is uniform.

DAHLIAS

Dahlias grown in this area have surpassed some of the finest grown anywhere in the country. They develop to perfection, in enormous size and with exquisite coloring, with very little effort. Good cultivation, staking, and disbudding are required for their success.

Numerous forms of the dahlia, in many sizes and many colors, are available. Unwin dahlias are grown easily from seed and they, as well as the miniature types, are excellent for cutting.

Don't be in a hurry in the spring to plant these flowers. April is time enough. The weather should be settled before the tubers, as the dahlia roots are called, are put into the ground.

Dahlias will tolerate an alkaline soil, and if their beds are well prepared with a mixture of compost, humus, or well-aged barnyard fertilizer, will require little more food. They like a sunny location, well drained and free from wind. Each tuber should be placed into its hole horizontally, its eye pointing slightly upward. Each hole should be deep enough so that three or four inches are above the tuber after it has been put into place. The soil is gradually filled in as the shoots come forth.

If the soil is rich in compost, it is not necessary to add fertilizer later, although a top dressing of manure or compost has been used to good advantage in my dahlia beds. Extra superphosphate is helpful. Water every four to seven days. Too much water causes the stalk and leaves to grow too fast, resulting in what is called "soft" growth.

Disbudding is necessary to secure the one large and perfect blossom on a stalk that is so desirable in dahlia culture. The unwanted buds should be picked off as they are forming.

Storage of the dahlia tuber sometimes is a problem. The tubers should be dug up just after the first killing frost. Lift them carefully from the ground so that the necks and stem ends are not broken. They should be dried off and stored in a cool place. Growers' methods vary greatly, but sand, peat moss, or vermiculite may be used to keep the tubers from drying. If the grower has a sandy spot, well drained and protected from cold, the tubers can be dropped into a hole and covered with sand.

Large types of dahlias, such as the cactus or decorative kinds, require plenty of space and do better if grown in beds by themselves. Allow two or three feet between each plant and four feet of space between each row.

Rich coloring, handsome and interesting shapes of the blooms, and the tall, woody green stalks of the plants themselves will lend the garden more fall variety. Since dahlias usually are tall, stakes should be inserted into the ground before the tubers are planted.

Literally thousands of dahlias are listed from which growers may choose. They range from the miniature, pompon, ball, and decorative through the singles, cactus, peony, anemone, mignon, and collarette groups.

Like any plant hobbyist, the dahlia fan should scour flower magazines to locate growers, get catalogues, study them, and make selections for color and form preference. Listed here are dahlias—a few I have grown, or would grow if dahlias were my particular hobby.

Descriptions to be found in catalogues: Amber Star, Arthur Godfrey, Avalon, Bertha Shone, Century of Progress, Cherokee Brave, Clariam Forever, Connie Casey, Croydon's Masterpiece, Danny, Drummer Boy, Frances S., Gerry Hoek, Gold Coin, Good Morning, Holland Festival,

Jane Lausche, Juanita Reedley, Lady Alice, Little Diamond, Lone Star, Mrs. E. J., Mrs. Thomas Edison, Mustang, Nepos, Nita, Orchid Lace, Perfectos Iva Jean, Pride of Holland, Priscilla, Val St. Lambert, Victory Maid, Vision, Wagschals Goldkrone, Yellow Spiral. Miniature (under four inches): Johnnie Casey, Animato, Maple Leaf, White Queen, Single: Jersey Maid, Kandy Korn. Collarette: Woody Woodpecker, La Cierva, Rococo, Pink Spangle. Orchid Flowering: Imp, Dandy, Twinkles. Pompon: Atom, Ted Thomas, Leslie Marks, Gold Dust.

CANNAS

A tall tropical herb, the canna is valuable for great splashes of color. Its foliage, especially the bronzy shades, is prized by flower arrangers. The plant needs plenty of room and does well without special attention if bed is enriched with compost and manures in preparation for planting. The roots are tuberous and in cold areas need to be stored over winter. Do not plant early as warmth is needed to promote growth and to mature. Spacing about twenty inches apart is sufficient. New varieties are a great improvement over the old and colors besides red, range from yellows through corals and rose. Pfitzer's new dwarf varieties are popular, and Primrose Yellow, Shell-Pink, and Porcelain Rose are examples. Other good varieties are Aida, Mme. Butterfly, and Rigoletto.

AMARYLLIS

When I wrote this book I had some amaryllis outdoors, and never dreamed they would winter so well. One clump is fifteen years old but it did suffer one winter with record low temperatures. Since then I have tried them in several spots in protected, partially shaded areas. When the new bulbs are purchased they are used for house plants, often bringing them into bloom for the Christmas holidays. After danger of frost has passed they are planted in the garden in well enriched light soil. When I get the bulbs in late fall they are set on top of quart fruit jars filled with water, with the roots hanging in the water, and left for a couple days. A large enough pot is selected for planting so that there is an inch between the bulb and the pot. A rich porous potting soil is used. When growth starts, a weak solution of plant food is used. It is continued every few weeks and after flowering to nourish the bloom for the next season. If kept for house plants it is still best to sink the pot in the soil outdoors and in late summer withhold water. When grown in the garden, cover with leaves for winter protection.

Roses

THAT THE DESERT SHALL BLOOM LIKE A ROSE is becoming literally more true of this area. Rose lovers are doing more each year to grow these blooms successfully. Though we have to adjust our soil conditions in many places, and although irrigation is bothersome, we do not have as many diseases and pests to fight as in other parts of the country.

To cover adequately the subject on how to grow roses in the arid Southwest would take a book. The area is one of the fastest growing in the nation and a large percentage of the residents are new gardeners— many have never grown roses before. Included here are many points elementary to the experienced grower. The chief differences from other sections of our country are: lack of rainfall, hot bright sun, strong winds, and generally an alkaline soil completely devoid of humus. It may be sandy, adobe, or (heaven forbid!) caliche. When roses are well-grown they will compare with any grown elsewhere—and their brilliance of color—Oh, so wonderful!

I have attended over twenty American Rose Society Conventions in the United States and have seen roses in Europe and Canada and there are few places where they grow better than here. Our foliage may have thorn pricks due to wind, but the texture and color of the blooms are superior. Several times our rosarians have taken top prizes from Californians in rose shows.

LANDSCAPING

(1) Have design in keeping with house. (2) The smaller garden should be simple in design. (3) Select colors to complement the exterior and interior of the house. (4) Grouping of colors, or tones of a color, are more effective from a distance. (5) Have little "personality spots" of outstanding plantings (just as a lovely grouping of furniture in a living room). (6) Use climbers for background planting or to trail over doorways or along the eaves. Pillars or Grandifloras for height. (7) Shrub and old fashioned roses make good backgrounds—Floribundas give mass color effects. (8) Roses should receive at least six hours sun a day (morning

sun, afternoon shade ideal). (9) Climbers should be placed at least a foot from hot south or west walls (on trellis, if possible). My climbers are tied to two inch pipes about eight feet high and set in cement. At the top there is an arc made of strap iron and the ends are set in the pipes. Pipes are about eight feet apart and surround the whole wall around the patio garden. Old nylon hosiery is cut up the back and then in strips crosswise, and these are then used to tie the climbers to the support. (10) Aeration is better if Hybrid Tea beds are not too close to garden wall or house. (11) Place where they can be enjoyed from important living areas, so windows frame a picture. (12) Plant far enough from "food robbing" trees and shrubs. (13) Make plan on paper first to see how it fits space. (14) Protect from winds with fences, trees, etc. (15) Beds should be small and narrow enough to work easily without stepping on soil around bushes. (16) Beds should be four to six inches lower than surrounding grass walks, etc. to hold irrigation water.

KIND OF ROSES TO PLANT

(17) Grafted stock superior to "own root." (18) Root stock of Dr. Huey (Shafter) or Ragged Robin is most satisfactory. (19) Hybrid Teas (our most beautiful roses). (20) Climbers for background, screening, over doorways trained along eaves. Pillar and Grandifloras for height. (21) Shrub, Moss and Musks for background planting—Miniatures can be used for borders or in planter boxes. (22) Buy good quality roses from reliable nurseryman or grower. Bargain roses—No! (23) On receiving roses put roots into thin mud or solution of foliar food or a little compost. (24) If planting must be delayed, "heel" them in a protected spot and wet down.

SOIL PREPARATION

(25) Soil preparation is of number one importance. Best done in advance. (26) Two inches manure or compost over area with three to four pounds each soil sulphur and superphosphate. (27) Spade deeply and irrigate well to be sure drainage is good—keep damp until planting.

PLANTING

(28) At planting time (January to March, depending on the area and before winds) dig generous pear-shaped holes 30″ to 36″ apart, and deep

enough so roots will not be crowded. (29) Top soil placed at one side—sub-soil on other. (30) Mix with top soil, a shovel of peat moss, one-fourth cup soil sulphur, one-half cup superphosphate. (31) Put shovel manure in bottom of hole, dig in, scooping out sides at bottom. (Growers disapprove of this but for thirty-five years it has worked for me.) (32) Make cone of top soil mixture—place rose, spreading roots over it. Fill with balance of top soil. (33) Tamp soil (not hard enough to tear roots). Water slowly. (34) The crown, or graft, should be ground level (or a little above as it may sink), and should face southeast. In warmer climates the graft can be an inch or two high and as much lower in mountain areas. Failures are often the result of placing the crown too deep. When settled, it should barely be covered with soil. (35) Hill the bush with sub-soil to protect from wind, or make a cylinder of roofing paper or use a heavy sack with the bottom removed and place over the rose. Fill with a mica product such as Terra-lite which has been saturated with water. (36) When buds start to break and weather is warmer, gradually remove this hill by washing it away with hose. Have boxes or sacks ready to cover a plant with tender young growth in case of a sudden storm. (37) Compost (if completely decomposed) may be used to fill in hole. Mix with top soil and some coarse sand. My best success from this. Every rose grower should make compost.

Preparing the hole
for planting a rose

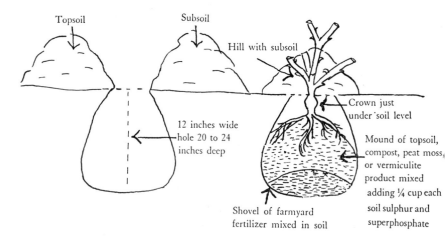

Topsoil

Subsoil

Hill with subsoil

12 inches wide
hole 20 to 24
inches deep

Crown just
under soil level

Shovel of farmyard
fertilizer mixed in soil

Mound of topsoil,
compost, peat moss,
or vermiculite
product mixed
adding ¼ cup each
soil sulphur and
superphosphate

FEEDING

(38) Continued feeding is important when plants are growing and established. Fertilizing after each cycle of bloom is good practice. (39) After pruning, add two inches manure which should be spread over the bed (use less of goat or sheep manure). (40) Because of the high pH I never use bone meal or wood ashes. (41) When buds appear, use my "rose brew," 100 pounds cottonseed meal, 10 pounds each superphosphate, ammonium sulphate, iron sulphate, magnesium sulphate, and soil sulphur. One-fourth to one cup per bush, depending on size, 5-10-5 or sewerage sludge may be used. (42) Foliar feeding every two weeks is fine. (It will never replace soil feeding.) (43) Additional manure or compost can be added as needed. (44) Add fertilizer when soil is damp. The day following application, irrigate thoroughly. (45) In early fall, use the "rose brew" again, and superphosphate. In ten year old gardens, use potash. (46) Because of frequent irrigation, more food should be used than in other areas. (47) An application of product of trace elements once during the year helps one of our big problems—chlorosis. This may be caused by nutrients being locked up due to high alkalinity and by too much water. Iron sulphate, applied after irrigation is helpful. Dissolve one-fourth cup in two gallons of water and pour it around the bush. The same amount of magnesium sulphate may be used. Iron chelate used on the soil or as a foliar food (if weather is not too hot) is preferred by some rosarians. Follow directions explicitly. (48) My best roses of all times were when I used an inch of manure each month from March to September. Prices now will not allow this. (49) Never get fertilizer on foliage or too close to plant.

How to plant a rose

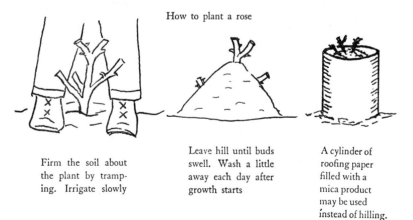

Firm the soil about the plant by tramping. Irrigate slowly

Leave hill until buds swell. Wash a little away each day after growth starts

A cylinder of roofing paper filled with a mica product may be used instead of hilling.

IRRIGATION

(50) Irrigate thoroughly and not too often. My average is each five to seven days. (51) Irrigate newly planted roses only enough to keep soil damp. (52) Overwatering can kill roses before roots are active. (53) Winter irrigation is essential when soil is dry. (Even in winter we have wind and sun.) (54) Irrigate in early morning to avoid mildew. (55) Do not

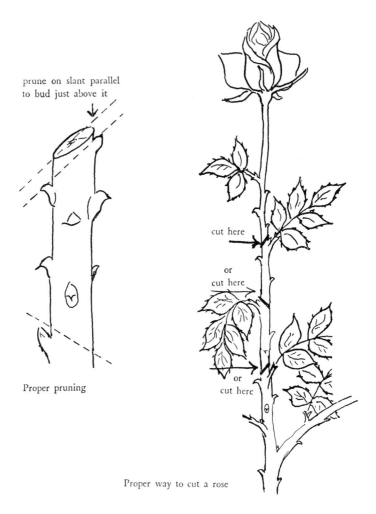

prune on slant parallel
to bud just above it

Proper pruning

cut here

or
cut here

or
cut here

Proper way to cut a rose

irrigate so much the food is washed to sub-soil. (56) More failures in rose growing in this area result from overwatering than any other cause. (57) Mulching conserves moisture—manure, compost, sawdust or dried grass clippings (use added nitrogen), buckwheat hulls (they do not stay put in heavy winds), peat moss and cottonseed hulls. (58) Every garden's soil is different and experience tells a gardener when to water. (59) Light and frequent irrigation causes feeder roots to grow close to surface and they are easily injured from heat and wind.

PRUNING

(60) Use sharp, clean pruning tools. A rosarian should own good pruning shears, a pruning saw (I like a key hole saw for narrow crotches), a lopper and a file to keep them sharp. (61) Delay pruning as long as possible in spring (around March). (62) When the buds swell—prune. (63) Prune oldest canes back to crown. (64) Open up center of plant. (65) This does not always work, but generally prune one-third number of canes and one-third height. (66) Make diagonal cut just above bud. (67) Select outside bud pointing away from the center of the bush. Experts advise using pruning paint to seal canes over a half inch. There are some new preparations that are colorless and claimed to be good. I boil thin mud and find this just as satisfactory in this dry sunny climate. (68) If bush has a sprawling habit, then prune to inside bud. (69) Remove twiggy growth and crossing branches. (70) Do not "whack" bushes. Some roses do not do well when pruned severely and the grower will have to learn from experience how a rose should be pruned. Peace is an example of a rose that should not be pruned too much. Grandifloras and Floribundas require little pruning. Some years weather will dictate how much a rose should be pruned. If the pith is brown, it is necessary to cut it back to white wood. (71) New bushes generally are pruned by growers. Wait until bush is established before pruning, if needed. (72) Do not prune roots of bushes to be planted unless excessively long, injured or broken. Some growers recommend pruning tops and roots of new roses quite a bit, but I have had poor results in trials. (73) Always keep in mind the shape of bush when cutting roses or faded blooms. (This is summer pruning.) (74) In fall, prune only very long canes that may be broken in the wind. (75) Prune climbers after bloom has gone. Very old, dead or twiggy growth may be pruned in February.

PEST CONTROL

(76) Wash dust from foliage weekly (and we do have dust!) (77) A clean-up spray after pruning most important of year. When mildew is exceptionally bad in the fall, this spray should be used in December or January. (78) For aphis, wash off with hose of cold water in heat of day. (Spray if you must). (79) Proper "morning" irrigation helps prevent mildew. (Of course, if we ever have rain, it's always late in the day or at night.) (80) Use insecticides from reliable dealers and manufacturers. (81) Remember birds, bees and helpful insects (yourself as well) when you use dangerous poisons. (82) Many bugs can be hand picked. (83) Blackspot is not a part of our problem yet (thank heavens!), although it has appeared in isolated cases. It is important to follow the irrigation schedule outlined. There is recent evidence that extra applications of potash are helpful in preventing plant diseases. (84) Dust only if the temperature is under 85°. (85) Spray only in cool part of day—the day following irrigation—burn from spray will do more damage than what you are after. See pests and diseases.

CUTTING BLOOMS

(86) Always leave two or three sets of leaves on stem. (87) Cut very few, with practically no stems, from newly planted bushes. (88) Cut short stems from first cycle of blooms. (89) Do not cut off at first set of leaves (usually a group of three). (90) Always cut above a five-leaf group. (91) Make the cut a diagonal just above the leaf in a parallel line to direction of leaf. (92) Never break off buds—cut properly. (93) Cutting faded blooms daily is desirable—(if we just had more time). (94) When cutting to arrange, slit stem end for an inch—plunge in hot water. (95). Cut in early morning, or best in late afternoon. Put in an inch of hot water. When cool, fill container with cool water. (96) Harden in a dark, cool closet (few of us have basements here) for several hours, or overnight. (97) If storing for several days is necessary, resort to icebox (it may change color).

GENERAL

(98) Belong to American Rose Society, Pacific Rose Society, and local rose or garden group—read all you can. (99) In winter, hill roses in cold yards for protection from winds—put a couple inches soil over crown in

My most efficient
insect eliminator

winter in warmer areas. I put six inches of leaves over the rose beds. Some disagree claiming this is a sanctuary of insects, but I cannot see this is true. (100) Disbud Hybrid Teas for finer specimens—collect vases to go with house and roses—have fun arranging this most perfect of all flowers.

Few roses fail to do well in the Southwest if they receive the proper attention. Some tender bushes, such as the Marechal Niel climber might winterkill in the northern sections but will carry over beautifully in southerly portions. Such a rose planted on my south wall died back to all but one or two eyes in eleven degrees below zero temperature that my garden experienced one winter. It did come back, even producing a few blooms the next season.

White roses seem harder to grow than others. The wind injures the blooms, but thrips are the chief enemy. The buds ball, brown about the edges, and fail to open. As for other colors, they run the gamut of the catalogues, rich velvety reds, salmons, rose, yellows, in dozens of shapes and varieties, until the heart melts with their beauty.

Floribundas are excellent for landscaping. They can be massed for effect as are azaleas in the South, with hedges of color along sunny lanes. Our arid regions can grow the Floribunda rose to flourish with beauty and satisfaction since this species is being developed rapidly. The Permanent Wave variety could, in the distance, be mistaken for an azalea. The Floribunda will bloom continuously until after the first frosts, and some have bloomed in temperatures as low as 26°. It needs no special care. Keep it in mind for low planting under windows or against fences.

The Grandiflora is a cross between a Hybrid Tea and a hybrid Polyantha or Floribunda. It grows taller than either parent generally and the flowers have a Hybrid Tea form. Recent introductions do not have the inflorescence that is characteristic of the Floribundas. The flowers have fine long stems which make excellent cut flowers even though the blooms may be smaller than a Hybrid Tea. In fact, it is becoming more difficult to tell this new race from the Hybrid Tea. I wish some varieties did not grow so tall. Queen Elizabeth sulks when I prune her to keep her from growing tall.

Miniatures are low-growing roses generally under a foot in height with eighteen inches permissible if other characteristics are present. Stems have short internodes and foliage is small and in proportion to the flower. The leaves have three to five leaflets averaging one-half to three-quarters inch or less. Flowers may be single or double and less than one-and-a-half inches in diameter. They are borne singly or in clusters that do not exceed ten buds or flowers. The past few years great strides have been made by hybridizers and these little roses are possessing all the beauty of form of the better Hybrid Teas. The color range has increased and with it added enthusiasm for these beautiful little flowers. They are hardy, but in this area they are growing so well the plant gets too large in many cases. In damper climates they are grown in pots, but here it is difficult to keep them watered. They come in tree form and these are very decorative. They are beautiful at the base of a piece of statuary, a bird bath, or in planters.

Many rose types should be encouraged in the Southwest. Grand-mother's garden will yield many choice species, such as the moss and musk roses. Some might say "yes, but they bloom only once," to which the reply might be that many of the best shrubs bloom but once, too, yet their beauty is worth the effort and space devoted to them. The foliage of these old-fashioned roses, properly fed, is green and shiny and lasts far into the late fall and early winter as a color contrast to our blue skies. Their fruit or hips are colorful, too.

Tree roses generally are not satisfactory here because of dry atmospheric conditions and winds. They can be grown in protected areas under tender care. During severe winters they must be bundled. Stakes supporting the tree rose detract from its appearance. For me a tree rose does not produce enough extra beauty to justify the grooming lavished upon it. Future rose growers may find a stock developed that will be strong enough to withstand some of these detractions, especially wind.

Improvements are being made consistently by hybridizers. Big winners sometimes do not stand up through the years. Some roses, that should be given more of a chance, are dropped from lists by growers. All in all, amateurs are fairly safe, however, in ordering most items in the catalogues.

Roses are the most versatile of flowers. Should I have a choice of one flower it would be the rose. It is not used nearly enough in landscaping. Its long periods of bloom, its harmonizing colors and interesting growth habits can make a garden beautiful with "only a rose."

The following list of roses includes those known to grow successfully in the Southwest. The rose varieties are listed in color groups according to types. My favorites are starred(*).

HYBRID TEA

White or Near White—Blanche Mallerin, Dresden, *Frau Karl Druschki (hybrid perpetual), Jackman White, John F. Kennedy, Matterhorn, *McGredy's Ivory, Pedrables, Rex Anderson, Sincera, Snowbird, Sweet Afton, Virgo, White Knight, White Queen.

Light Yellow—*Burnaby, Joanna Hill, Lemon Spice, McGredy's Yellow, *Mme. Chiang Kai-Shek.

Medium Yellow—Arlene Francis, Debonair, *Eclipse, Golden Masterpiece, *Narzisse, Soeur Therese, Sunlight.

Deep Yellow—Amarillo, Golden Rapture, *Golden Scepter, Isobel Harkness, *King's Ransom, *Lowell Thomas, San Luis Rey, Summer Sunshine.

Yellow Blend—American Heritage, Butterscotch, *Champagne, Chief Seattle, Diamond Jubilee, Fred Howard, *Grand-mère Jenny, *Joanna Hill, *Lady Elgin, Mme. Joseph Perraud, *Peace, *Personality, *Sutter's Gold.

Apricot Blend—*Angels Mateau, Apricot Dawn, *Invitation, McGredy's Salmon, Moonlight Sonata.

Orange & Orange Blend—Autumn, Bettina, Condesa de Sastago, *Duquesa de Penaranda, *Fred Edmunds, Girona, Horace McFarland, *Lady Elgin, Mark Sullivan, McGredy's Sunset, Mojave, *Mrs. Sam McGredy, *Pilar Landecho, Signora, *Tanya.

Light Pink—*Blithe Spirit, Dame Edith Helen, Eternal Youth, *First Love, LaFrance, Lucky Lady, Memoriam, *Mme. Butterfly, *Mrs. Chas. Bell, Nobility, *Ophelia, *Picture, Pink Princess, Radiance, *Royal Highness, Susan Louise, Suzon Lotthe.

Medium Pink—Bewitched, Bermudiana, Capistrano, Columbus Queen, Curly Pink, *Duet, Editor McFarland, *Eiffel Tower, Henry Ford, Juno, J. Otto Thilow, Katherine T. Marshall, Lulu, *Mary Margaret McBride, Pink Favorite, Pink Frost, Pink Lustre, Pink Peace, Santa Anita, *Show Girl, South Seas, *The Doctor.

Pink Blend—Allure, Angel Wings, *Anne Letts, Chicago Peace, *Confidence, *Comtesse Vandal, Edith Nellie Perkins, Fantastique, Gail Borden, Good News, *Granada, *Helen Traubel, Isabel de Ortiz, Kordes' Perfecta, La Jolla, Las Vegas, Los Angeles, Love Song, *Michele Meilland, *Mme. Cochet-Cochet, Mrs. Lovell Swisher, Pink Masterpiece, San Gabriel, Silver Lining, Sonata, Swarthmore, *Sweet Sixteen, Taffeta, Talisman, *Tiffany.

Light Red and Deep Pink—*Applause, Best Regards, *Charlotte Armstrong, Eden Rose, Paris Match, Red Radiance, *Rubaiyat, Tallyho, Texas Centennial, Tom Brenneman.

Orange Red—*Aztec, Hawaii, Polynesian Sunset, *Simon Bolivar, *Tropicana, Valencia.

Medium Red—Bob Hope, *Bravo, Christian Dior, *Christopher Stone, Ena Harkness, Etoile de Hollande, Grande Duchesse Charlotte, Grand Slam, Hallmark, Jamaica, Lotte Gunthart, Mr. Lincoln, New Yorker, *San Fernando.

Dark Red—American Flagship, Ami Quinard, Avon, Charles Mallerin, *Chrysler Imperial, *Crimson Glory, Hearts Desire, *Midnight, Mirandy, Night, *Nocturne, Oklahoma, Papa Meilland, Red Talisman.

Red Blend—Aztec, Flaming Peace, *Forty-niner, Hector Dean, Living, Mexicana, Mme. Henri Guillot, *Opera, Rose Gaujard, Saturnia, Suspense, The Chief.

Singles—Cecil (Yellow), Collette Clement (Coral), Dainty Bess (Pink), Golden Wings (Yellow), Innocence (White), Isobel (Apricot Blend), Oriental Charm (Red), White Wings (White).

Mauve—Lavender Charm, Lavender Queen, Song of Paris, Sterling Silver.

FLORIBUNDAS

White—Dagmar Spath, Irene of Denmark, *Ivory Fashion, *Saratoga, Summer Snow, White Bouquet.

Pink—*Betty Prior, Cecile Brunner, China Doll, County Fair, *Else Poulsen, Frolic, Gay Princess, *Pink Bountiful, *Pink Chiffon, Pinkie, Pink Rosette, Rosenelfe, *The Fairy, *The Farmer's Wife.

Yellow—Gold Cup, Goldilocks, Starlet, Yellow Pinocchio.

Blends—Apricot Nectar, Betsy McCall, Circus, Easter Parade, Fanfare, *Fashion, Fashionette, Fusilier, Golden Slippers, Jiminy Cricket, Ma Perkins, Little Darling, Margo Koster, Masquerade, Pinocchio, Roman Holiday, Sarabande, Siren, Vogue, Winifred Coulter.

Orange Red—Ginger, Heat Wave, Woburn Abbey.

Red—Alain, Baby Blaze, *Chatter, Crimson Rosette, Donald Prior, Eutin, *Floradora, Frensham, *Garnette, Lilli Marlene, *Permanent Wave, Redcap, *Spartan, Tom Tom, Valentine, *Wildfire, World's Fair.

Mauve—Lavender Princess.

Leave paths wide enough for the lawn mower

GRANDIFLORAS

Buccaneer (dark yellow), Camelot (pink), *Carrousel (dark red), Dean Collins (light red), El Capitan (red), *Gov. Mark Hatfield (red), John S. Armstrong (dark red), June Bride (white), Merry Widow (dark red), *Montezuma (orange), Olé (orange red), *Pink Parfait (pink), *Queen Elizabeth (medium pink), Roundelay (dark red), Starfire (red), Yellow Queen Elizabeth (medium yellow).

MINIATURES

Baby Betsy McCall, Baby Darling, Baby Masquerade, Beauty Secret, Bit O'Sunshine, Cinderella, Coralin, Dian, Dwarfking, Eleanor, Jet Trail, June Time, Little Buckaroo, New Penny, Pink Cameo, Red Imp, Sweet Fairy, Yellow Doll.

CLIMBERS

White or Near White—*City of York, McGredy's Ivory, *Silver Moon, Lemon Pilar.

Yellow—Golden Emblem, High Noon, Mrs. Pierre S. du Pont, Royal Gold.

Blends—*Bloomfield Courage, *Frances Lester (Musk), Gloire de Dijon, Mme. Henri Guillot, Mrs. Sam McGredy, Peace, *Reveil Dijonnais, Royal Sunset, Sierra Sunset, Talisman, Wind Chimes (Musk).

Pink—*Chaplin's Pink, Dainty Bess (single), Dame Edith Helen, Ednah Thomas, *Kitty Kinnimonth, *Mme. Gregoire Stachelin, New Dawn, *Picture, Sparrieshoop.

Red—Blaze, Chrysler Imperial, *Crimson Glory, Don Juan, Dr. Huey, *Etoile de Hollande, *Paul's Scarlet.

Note: Many Hybrid Teas can be had in climbing form—they produce beautiful flowers but do not put on the great show that true climbers, such as Paul's Scarlet, do in the early spring.

SHRUB ROSES FOR BACKGROUND

Austrian Copper, Harison's Yellow, Lipstick, R. Hugonis (Father Hugo's Rose), R. Rubrifolia (noted for beautiful foliage and hips), Therese Bugnet (red).

OLD-FASHIONED TYPE ROSES

Roses grown prior to La France, the first Hybrid Tea, are now considered old fashioned. However, there are many fine old ones of a later date, not found in nurseries or catalogues, but may be secured from specialists. Those of us who grow them believe they add much to the garden used as shrubs or background plantings. Some may be disbudded for better specimens or to use in bouquets.

Moss Roses—Crested Moss, Gloire Des Mousseux, Jeanne de Monfort, Pink Moss, Salet, Archduke Charles (pink), Baronne Prevost (rose pink), Baroness Rothschild (pink), Black Prince (red), Camaieux (pink and red striped), Catherine Mermet (pink), Duchesse de Brebant (pink), *Frau Karl Druschke (white), *Georg Arends (pink), Henry Nevard (red), Jeannette (rose pink), Koenigin von Daenemarck (pink), La Marque (white), La Reine Victoria (rose-pink), *Madame Hardy (white, Damask), Maman Cochet (white), Mrs. Dudley Cross (pale yellow), *Mrs. John Laing (pink), Paul Neyron (rose-pink), *Roger Lambelen (red with white edges), Souvenir de la Malmaison (pink), Ulrich Brunner (red).

It is like trying to name my favorite child when asked to give my favorite two dozen roses. Usually the list will vary some from year to year or there may be some new rose that I am in love with, but fails to continue to perform to its first standard. My present list includes Anne Letts who is stingy with her blooms but when they come they are so perfect I think I would always want her—this is the way we rosarians react to a beautiful rose. Favorites are: Anne Letts, Champagne, Charlotte Armstrong, Chrysler Imperial, Comtesse Vandal, Confidence, Crimson Glory, Duet, Eclipse, First Love, Granada, Jamaica, John F. Kennedy, King's Ransom, McGredy's Ivory, Mexicana, Michelle Meilland, Peace, Pink Parfait (Grandiflora), Pink Peace, Royal Highness, Saratoga (Floribunda), Tiffany, Tropicana.

A variety of
rose beds

Iris

IRIS are among our most beautiful flowers. Many rival the orchid for distinction. In fact, I sometimes feel the iris ranks above the orchid for sheer line and color. And, iris are so much easier to grow.

Iris grow from rhizomes (thick, fleshy roots), but it is not difficult to grow them from seed. In this area, iris are easily grown, and thrive with little attention.

Cooler areas, such as about Santa Fe, Los Alamos, and similar localities, grow iris to peaks of true perfection.

Soil requirements of the iris are not nearly as exacting as for other flowers. More neglect can be piled upon an iris than almost any other specimen, and results will be cause for rejoicing.

As with any plant, the handsome iris is the one which has received care. Yet, if an attractive garden is desired without much time, expense, irrigation, or culture, pick the iris.

Beds should be well drained, in sunny positions, and prepared in the usual way. Try not to place iris where sprinkling systems will hit or injure the flowers when in bloom. Water will spot and tear the delicate flower tissue. Irrigation need not be frequent. This is one reason why the iris aren't as happy in a perennial border, where much water is required.

At the same time, any border is enhanced by the beauty of the blossoms. Many superb combinations can be planned with the iris and other flowers.

When planting, a shovel of well-rotted manure and compost in a generous sized hole, covered with top soil, is suggested.

Place the plant in position, trimmed of its leaves. Roots are spread carefully over a little mound of soil. The rhizome is covered one-fourth of an inch with soil, tamping the soil well as in planting a rose bush.

Pointing the "toes" of the rhizome outward allows plenty of room for new growth. This is particularly good when planting several of one kind in a site, preferable for effect (if the plants are not too costly). Spacing need not be as far apart as most growers recommend if the soil is well prepared. Eighteen inches between plants or clumps is sufficient under these circumstances.

The only fault with growing iris is that the hybridizers are so busy developing lovely new varieties that an iris garden (on which considerable money could be spent) is completely out of date in three to five years. Iris purchased a few years ago as "something special" often is not even listed in today's catalogue.

Really keeping up with iris is expensive, and sometimes aggravating. Since I like to know all the names of plants in my garden, trying to keep up with all the new names and varieties is an added irritation. However, I have learned to be happy with plants about three years old, since they drop in price in the catalogue as the variety becomes more popular. It is not unusual to see a new iris listed at twenty-five dollars the first year, then drop to seventy-five cents the third year.

Color, form, and substance are the trinity to find in an iris. I find I love the older iris just as much as always when they bloom in the spring, generous with their fragrance and beauty. For instance, I am still in love with Jean Cayeux, and will always have this graceful tan, blue-traced iris in my garden, with blue columbine alongside the clump when possible, but it is seldom found now.

Hybridists are obtaining exquisite colors, particularly in pinks and oranges. Some of the new ones appear to be covered with a thin layer of frost. There is more substance in new varieties and many are quite ruffled. Beginning gardeners will get better values by selecting growers' collections, which are always well chosen with an eye to mixture in colors.

Iris do not require as much fertilizer as most flowers. When planted well, the clump often will get by with no added food until it is divided, three to five years later.

Still, a little compost or all purpose food right after blooming is small reward for their contribution. More water is given just before the blooming period. In fact, leaves can be washed frequently on warm, sunny days to help control thrips and aphids which often are harbored in the crevices. Thrips do not damage the iris much, but they transfer their affections to the rose, with damaging results.

Disease in iris is not common. The chapter on pests and diseases touches on this, however. Cleanliness is important in the culture of iris. Always remove browning leaves, and keep beds clean. Winter leaves are removed, since protection in this area is not necessary for most varieties. Being covered with too many leaves may be a factor in causing crown rot or botrytis.

Mention should be made that iris foliage should not be cut back as the broad leaves nourish the rhizome. An exception is made when transplanting.

Should the iris bed appear unsightly, a few zinnia seed may be planted in between as a cover. Hold back water as much as possible, and do not plant the zinnias thick enough to create a dense shade as sun is necessary for healthy iris after blooming and before.

Flooding the iris bed with deep irrigation is disapproved by some growers. The method of morning irrigation that I use has not caused any damage with flooding. However, when planting iris I do plant them a little higher than the surrounding clumps of flowers so that water draws away from the rhizome.

Division of rhizomes for transplanting may be made at any time. Right after the blooming period is a good time, although August is recommended. Even December transplanting has brought good blooms. One year my iris were transplanted in February onto our new lot where our new home was to be built. The amount of blooms that came through, with beauty and substance, was remarkable.

All this proves that the iris is one of the easiest of all flowers for handling and growing in this area, with the greatest amount of return for

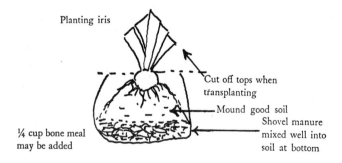

Planting iris

Cut off tops when transplanting

Mound good soil

Shovel manure mixed well into soil at bottom

¼ cup bone meal may be added

To get mass effect
quickly plant several
iris in circle with
toes pointing out

the trouble involved. Be reminded, too, that the lovely iris is wonderful for cutting, with long stems for church and hospital decoration. For landscape purposes, no flower other than the rose can equal it for show.

When iris are used for perennial borders, mention must be made that true colors are more effective than the blends. When well planned, the perennial border may be at its most glorious stage during the iris season. A few combinations might be yellow iris before the Austrian Copper rose. The frilled yellow Ola Kala surrounded by pink columbines is breathtaking. Yellow Happy Days combines with the watermelon-colored oriental poppies. A pink iris looks well with the orchid sweetrocket or Hesperis. Try Sierra blue with peony, Mons. Jules Elie, Missouri, a blue, can be combined with a contrasting rose, the Harison's Yellow.

Pansies are a colorful border for iris. Alyssum saxatile and blue iris make a picture.

Iris are fragile, and a drawback is their inability to stand the high winds in this country. Their only protection is that of the gardener himself, who should see that the iris get the wind-protected spots in the garden.

When iris are mentioned, most gardeners think of the bearded variety, but now the onco-breds are becoming better known and they do unusually well in our area. The name "Mohr" has become synonymous with them since William Mohr produced the first hybrid. The onco-breds are characterized by artistic veining throughout. They at first seemed a little less hardy, but since becoming acclimated they have increased in hardiness. New varieties of Dutch, Spanish, English, Siberian, Spurias, Arils, Louisiana, medians and dwarfs, are introduced each year. Space does not allow listing these, but any member of the American Iris Society has information where to get catalogues of these specialties. The iris fancier can have a hobby garden from any one of these species.

Listed here are varieties popular in all sections—many of them from the "100 best" popular vote list of the American Iris Society. The expensive varieties listed will be cheaper in a couple of years.

These fine iris, favorites all over our land, include some old and new. Color descriptions may be found in growers' catalogues which the hobbyist will love studying and seeing the exquisite color plates.

Allegiance
Amandine
Amethyst Flame
Argus Pheasant

Ballerina
Belle Meade
Big Game
Black Castle
Black Forest
Black Hills
Black Swan
Black Taffeta
Blue Chip
Blue Hawaii
Blue Rim
Blue Rhythm
Blue Sapphire
Blue Shimmer
Blumohr
Bryce Canyon

Casa Morena
Cascadian
Cascade Splendor
Cayenne Capers
Celestial Snow
Cherie
Chiquita
Cliffs of Dover
Cloth of Gold
Cloudcap
Colonel Primrose
Color Carnival
Crispette

Dancing Tiger
Dark Mood
Deep Black
Desert Song
Dream Castle

Eben
Ebony Echo
Edenite
Elmohr
Elsa Sass
Extravaganza

Fire Dance
First Violet
Fluted Haven
Foxfire
Frances Craig
Frost and Flame
Frosty

Garnet Glow
Gene Wild
Gold Cup
Golden Fleece
Great Lakes
Golden Hawk
Golden Majesty
Golden Ruffles
Golden Russet
Gold Sovereign
Grand Canyon
Great Day
Gudrun

Happy Birthday
Happy Days
Harbor Blue
Helen McGaughey
Helen McGregor
Henry Shaw
High-Tor

Illustrious
Inca Chief

Jane Phillips
Joseph's Mantle
June Meridith

Lady Elsie
Lady Ilse
Lady Louise
Lady Mohr
Licorice Stick
Lavanesque
Limelight
Lothario
Lynn Hall

May Hall
Mary Randall
Masked Ball
Minnie Colquitt
Mohr Affair
Montecita
Mulberry Rose

Native Dancer
New Look
New Snow

Ola Kala
Ormohr
Orange Parade

Pacific Panorama
Palomino
Pianissimo
Pierre Menard
Pink Enchantment
Pink Formal
Pink Frost
Pinnacle
Prairie Sunset
Pretty Quadroon

Ranger
Raspberry Ribbon
Raven Wing
Rippling Waters
Rehobeth
Rococo
Ruffled Organdy
Ruffled Taffeta

Sable
Sable Night
Sierra Blue
Sierra Skies
Snow Flurry
Snow Goddess
Solid Gold
Solid Mahogany
South Pacific
Spanish Peaks
Spring Romance
Spun Gold
Swan Ballet

Tabasco
Techny Chimes
Temple Bells
Thotmes III
Toast'n Honey
Top Hat
Truly Yours

Ultrapoise

Vatican Purple
Veri-gay
Violet Haven
Violet Harmony
Vivezia

Wabash
Wedding Bouquet
Wheelhorse
White Heron
White Peacock
White Ruffles
Whole Cloth
Wild Ginger

Zantha

Iris

Chrysanthemums

CHRYSANTHEMUMS are among the most satisfactory of all garden flowers in this region. The cool nights seem to be a main factor in their success.

More than five hundred cultivars of the chrysanthemum have been counted. It is a flower that has been cultivated for centuries and one of the earliest mentioned in history.

Present exhibition varieties are typical examples of perfection in the work of hybridists. The flowers range in size from less than an inch to twelve inches in diameter. There are buttons, pompons, cascades, large perfect globes, incurved, singles, anemones, cushioned, and other shapes.

Such members of the chrysanthemum family as the shasta daisy, pyrethrum, and marguerite will not be discussed in this chapter. Only those flowers which are commonly thought of by the general public as chrysanthemums will be considered. The other flower varieties are described under the perennial section.

Few realize it is almost as easy to grow the large exhibition or "football" variety of chrysanthemum as the common or hardy types. With all of them, good flowers are the result of fairly rich soil, plenty of water, and extra food right before the blooming period.

Location of the bed is important. It needs plenty of sun, but also must be where plants will receive fewer hours of daylight. Tests show that shortening days are a factor in producing early buds. I prefer an eastern exposure, one where the house, a fence or a tree will shade the bed from the late afternoon sun.

In preparing beds, dig deeply and incorporate plenty of compost or well-rotted manure into the soil. If the ground is heavy or sandy, peat moss may be added to advantage. I have found a manure mulch valuable after the plants are growing. This consists of an inch put on about June, another in July, and a final inch layer in August, until finally a three-inch mulch covers the ground. This may be supplemented with a good commercial fertilizer, particularly one containing plenty of nitrogen. Chrysanthemums prefer a slightly acid soil, so buy fertilizer with this in mind. Several weeks before blooming, a light foliar feeding once or twice a week is advisable.

Extra superphosphate is valuable for chrysanthemums. A thin sprinkle between rows will improve the quality of the stems and aid in producing earlier blooms. An excellent "tonic" is a small handful of ammonium sulphate in two and a half gallons of water, sprinkled on the soil when damp. All feeding should stop when the buds show color. This feeding program is the same for the large flowering type as for the hardy varieties.

Hardy garden types, such as the Korean hybrids, are grown easily from seed. They are a daisy type flower, with a fine color range, keep well, and handle nicely in arrangements. Others range from the small, round, compact ball to blooms three and four inches across. The form may be compact or loose and feathery. When growing this type it is desirable to pinch out the main stem when the plant is eight or ten inches tall. From each leaf will spring a new stem. When this stem grows a set of true leaves, pinch back again just above these leaves, and so on until August. Such treatment will result in a round, bushy plant. Remember when working with large beds of these plants they can be cut back just as successfully with hedge shears.

Large flowering types of chrysanthemums include the exhibition, commercial, spidery or threadlike, and other odd forms. They are planted in rows, not more than four rows to a bed, so each row can be reached easily to remove lateral growth and for disbudding. The plants are grown ten to fifteen inches apart.

Staking is necessary for these larger flowers. A simple method is to put a strong stake (redwood is preferred), about six feet tall at the end of each

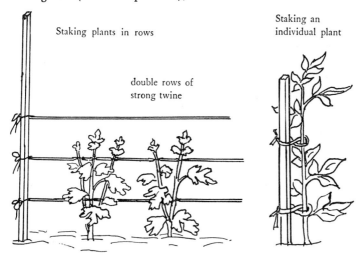

Staking plants in rows

Staking an individual plant

double rows of strong twine

row. Double rows of strong twine are stretched between the stakes, starting eight inches from the ground and at a distance of twelve inches from one another to the top of the stake. As the plants grow, insert their tops between the double strand of twine, sometimes giving the twine a little twist about the plant to better hold it in place. Some growers use wire between the stakes and tie the stems to this with raffia. The heat from our hot sun can be absorbed by the wire, so I prefer twine. (See illustration.)

Pinching or stopping the main stem is done for these exhibition varieties as for the hardy types. Only two to five stems are retained with the others pinched off. Lateral shoots are pinched off, too, and disbudding is severe. Proper disbudding leaves one perfect bud that will produce the prize bloom on each stem.

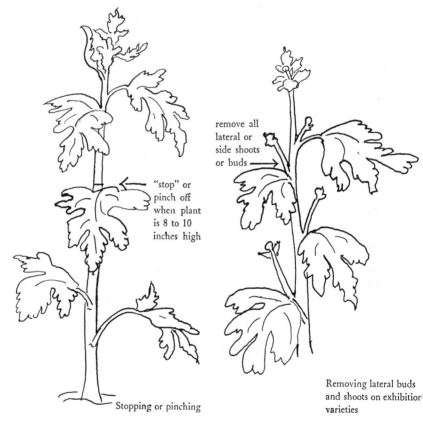

"stop" or pinch off when plant is 8 to 10 inches high

Stopping or pinching

remove all lateral or side shoots or buds →

Removing lateral buds and shoots on exhibition varieties

As each plant is put into the bed, a trowel of soil mixture consisting of sand, peat moss, manure, compost, and vermiculite is put into the bottom of the hole. Chrysanthemums appreciate a little extra richness, so fertilizer, humus, or compost can be increased in the proportions of the mixture. Mix this well into the soil that will receive the plants. Their best root development comes through while the weather is fairly cool, and their greatest period of growth comes in the fall just before blooming. Hardy chrysanthemums can be set out after the weather is settled, from the middle of March to the middle of April. Exhibition varieties should be planted as early as possible for best results, usually soon after March fifteenth. May and June are late. Since these prize types are less hardy, the hot and dry air seems to retard their development.

Beginners worry about the proper way to disbud a chrysanthemum plant. It is quite simple. There are two types of buds, the crown and the terminal. The crown is the first or middle bud and its selection is determined easily after a little practice. Growers, in their catalogues, sometimes indicate which bud will produce the best bloom. Generally it is conceded that the

Disbudding

disbud for
good blooms

crown buds are best for most early types. Terminal buds are left on for the later varieties. The crown bud has a vegetative growth or grass-like leaf. Terminal buds have a true leaf or a cluster of buds surrounding them.

When choosing which bud will remain it is wise not to select any before August twentieth. These are truly fall flowers, so do not hasten to remove any buds until you have examined all of them. Those that are to remain should have a round and healthy form. Some growers leave two buds for a period to be sure and have a second good one—grasshoppers love those tender morsels, and the second bud is a gardener's protection.

This leads us to pests. Fortunately, in this area we are not too troubled with pests and diseases. Aphids are the most common nuisance and can be controlled easily with a strong spray of cold water in midday, once or twice a week. For a serious infection, use the cold water treatment for several days. Insecticides can be used for grasshoppers and cabbage worms, both of which do enjoy chrysanthemum diets. An early morning round of the beds will find the pests at work then, enjoying their tender bud-and-leaf breakfasts. They can be caught easily and destroyed.

When irrigating chrysanthemums, light applications of water at frequent intervals is the best practice. They like daily baths, and on hot days a light spray of water revives their wilted leaves in about ten minutes. The transpiration of moisture on the chrysanthemum leaf is greater than in most other plants. As with other plants, late day irrigation is harmful. Wilt can develop from this practice. This wilt is similar to the type that attacks tomato plants. When it is noticed, the plant should be pulled up immediately and discarded to save its neighbors from destruction from this disease.

An endearing trait of the chrysanthemum is its long-lasting and long-keeping qualities. Often I have these flowers into early December by cutting them off the parent plant and bringing them inside to be kept in a cool place. One year I brought out splendid chrysanthemums from their storage place for the New Year holiday.

Slit each stem several inches upward after harvesting or pound the ends with a mallet or hammer to break down the woody texture, thus allowing water to be absorbed more rapidly. Remove those leaves which would be under water, since they would decay rapidly. When cutting the blooms for arranging a bouquet, gather them at least eight hours before and plunge them into cold water to harden.

The most beautiful chrysanthemums bloom dangerously close to frost time, so bringing the buds into blooms as early as possible is important. It is wise to have shelters of cloth-covered frames or cloth houses if you plan to "go in" for chrysanthemums. Wind and weather changes make this added protection desirable. It is not a necessity, and don't let this suggestion discourage you from growing chrysanthemums. Just select your more sheltered spots and proceed as directed.

If you want still later blooms, use a glass type covering. This may be a glass substitute, plastic or similar material. This usually is purchased in rolls or by the yard. The partial shading thus achieved hastens blooms and protects the plant from the bright sun enough to produce finer colors. Pink varieties seem to fade in the sun more than others. Should you use the protective shelters or houses, don't put them up until the buds start to form.

Blooming times must be considered when the large mums are bought. Learn the time of frost in your community from the weather man, and select plants accordingly. If frost dates are around mid-October, pick plants scheduled to bloom before that. Blooming dates in catalogues listing chrysanthemums vary only a few days from our periods of blooming.

Propagation of chrysanthemums is by root divisions or cuttings from the parent plant. The finer the flower the more tender it seems, and the more difficult to carry it through the winter. Unless shoots are strong and healthy looking, they should be discarded. Inferior shoots may not recover enough to produce a good bloom. For those chrysanthemums hard to winter, a wise gardener will insure their well-being by taking up the entire clump, or by taking cuttings from it for the cold frame or for some protected spot in the garden until spring planting time.

Usually the best time for this is after the blooms have died out and the flowers have been cut. Plants are placed in the cold frame. Use sand and peat moss for the soil mixture in the cold frame for the cuttings, wetting the

Chrysanthemum
cutting rooted

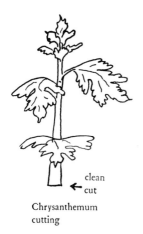

clean
← cut

Chrysanthemum
cutting

mixture thoroughly. Use a knife to cut a trough in the soil, inserting the plants close together and firming them in well. Water again thoroughly when finished. They'll need occasional watering through the winter. Lift the cover of the flat several times a week on warm days to aerate the plants.

When pinching back plants during their growing season, the tops thus taken out can be used as cuttings. The bottom ends are cut cleanly across with a sharp knife, and several leaves are removed. (See illustration.) They should then be treated as the shoots that appear in the fall. Some use a preparation to hasten the rooting process, but chrysanthemums take root so easily that I never bother.

After the divisions and shoots have been established they can be kept a little on the dry side to avoid too much soft growth and to prevent rot. The leaf can be watched to signal watering time.

Covering beds with leaves or straw is not too wise, unless the covering is very light. Plants rot easily in the late fall and winter. Don't cut back the old stock too soon after the flowers are gone, for the leaf and stem continue nourishing the root until completely frozen back.

Those cuttings rooted during the earlier growing season can be put into their permanent beds when the roots are fairly well developed. I usually put extra plants in my cutting garden to fill in the bare spots left by bloomed-out early annuals. Chrysanthemums can be transplanted at any time. Often I have placed full grown or blooming plants into a spot which called for a lift. I always am careful to keep the soil intact about the roots when transplanting, then shade and water the plant well. Usually it doesn't even show it's been moved.

Chrysanthemums can meet nearly every taste in color and in the variety of shape and style. Men are partial to the big round ball exhibition variety. Women interested in flower arrangement find the fragile spiders, the singles, and the button types produce unusual effects. There is not as much change in the chrysanthemum field as in the iris or gladioli varieties, but nearly every year some fine new types are added to the list.

Few flowers have more of a range in form and color than chrysanthemums. Classes include the single, semidouble, regular anemone, irregular anemone, pompon, regular or Chinese incurve, reflexed or decorative, aster flowered, reflexes, regular Chinese reflexes, irregular or Japanese reflex, spoon, semidouble and double spoon, quill, thread, and spider. Most colors are represented except blue.

For landscape value the hardy cultivars are more satisfactory. The large disbuds that need to be staked are best planted in the cutting garden. In a former garden I did grow them in the patio area with a border of cushion chrysanthemums and they finished the bed. Reinforcing rods were used for stakes.

Chrysanthemum impractical for outdoor culture are not listed here, nor are the hardy varieties which are easily obtained from most growers in a nice range of color. Korean hybrids are raised easily from seed packets, and are not listed for that reason. Although I grow other varieties in my garden I have not attempted to name them all. What follows is a general listing serviceable for the average gardener.

Chrysanthemum

CHRYSANTHEMUM LIST

Pompon or Miniature

Variety	Blooming Date	Remarks
White—		
White Jewell	Oct. 5	Low growing, good, trace of pink
Irene	Oct. 15	One of best, dependable
Margot	Oct. 15	Low growing, very small flowers
Pinocchio	Oct. 25	Uniform flowers, full and perfect on a tall plant
Silverbells	Oct. 25	Ball-like and compact
Snow Drops	Nov. 1	Tiny and long lasting
Yellow—		
September Gold	Oct. 6	Brilliant and small, medium sized, excellent
Baby	Oct. 22	One of smallest buttons
Judith Anderson	Oct. 10	Lemon yellow, good producer, stands wind
Golden Bantam	Oct. 26	Produces fine terminal sprays
Yellow Irene	Oct. 20	Compact
Nuggets	Oct. 25	Rich yellow, one of best
Pink—		
Pink Jewell	Oct. 15	Excellent
Trinket	Sept. 28	Lavender pink
Annette	Nov. 1	Mauve pink, perfect ball
Pinkdot	Oct. 25	Light pink, deeper center
Isobel	Oct. 25	Deep pink, slightly cupped petals
Bronze—		
Early Bronze	Oct. 5	Short, orange bronze
Little Bob	Oct. 5	Red bronze, more azalea type mum, a favorite with me
Bonnibel	Oct. 20	Good form and substance
Clare Jameson	Oct. 20	Small bronze, good substance
Ethel	Oct. 25	Low, reddish
Dark Red—		
Patsy Dowd	Nov. 11	

(Later dates are listed in the dark red and bronze varieties since they take more frost than the whites and pinks.)

Commercial Varieties

Variety	Size	Height*	Date	Remarks
White—				
Quakermaid	6 in.	Medium	Oct. 1	Good grower without much form in flower
Albatross	7 in.	Tall	Oct. 10	Good early variety; dependable, strong grower
Ambassador	7 in.	Medium	Oct. 15	Excellent form in flower head, though foliage and stem tend to crookedness
Silversheen	6 in.	Tall	Oct. 20	Good, dependable, firm, straight stalks
Betsy Ross	6 in.	Tall	Oct. 20	Incurved, good form, good foliage
Indianapolis	7 in.	Medium	Oct. 20	Good form, healthy stemmed foliage, dependable
Sterling	7 in.	Medium	Nov. 5	Good form, pure white
Pink—				
J. W. Prince	6 in.	Medium	Oct. 25	Good grower, fair form
Major Bowes	6 in.	Medium	Oct. 25	Rose pink, good form and stem
Pinkchief	6 in.	Medium	Oct. 5	Orchid pink, good
Yellow—				
Blazing Gold	7 in.	Medium	Oct. 10	Good substance
Butterball	6 in.	Medium	Oct. 1	Good form
Friendly Rival	7 in.	Medium	Nov. 1	Pale yellow, good
Gold Lode	5 to 6 in.	Short	Oct. 1	Don't care for form, but like its early blooming date
Mrs. H. E. Kidder	7 in.	Medium	Oct. 15	An old favorite, with good foliage, one of the most popular varieties throughout the country
Bronze or Red—				
Alameda	6 in.	Medium	Oct. 5	Good
Hilda Bergen	5 to 6 in.	Tall	Oct. 15	Hard to get good size, form only fair

(* "Medium" designates plant three to four feet high. "Tall" designates plant five feet and over.)

Variety	Size	Height	Date	Remarks
Garnet King	6 in.	Medium	Oct. 25	Good red reflexed type, stands frost, beautiful color
Mrs. D. F. Roy	7 in.	Medium	Oct. 20	Crimson and gold, good form and color
Shirley Beauty	6 in.	Medium	Oct. 25	Rich in color; good stem and foliage

Exhibition

White

June Bride	7 in.	Medium	Oct. 20	Beautiful incurve
Sterling Silver	6 in.	Tall	Oct. 20	Pure white, good Symmetry
Snow Man	7 in.	Tall	Oct. 25	Round pure white incurve
Snow Ball	7 in.	Tall	Oct. 25	Well named, good grower
Eclipse	6 in.	Medium	Oct. 15	Excellent form
Stromness	7 in.	Tall	Oct. 25	Reflexed flower, with swirled center
William Turner	8 in.	Tall	Nov. 1	Excellent form and popular all over. Should be protected from frost
Watanabe	7 in.	Medium	Oct. 5	Very good

Pink

Angeles Belle	7 in.	Medium	Oct. 25	Beautiful and multiplies well
Otome Pink	6 in.	Medium	Oct. 25	Beautiful color, decorative form
Pink Chief	6 in.	Medium	Oct. 10	Incurve and dependable
Floral Queen	6 in.	Medium	Oct. 25	Soft pink which I think can be grown very large
Tone Beauty	7 in.	Tall	Oct. 25	Very symmetrical and fine form and color
Seiko Giant	7 in.	Medium	Nov. 1	Rose pink and claimed to be very large
Pink Perfection	7 in.	Tall	Oct. 25	Excellent grower with good form and clear color
Portrait	7 in.	Tall	Oct. 20	Wonderful, vigorous; globular in form; nonfading

Variety	*Size*	*Height*	*Date*	*Remarks*
Greer Garson	6 in.	Tall	Oct. 25	Soft pink, reflexed, swirled center; lovely in arrangements
Yellow				
Big Time	8 in.	Tall	Oct. 20	Excellent
Century	6 in.	Medium	Oct. 25	Rich orange yellow
Garden State	7 in.	Medium	Oct. 20	Incurve, strong stem and good foliage
Mountaineer	7 in.	Medium	Oct. 25	One of my favorites
Kikubiyori	7 in.	Medium	Oct. 28	Can be perfect, will grow five large flowers per plant
Monte Vista	6 in.	Tall	Oct. 25	Beautiful form, strong stems
Triumphant	7 in.	Medium	Oct. 5	
Bronze				
Bronze Prince	7 in.	Medium	Oct. 20	Excellent form
Muto's Crimson	6 in.	Tall	Nov. 1	Red and gold reverse
Zigzag	6 in.	Medium	Oct. 20	Fine bright bronze with gold tips
Gloria Deo	7 in.	Medium	Oct. 25	Dark red with lighter reverse
Sancho	6 in.	Medium	Nov. 1	French import of bronze and gold
Stadium Queen	6 in.	Medium	Sept. 5	
Country Maiden	8 in.	Medium	Oct. 25	Broad petaled, incurved soft light bronze
Appert	7 in.	Tall	Oct. 28	Pale bronze and exquisite when at its best
Mikado (Improved)	6 in.	Medium	Oct. 25	Stem and foliage fair, loosely incurved, gold and bronze
Other Colors				
Grace Sturgis	8 in.	Medium	Nov. 1	Cherry and silver, good stem, foliage stands frost
Ben Leighton	7 in.	Medium	Oct. 15	Wine, with little lighter red outside petals, good form
Agina Purple	6 in.	Medium	Oct. 28	Rosy purple — very dependable
Cover Girl	7 in.	Medium	Oct. 25	Rich wine red with lighter reverse

| Miss Frances Lowe | 8 in. | Medium | Nov. 1 | Odd shade of buff pink, one catalogue describes it as crushed-raspberry bronze |
| Dr. J. M. Inglis | 7 in. | Tall | Nov. 1 | Wine and silver |

Spider chrysanthemum

Spider or Threadlike

Yellow—Albert Witt, Crescendo, Garden Glory, Golden Splendor, Lorraine, San Gabriel

White—Alice Tashima, Bridesmaid, Bride's Veil, Dainty White, Maria, Morgan's White, Pinnacle, Silver Lace, Swan Ballet, White Rayonnante, and Youth

Green or Chartreuse—Dr. Ira B. Cross, Emerald Isle, Nightingale

Orange—Mamoru

Bronze—Bess Witt, Gena Harwood, Miss Dorothy P. Tuthill, Waikiki, Warrior

Pink or Lavender—Ballerina, Bunbu, Calypso, Classic Perfection, Georgina Hedinger (must be shaded for best color), Lavender Dream, Peggy Ann Hoover, Pink Exquisite (swirled center), Rayonnante, Roulette, and Sarah Morasch

Wine or Red—Cathy, Diablo, Mauve, Unique and Universe

Anemone
Angel Face, Daybreak, Joan Castle, Powder Puff, Sincerity

Single
Broadacre, Golden Anniversary, Potomac, Silver Lining, Toreador

Cascades
Bronze Charm, Cherry Blossom, Crimson Tide, Imp. Shiratsuru, Liquid Amber, Maiko, Moonbeam

Cushions
Amelia, Bronze Queen, Cochise, Forest Fire, Golden Carpet, Lipstick, Mischief, Wee Willie

Tree Mums
(Cultivars that can be grown as a small tree)
Magic Carpet, Magic Cushion, Magic Dot, Magic Light

Vines, Hedges, and Ground Covers

VINES

Quick shade and ornament are desirable features of the vine. Vines are helpful, too, in screening service areas, a trash can, compost box, and the all-too-prominent telephone pole.

For very quick results the morning glory is a favorite, with the white and blue varieties most popular. Home owners are grateful for this quick-growing annual vine that will serve adequately until a tree grows to the proper size to shade a window.

Silver lace is a good vine for such problems as the telephone pole, since it grows quickly and spreads generously. Too generously, some gardeners believe, as they tediously trim back its long tendrils and hack out its abundant suckers that soon travel far out of bounds. The trumpet vine, with the orange-red blossoms that give the vine its name, is effective against native homes. Either of these thrive well in nearly any position, but will bloom more profusely if they are in spots where the sun strikes them.

Wistaria is beloved by all gardeners, but is stubborn about blooming in this area. It suffers shock on transplanting and often will not bloom for years. It is important to buy stock that already has bloomed. Careful pruning encourages bloom.

Boston and English ivy are popular and are attractive when trained on areas of brick. The Queens Wreath is another fine vine, but grows mostly in the warmer areas of our region. I have never been able to grow it because of our low temperatures.

Clematis will do well if planted in a lightly shaded spot, given good soil and food, and protected from extreme heat. It can be planted on the north with success. Jackmani is a deep purple variety, Henryi is white, Crimson King, and Ramona, blue, are good. Also successful are Duchess of Albany, Duchess of Edinburgh, Comtesse de Bouchard, Lanuginosa Candida, Mrs. Chomondeley, Nellie Moser, Mme. Édouarde André, Ville de Lyon.

Honeysuckle is another vine that does well in our area. Gold Flame, Hall's Yellow, and Scarlet Trumpet are excellent.

Virginia Creeper, sometimes called the woodbine, provides splashes of red and bronze color in the fall, besides giving good covering for house and fence. Its vigor is desirable. Small blue berries in clusters are attractive.

Often an edible grape vine can be trained for attractive covering on a lattice or fence. Several good varieties will please the family taste.

HEDGES

Hedges are attractive when well kept. The gardener must remember when planting a hedge that clipping it and otherwise keeping it in good condition will be extra chores. Another aspect sometimes not considered is that the hedge becomes a paper and leaf catcher and, with our windstorms, removing the captured debris becomes a regular cleanup job.

Hedges do define garden areas, separate sections of the yard and otherwise perform the double duty of utility and trim beauty.

Rural gardeners find the Russian olive, cut and shaped as a hedge, as satisfactory as any type hedging.

Privets are fine for summer hedges, but in our colder areas they are ragged and bare during the winter. Euonymus is satisfactory, with its rich-green, glossy leaves, but will freeze in colder areas. This plant often will grow back from the root.

Santolina is one of my favorites for low hedges, but it, too, will winter-kill in colder areas. The Lodense privet probably is our most satisfactory low hedge. It also is pleasing when grown as an individual mound, neatly pruned and shaped to add a nice touch to the landscape.

Floribunda roses are becoming popular as hedging material. They sometimes retain their leaves until spring. Thorns on the plants keep children and animals from passing through them.

Other hedges often used are the Amur River privet, *Buxus japonica* (a boxwood), California privet, Chinese privet, and Redleaf barberry. Crimson Pigmy barberry is dwarf.

GROUND COVER

Nearly every garden presents areas here and there that require what is called "ground cover." Narrow spaces between walks and buildings need it. Sometimes the lawn, with its edging of shrubs, develops bare strips where the shade from the shrubbery covers the ground. Then it is that these little, low plants, sometimes with appealing little blossoms, perform a valuable service in our gardens.

Planned flower beds, too, can be given a carpet of contrasting color by ground cover which ties massed effects together. Of course, rock gardens demand cover, and great varieties are provided for them.

Home owners who do not want to be troubled with perennial borders often use cover plants as transition between flower beds and lawn or shrubbery. For small home grounds, ground covers replace lawn. Ranch homes with patio gardens improve entryways with such plants.

Numerous people, discouraged with grass and wanting to substitute a ground cover, have called on me for advice. I hasten to warn them that these can be problems, too. Anyone living in the Southwest, or Rocky Mountain area, is familiar with wind-blown trash, and areas with ground covers cannot be raked. Weeds, also, will get a start hidden beneath them and often will go to seed before they are discovered, or roots have such a tenacious hold they are difficult to pull. Ground covers in large areas do not have the even, neat look of a well-mowed lawn. For "islands" in a restricted or paved area they work out well, but as a setting for a home nothing is so beautiful as a fine lawn.

Ground covers vary in height from an inch to a foot, and their variety is infinite. Those listed here are among the most common, some creep and some do not, but all provide excellent cover material, and all are perennial.

AJUGA *(repens)* or CARPET BUGLE.

ARMERIA ALPINA.

ARABIS or ROCK CRESS.

AUBRIETA, common, *Leichtlini* variety.

BUTTERCUP—*Ranunculus acris* is the single variety. *Ranunculus repens florepleno,* double.

CAMPANULA *(carpatica).*

CANDYTUFT—A hardy variety is Evergreen.

EUONYMUS *(radicans).*

LILY-OF-THE-VALLEY

NEPETA (Catnip)—*Hederacea* or ground ivy (becomes a nuisance because of its rapid spread). *Mussini.*

OXALIS or WOODSORREL—Violet. Not hardy in colder areas.

PERIWINKLE—Both the minor and the major are desirable, with their little, blue, star-like flowers.

PHLOX—Blue Hill, Crimson Beauty, and Vivid varieties.

SOAPWORT—*(saponaria ocymoides).*

SNOW-IN-SUMMER *(cerastium tomentosum)*—Its woolly, gray leaves when in bloom make a mass of white.

STONECROP—*Sedum spurium* and *S. sieboldi,* among others.

TROLLIUS—Globeflower, *Trollius ledebouri.*

VERONICA—*Veronica latifolia prostrata.*

VERONICA—*Veronica repens.*

House Plants

OUR OVERHEATED HOMES, coupled with the natural lack of humidity in the Southwest, are drawbacks to the culture of a great many house plants and even to the perfection of those we do grow here.

Yet, every home is the more attractive for its accessory indoor plants. Even the humble adobe homes in rural and suburban areas are brightened by the truly fine geranium plants that crowd their windows. These rich-blooming, healthy specimens sometimes are my despair for they appear to be so happy and content in their extremely simple surroundings. My theory is that these native window plants are protected by the thick adobe walls that retain coolness in summer and are only moderately heated in winter. Too, perhaps the tin cans they're planted in give them an additional reservoir of mineral food. These windows usually are lightly curtained, if at all, and the sills are just wide enough for such a "conservatory."

Sunny windows are an asset in growing house plants. Windows admitting a great deal of light are fairly good substitutes. Lacking these, select such plants as the philodendron, with its many varieties, which requires much less light or sun. Even these produce the best specimens if they are grown in very light windows. African violets are my winter hobby and I have found, contrary to most advice, that they do well with as much as a half day's sun in winter—but never after March first.

House plants need food just as garden plants. A very light feeding once a week is not too often. Liquid manure or compost water are excellent for indoor plantings as well as the commercial preparations. Watering is most important. More failures occur from too much water than from too little. Most plants prefer being fairly dry before they receive their next drink. When I instruct a helper to take care of my plants while I am away I find it hard to say something simple such as "water every other day," because outdoor weather plays a part in how fast indoor plants may dry out. If the weather is very cold and the furnace has been going day and night the indoor air may be much drier than usual. Windstorms, too, reduce humidity. Cloudy weather tends to keep plants moist. So, plain common sense is used handily.

Always use tepid water on house plants. Alkali and chlorine are hard

on plants and it is helpful to draw water and let it stand overnight. When (if ever) it rains, I save rain water—it will keep for a month.

Potting mixtures require peat moss, garden soil, compost, and sand or vermiculite. Compost and garden soil should be sterilized for African violet mixes. Usually each plant requires its own type of mixture with proportions varying accordingly. Good drainage and good soil are most important.

An occasional bath is welcomed by plants. Again, don't use cold water. A little vinegar in the water can be used with a soft cloth for wiping away alkaline spots or dust on foliage. Never oil foliage to make it shine. There are preparations on the market for this purpose, but I use them only as "party make-up" and not as regular routine. When the humidity reading is extremely low, plants enjoy being sprayed with a fine mist.

Insects and diseases in house plants need not be bothersome if cleanliness is practiced. Mealy bugs sometimes are troublesome, but a small swab of cotton on the end of a toothpick can be dipped in rubbing alcohol and touched to each bug lightly. This will eliminate them. Sometimes my plants are troubled with what appear to be little gnats or fruit flies. I think these might come from the compost used for the plants. Generally they disappear in a day or so. I don't worry about them, and a little fly spray applied around the outside rim of the flower pot or the window sill near the plants is a good eliminator. Heat treated manure doesn't bring the flies into the house and is excellent in soil mixtures.

Many house plants may be increased by cuttings. Here, too, I use the easy way. The pots are filled to just below the usual height with the proper mixture. Then I stick my finger down the middle and fill this hole with sand or vermiculite. Now the cutting pruned from the plant is inserted. The cutting shouldn't be too large and not have too many leaves left on it. The soil is firmed about it and the pot watered. Do not over water for this might rot the plant. Faster rooting might be induced by dipping the end of the plant into a root hormone preparation, but this isn't necessary. Shade the cuttings until they are well established.

House plants can be benefitted in many cases by putting them out in the garden during the summer. Be sure the spot is partially shaded and protected from the wind.

Naturally, those who want to grow house plants should have a proper place for them. Makeshift situations always result in poor plant culture and require extra work and care from the gardener.

Fruits and Vegetables

NO HOME GARDENER can resist planting a few vegetables, for several reasons. First of all, the pleasure in gathering truly fresh vegetables for home use is most satisfying. Second, vegetables can be gathered in the amount needed, a carrot or two for stew, a small handful of parsley for garnishing, a few thin spears of chives to flavor a dish of cottage cheese. Thrifty housewives don't like to bring home a large bunch of parsley from the market to see it languish in the refrigerator, nor do they enjoy preparing a wilting bunch of carrots.

Another good reason for vegetable gardening is the actual attraction they add to the garden itself, in borders or in a plot by themselves. They seem so tidy and snug that they give the gardener a sense of well-being, an instinct hangover, no doubt, from the early days when we all depended on our own hands for gathering food from the plants around us.

Tomatoes seem to be the choice of nearly all gardeners when they relent and consider "a few vegetables" along with their flowers and shrubs. Parsley, lettuce, radishes, and then a few additional "favorite" vegetables find their way into separate rows or are tucked here and there in borders and in spare parts of flower beds.

With the use of the cold frame, the home gardener can put out plants much earlier than by planting the seed in open ground, thus providing the family with succulent, crisp vegetables often some time before they appear as "locals" on the market.

Since a vegetable, after all, is a garden plant, there is little difference in the general culture of the vegetable plot and the flower bed. All like good soil and proper irrigation, although, as a whole, vegetables do not require as much water as flowers.

Lettuce makes an attractive flower border, particularly if it is the leafy kind that now comes in several color shades, including that which is tipped with bronze. However, the vegetable plot itself can be most attractive, with curly parsley borders, the red-stemmed "beet chard," and crisp turnip tops. One of my flower beds is edged with a thick row of strawberries, whose leaves remain green far into the fall and then turn later into all shades of yellow, red, and brown.

Fruit trees add beauty to the general garden landscape for their graceful branches, their springtime flowering, and the richness of the laden tree in fall. The leaves of the apple, cherry, and apricot trees remain green and glossy long after most trees have become bare. Dwarf fruit trees lend themselves to the small home plot and their fruit often is superior to the ordinary fruit tree.

Tree-ripened fruit tastes so much better than that which is picked almost green in order to insure safe transportation from orchard to market to consumer.

An objection to fruit trees of course, is the unsightly fallen fruit and the attraction of insects to the ripened fruit. I made the mistake of placing them in view of the street. Boys stealing fruit break branches and injure plants beneath the trees.

Seeds are available for dwarf varieties of cantaloupes, corn, cucumbers, and melons, and these can be grown in a small space.

I avoid chemical fertilizers and poison sprays for vegetables, though when preparing the soil I use soil sulphur, iron sulphate, and superphosphate, in addition to compost and manure in the fall prior to spring planting. As extra feeding for the growing plants I use only manure or compost. A constant mulch of compost gives excellent, tender growth. The wells around fruit trees always are kept full of compost. Foliar feeding has proved very helpful, especially for fruit trees. Peach and cherry trees always are treated for borers spring and fall. Members of the cabbage family generally seem to have cabbage worms—these I hand pick, as I do the grasshoppers that may be damaging plants.

Irrigation twice a week is enough for young vegetables, and once a week for older plants. Fruit trees get along with water every two to four weeks—peaches especially may die if irrigated too much. A root feeder is excellent to irrigate them.

Reaping the Reward

FINALLY comes the thrill of the use of flowers beyond their beauty of growth and maturity in the garden. The generous gardener finds hundreds of occasions for which a bouquet is just the right gift or addition. The beauty of flowers alleviates grief and comforts the sick. Any occasion can be made more festive with the addition of floral arrangements, within the home, the clubhouse, or in public buildings.

All children love to take teacher a bouquet. Teach your child how to cut a flower instead of pulling it off by the head. Show him that to cut the flower allows a longer stem for carrying the bouquet to teacher. Give him a piece of waxed paper, or foil, to wrap the stems of the flowers instead of putting them in a hot little hand to be clutched all the way to school.

Often the schoolroom bouquet suffers on arrival because there are no containers. A simple can or jar painted or covered with a colorful bit of paper serves well. This is also a good idea for bouquets that will be carried to the hospital for a sick friend, or for a member of your club or church group. Anyone who is ill loves to receive flowers. My own experience has taught me that a bouquet arriving at a dull hour will brighten the entire hospital day. Flowers on the church altar are admired, and comfort those who stop by for a casual visit. Formal church services demand the addition of the flower's beauty and dignity. The practice of taking church flowers to the sick and the bereaved after the service is a beautiful one.

Parties demand flowers and rival the clothes and party atmosphere in gaiety and beauty. It is such a thrill to present a beautifully arranged bouquet to your hostess. Just a word of advice here. Do take flowers that will fit the hostess' decorative scheme or the occasion. Remember, too, if the party is at a time when flowers are plentiful, ask the hostess if she could use another bouquet. Nothing looks more overdone than a room heaped with flowers. Most hostesses feel they shouldn't hurt the giver by failing to use all the floral gifts.

Naturally, the pleasure of flowers for your own home and for your family is boundless. Minimize worn rugs, faded upholstery, the wear and tear in a home, by charming floral arrangements that will take the eye. It needn't be a large bouquet. A few violets or pansies will do, or a single rose in a bud vase. Sprigs from a flowering tree in a colored glass container can work a miracle if they are planned to be in keeping with the color tones of the room. Sprays from flowering trees can be cut as though they are an extension of the pruning job, thus relieving the conscience of cutting fruit branches. Leaves from house plants combine nicely with these, also with pussywillow, forsythia, and other early-blooming shrubs and plants.

If your house is informal in style, don't grow lilies for its decoration. If the house is modern, modern arrangements can be evolved, for that is the trend. Should you live in a Pueblo or Spanish Colonial architectural atmosphere, plant zinnias, marigolds, and calendulas for cutting. Blue and green glass bowls are perfect for these, as well as the black Indian pottery vases. Remember pottery allows water to seep through, so put your bouquets in glass containers before resting them in a pottery bowl. Place your flower bouquets near a window where light can reflect through glass containers for added beauty. A colonial type of home will accept mixed bouquets and roses, particularly when antiques and figurines are part of the interior decoration.

Plan your garden so that it will produce the grace notes of living through the year for you and your family. Select and grow those flowers that will be used to decorate your home for special occasions such as anniversaries, birthdays, luncheons, and dinner parties.

At one time my home was a huge old-fashioned house, with high-ceilinged rooms. At that time I planned flowers that grew tall, to fill large spaces. My vase collection corresponded. My next home was smaller, a modified version of the Georgian style of architecture. Floral arrangements and containers tended toward the small and exquisite rather than the showy. Line arrangements became important, and tiny bouquets. When I planned my new home that we now enjoy I included room for many types of arrangements of flower and color combinations.

Red flowers are a weakness with me, but my kitchen is the only room where flagrant red is used for decoration. My breakfast room blazes with tulips, geraniums, pompon zinnias, and deep tones of nasturtiums and allied flowers that are perfect for the crisp, neat atmosphere of our pleasant, roomy kitchen. The nook has, in fact, become the family sunroom, where we linger over the morning paper and that final cup of coffee.

Soft, pink chrysanthemums are in my garden, planted specially for my bedroom, where they will be combined with a turquoise vase to tie in with the wallpaper and drapery. Pale, peach-pink walls tone in well with the mums.

Hollyhocks against a turquoise sky are brought into the living room in a painting. The hollyhocks are in rose tones, and so, just underneath, a little purple glass pitcher finds itself very much at home. Particularly if it bears a spray of Cardinal peach blossoms in the spring. Or, a floribunda rose in the Permanent Wave variety and sometimes a line arrangement of flowering plums. When the fall season comes around I look forward to arranging three pink spider chrysanthemums, one fully opened and the others half opened and budding.

Good flower arrangements depend a great deal on the proper containers. Select those suitable to the style of your home. Have plenty of good anchors in frogs of various sizes. The needle type is excellent. Floral clay holds the frog to the dish. Paraffin serves better in some bowls. Chicken wire folded into the vase provides a good base. Some people use stems to anchor an arrangement, but when the plant material decays it presents an unpleasant mess that hastens the withering of your flowers themselves. Good scissors or clippers are a necessity.

Roses, some iris, and other fine flower types require silver containers, good glass vases, and better types of pottery and other ceramic dishes, always appropriate in color, line, and size. Zinnias need bronze holders, metals, and heavier potteries, as do marigolds. Flowers should have a definite relationship with their containers and both should be planned for their position. A flower with a sheen or satiny finish needs the complement of a container in the same textured surface.

Do not arrange flowers immediately after cutting. Let them soak up water or "harden" for several hours, plunged deep in warm water. Early morning or late afternoon cutting is best. I prefer the late afternoon so the flowers can stand overnight in water. I cannot bear to cut flowers in the heat of the day.

Some blooms need special attention on cutting. Those with a milky substance in their stems, or with coarse hairs along their stems must have their cuts sealed. Scrape hairs from cut end two or three inches back. A dahlia or a poppy needs to be sealed, also such hollow-stemmed plants as the delphinium do better when so treated.

Hold the stem over a flame or plunge it into boiling water for a minute. The stem should be held on a slant so that the steam or heat will not reach the flower to injure it. Short-stemmed flowers can be protected by a cone of paper. Roses and chrysanthemums do better if their stems are split or mashed with a hammer. A sharp knife can be used to split the stems three or four inches from the cut. Roses, and flowers with tough leaves, should be plunged in tepid water right up to their necks. Chrysanthemums have soft leaves that decay under water, so the foliage should be stripped away to avoid the unpleasant odor, and damage from decay.

Putting flowers into the refrigerator where the temperature is quite low isn't wise, unless the flowers are being stored for use at a later date. When flowers emerge abruptly into warm air from cold storage they seem to wilt faster and often they undergo a color change. We who do not have cellars, and in the Southwest few possess them, can keep our flowers in any cool, dark place. Mine happens to be a clothes closet on the north side of the house. Inconvenient at times, of course, but worth the effort. Flowers don't like drafts and bouquets placed where they are in a draft succumb. Outdoors, they can take it. Brought indoors, they become sensitive bits of color.

Remember when arranging flowers to place the larger and darker-colored blooms at the bottom. Finer and lighter material is inserted around the top. Break the rules occasionally, as I did when I put three madonna lilies in a shallow white pottery dish with low lines. I tucked foliage about their base, then allowed a stalk of blue delphinium to rise quite high. The arrangement was too high for the container, the dark color was at the top, but the lines swept the eye to appreciation of beauty. Usually a bouquet should be one and a half or more times the height or width of the vase. Height must be avoided at the dinner or luncheon table so that guests needn't peer at each other through flower masses.

Tones of one color can be very effective and I use this treatment often. Reddish bronze tulips are fitted into the bottom of an arrangement in a yellow pottery vase. Lighter bronze tones of tulips range upward, and then deep yellow ones are inserted, with pale yellow blooms rearing their graceful heads at the top. A few mahonia leaves are arranged at the base for accent. Or, if you have purple tulips, range through into lavenders and pinks in a pink or rose-colored bowl. How about bronze chrysanthemums in a copper bowl, with lighter bronze tones graduating into yellows? They'll bring comments of sheer delight.

Startling contrasts can be effective. I like to put white chrysanthemums into combination with bright red zinnias in a white container. Pink goes very well with purple. Two colors often can be arranged more effectively than several colors together.

One-color arrangements depend on the texture of flowers as well as contrasts in size. A couple of the flowers should be large enough to give contrast. Large leaves may do it.

Leaves sometimes give a bouquet the spark that touches off a beautiful reaction. When you receive a dozen red roses on your next anniversary, cut some of the stems shorter and do a line arrangement. At the base put a few philodendron leaves, or large garden leaves, using your ingenuity.

Early forcing of flowers brings beauty into the house soon after gray winter skies. Crab apple, flowering quince, jasmine, forsythia, pussywillow, and pruned fruit tree branches make exquisite arrangements. Greenery can be added by choice geranium, philodendron or other available large leaves. The branches are "forced" to bloom by bringing them in or cutting when budded and placing in deep water in a cool dark place for several days. Bring them into a light and bright room for another day or so. Arrange when in blossom.

A beauty spot in my new home is the niche I planned in our informal living room, or "den" as that room has been named by architects. This year it has paraded a number of arrangements in suitable vases. Surprising combinations have turned up in scant seasons, until it has become a game that all the family plays by joining in suggesting and guessing at what mother will do next. I would like to make my comment here about the trend of arranging just about everything into a "still life" and calling it a flower arrangement. It is more appropriate that they are now called abstract or modern and results are handsome and exotic to the extreme. I am old-fashioned enough to love flowers so much that my arrangements don't find a place for driftwood, Chinese masks, or grandfather's old pipe. Japanese arrangements are very popular and clubs organized to study this style are found in almost every city. These arrangers have produced many artistic arrangements for flower shows and reflect the Japanese devotion to nature.

Flower shows and garden club schools teaching arrangement have done much to improve this art for the general public. They stress principles of design—balance, dominance, contrast, rhythm, proportion, and scale.

As competition becomes keener, the tendency to "overstylize" should be avoided. The effort to be original often leads to arrangements or compositions that are too stiff, with flowers arranged like peas in a pod. Many arrangers are not interested in horticulture and, lacking lovely specimens, make arrangements almost without flowers, or with any flowers that may be available. They often frown on the Flemish or Victorian styles of arranging, believing these with their masses of flowers poor art. The height of any art is yet to be attained, and who are we to judge which is the best? The fact still remains that the real beauty of flower arranging comes with lovely flowers arranged in a pleasing, natural manner. From comments I hear at flower shows, the general public will be pleased when emphasis is on color and naturalness instead of line and design.

In flower-show judging, the scale of points differs with types of arrangements and specialized societies vary on judging, but generally 30 points go for design; 20 for color; 20 for suitability of relationship of all materials; 10 for distinction; 10 for originality, and 10 for condition of materials. In noting these, originality has only 10 points, so there is no need for overemphasis here. In general, this is an excellent system and as judges and exhibitors become more experienced, they will not be so impressed with the bizarre and fantastic. No other affair in civic life seems to create more interest than a flower show, as evidenced by great attendance.

Plants for Special Purposes

LISTED here are plant materials for special purposes that should be helpful to the beginning gardener. See garden catalogs for description.

FOR THE HOBBYIST GARDENER—Chrysanthemum, daffodil, dahlia, delphinium, gladiolus, herbs, iris, lily, peony, rose, tuberous begonia.

SHADE—Aucuba (shrub), caladium, campanula, clematis, (vine), coleus, delphinium, dogwood (shrub), forgetmenot, holly (shrub), lily, pansy, redbud (tree), tuberous begonia, violet, tree peony (light shade).

SUN—Alyssum saxatile, aster, babysbreath, bachelor's-button, chrysanthemum, daffodil, dahlia, daisy (all types), daylily, gladiolus, iris, marigold, zinnia.

WATER REQUIREMENTS LESS—Cactus, cosmos, gaillardia, iris (except just before blooming), marigold, oriental poppy, petunia, succulent.

PLANTS THAT DO NOT REQUIRE DIVIDING—Alyssum saxatile, bleeding heart, delphinium, lythrum, oriental poppy, painted daisy, sweet rocket, tuberous begonia.

TALL PLANTS FOR BACKGROUND—Campanula (gargantea pyramidalis), cosmos, daylily, delphinium, eremurus, false dragonhead, iris ochroleuca, lily, lythrum, marigold, peony, perennial phlox, sweet rocket.

INTERMEDIATE PLANTS FOR BACKGROUND—Babysbreath, baptisia, chrysanthemum, daffodil, daisy, feverfew, oriental poppy, peony, sea lavender, tulip, zinnia.

LOW PLANTS FOR FOREGROUND—Alyssum saxatile, candytuft, catnip, cerastium tomentosum, chrysanthemum (cushion and button), jonquil simplex, nierembergia, pansy, petunia, phlox camla, phlox stolonifera (Blue Ridge), pinks.

EDGINGS—Ageratum, alyssum saxatile, babyblue-eyes, chrysanthemum (Dorothy Nehrling), dustymiller, dwarf barberry (Crimson Pygmy), grapehyacinth, lobelia, oxalis, pansy, petunia, santolina, teucrium.

GROUND COVERS—Arabis, ajuga, buttercup, cerastium, euonymus radicans, ground ivy, myrtle, plumbago.

SPRING COLOR—Alyssum saxatile, bulbs, flowering trees, forsythia, iris, lilacs, pansies, phlox subulata, violets.

MIDSUMMER COLOR—Crapemyrtle (shrub), dahlia, daisy, daylily, gladiolus, lily, nierembergia, petunia, rose, sweet alyssum, vitex (shrub), zinnia.

FALL COLOR—Ageratum, alyssum (Royal Carpet), butterfly bush, chrysanthemum, dahlia, gladiolus (if planted late), marigold, rose.

ANNUALS—Ageratum, aster, calendula, cornflower, cosmos, larkspur, marigold, nasturtium, petunia, phlox, sweet pea, zinnia.

PERENNIALS—Alyssum saxatile, anchusa, baptisia, chrysanthemum, daisy, delphinium, gaillardia, hardy aster, lythrum, phlox, pyrethrum, sweet rocket, veronica.

Dependable Varieties

THESE plant lists of dependable varieties will aid the beginning gardener in making selections.

DAYLILY—Autumn Daffodil, Black Falcon, Coral Mist, Glory, High Noon, Honey Redhead, Hyperion, Linda, Mrs. B. F. Bonner, Painted Lady, Pink Dawn.

LILY—Auratum, Aurelian, Centofolium, Fiesta Hybrids, Green Mountain hybrids, Mid-century hybrids, Regal, Shuksan, Speciosum, Testicum.

DAFFODILS AND JONQUILS—Beersheba, Cheerfulness, Duke of Windsor, Early Perfection, Green Emerald, jonquilla simplex, jonquilla Triviathian, King Alfred, Lord Nelson, Mount Hood, Romaine, Triandrus Thalia.

OTHER BULBS—Chionodoxa, crocus, grapehyacinth, hyacinth, ixia, scilla, snowdrops.

DAHLIA—Arthur Godfrey, Avalon, Century of Progress, Cherokee Brave, Clariam Forever, Connie Casey, Gold Coin, Jane Lausche, Lady Alice, Little Diamond, Lone Star, Mrs. E. J., Mrs. Thomas Edison, Pride of Holland, Vision.

GLADIOLUS—Apple Blossom, Caribbean, Elizabeth the Queen, Golden Arrow, King David, Maytime, Mother Fisher, Picardy, Red Wings, Royal Stewart, Sparkling Eyes, Spic and Span, White Goddess.

TULIPS—Aristocrat, Bandoeng, City of Haarlem, Eros, Glacier, Ibis, Marietta, Mount Tacoma, Mrs. John T. Scheepers, Queen Elizabeth, Queen of Spain, Queen of the Night, Red Ace, Red Emperor, Therese, Uncle Tom.

SHRUBS—Bridal Wreath, butterfly bush, caryopteris, crapemyrtle, euonymus, flowering quince, forsythia, gold-dust plant, holly (Wilson's), Oregongrape, privet, pussywillow, vitex, weigela.

ORNAMENTAL TREES—Chinaberry, flowering crab (many varieties), flowering peach (several varieties), flowering plum (several varieties), golden chain tree, goldenrain tree, hawthorn, mountain ash, redbud, silk tree (mimosa), smoke tree, sweet gum, weeping mulberry, wistaria.

SHADE TREES—Apple (fruit), apricot (fruit), ash, cottonwood, hackberry, locust, mulberry (fruitless), pecan, Russian olive, sycamore, weeping willow.

HOUSE PLANTS—African violet (Saint Paulia), begonia, cactus, coleus, dieffenbachia, dracaena, geranium, Norfolk Island pine, philodendron (many varieties), rubber plant, sansevieria.

PEONY—Albuquerque, Chocolate Soldier, Doris Cooper, Elsa Sass, Felix Crouse, Festiva Maxima, Gay Paree, Isani-Gidui (Japanese single), Le Cygne, Longfellow, Loren Franklin, Martha Bullock, Minuet, Mons. Jules Elie, Nick Shaylor, Solange, Westerner.

VINES—Boston ivy, clematis, climbing roses (must have support), English ivy, grape, honeysuckle, silver lace, trumpet vine.

Calendar

EXACT TIMES for garden chores cannot be stated for the entire area, since sections farther north, such as Taos, Santa Fe, and southern Colorado, will develop seasonally considerably later than portions as far south as El Paso. A difference of from two to three weeks sometimes is noted from year to year, even in the same locality, due to climatic changes. However, for most practical purposes, this calendar can be followed generally.

January

BUDDLEIAS — Prune.

EQUIPMENT — Repair, sharpen, and paint handles. Check sprays.

GARDEN PLANNING — It's a good time to do some quiet planning for the coming year. The post-holiday doldrums have set in and it is too cold to be outdoors, so study the catalogues and place orders.

HOUSE PLANTS — Since this is the month they are enjoyed the most give them a little extra food and attention.

IRRIGATE — At least once during the month.

POTTED BULBS — Check bulbs that are being forced. If roots show through the drainage hole place the pots indoors in a cool, dark corner. When the green shoots are an inch high, put them out into the light.

ROSES — Plant dormant roses.

SEED FLATS — Plant indoors.

TUBEROUS BEGONIAS — Start indoors.

February

BULBS — Give forced bulbs plenty of sun and enough water to encourage their blooms.

COLD FRAMES — Start late in month.

EVERGREENS — Give good washing with the hose.
— May be planted as they become available.

GENERAL — Apply agricultural sulphur to combat alkalinity.
— Dig flower and vegetable beds and prepare for planting in March.
— Remove dead leaves and debris, but leave enough to protect tender shoots during any cold spells to come.

LAWN — Fertilize when lawn shows touch of green. Valuable nitrogen is lost if lawn is fertilized before roots start activity.

PANSIES — Plant.

PERENNIALS — Transplant hardy.

PLANT — Pansies and other hardy plants.

PRUNE — Fruit trees, flowering fruit trees, and evergreen branches that have grown out of bounds.
— Roses late in the month if buds appear ready to leaf. Do not be in a hurry, however. It is better to prune a little late than too early.

ROSES — Plant new.
— Fertilize as growth appears.
— See "Prune."
— In warm sections gradually wash away the hills of soil.

SEED FLATS — Start late in month.

     — Harden off fall-planted seed flats by giving them sun and allowing them to remain out overnight when nights are mild.

SHRUBS — Plant as they become available.

SPRAY — Buds are beginning to swell, so use the cleanup (dormant) spray, which is the most important spray of the year.

SWEET PEAS — Plant between the "presidents' birthdays."

TREES — Plant as they become available.

March

CHRYSANTHEMUMS — Prepare beds for planting late this month or early April.

COLD FRAMES — Harden off plants in cold frames.

FERTILIZE — Use compost around special plants such as the favored delphiniums.
— Put first manure mulch on roses.
— Fertilize lawn if you haven't done so.

FLOWERING SHRUBS — Bring in branches to force for attractive home display.

GENERAL — Give flower beds final cleanup.
— Dig grass from around flower beds and edge lawns around them.
— Protect small plants from wind and irrigate after severe windstorms.

GLADIOLI — Plant a portion of your gladioli.

IRIS — Clean up. Remove dead leaves.

LAWN — Fertilize if you haven't done so.

PERENNIALS — Plant and transplant. Fertilize.

PLANT — Hardier vegetable and flower seed.
— This is last month advisable to plant roses, shrubs, trees, and other large plants. If available in containers they may be set out later than this month.

ROSES — Last month advisable to plant, except in high altitudes.
— Put first manure mulch on roses.
— Prune and use cleanup spray if you neglected it last month.

SHRUBS — Last month advisable to plant.
— See "Plant."

TREES — Last month advisable to plant.
— See "Plant."

VEGETABLES — Plant seeds of hardier vegetables.

April

ANNUALS — Seeds may be planted in mild weather.

DAFFODILS — Feed those that have finished blooming. Remove faded heads, but leave stems.

IRIS — Wash aphids off plants by streams of cold water, on sunny days. Use chemical spray if necessary.

— Clumps will be more tidy if bloomed out stalks are cut away.

JONQUILS — See Daffodils.

PANSIES — Keep picked for longer blooming period.

PRUNE — Hedges, santolina, nierembergia, and similar plants, also crapemyrtle.

ROSES — Disbud and give a little extra food.

— Wash aphids off plants as with iris.

TUBEROUS BEGONIAS — Set out if weather seems settled.

VEGETABLES — Seeds may be planted in mild weather.

VIOLETS — Keep picked for longer blooming period.

TREES AND SHRUBS — Container stock can be planted.

May

ASTERS — May be cut back to encourage branching.

CHRYSANTHEMUMS — Usually need their first pinching back this month.

DELPHINIUM — Have finished blooming and should be cut back part way. Finish the cutting-back process next month to diminish the shock.

GENERAL — Faded blooms should be cut away from spirea, lilac, and forsythia, and all other plants. Seed pods should not be allowed to develop, as seed from such flowers as the larkspur, bachelor's-button, and poppy will crowd out other desirable garden plants in later seasons. I do pick out the very best flower specimens and allow them to reseed.

— Plants that multiply rapidly should be kept within bounds.

ORIENTAL POPPIES — Should be cut back some now and the cutting-back process finished next month.

PHLOX — Cut back to encourage branching.

ROSES — Do not cut long stems when gathering the first roses. After the first cycle of bloom give the plants extra food or a manure mulch.

SEEDS — Finish planting annual and vegetable seeds.

TOMATO PLANTS — Put out.

TULIP BULBS — Feed; plant annuals nearby to fill in spots with future blooms.

June

BULBS — Order. Many growers give discounts for early orders.

CHRYSANTHEMUMS — Pinch off side shoots of exhibition chrysanthemums.

— Stake.

DAFFODILS — See tulips.

DAHLIAS — Stake.

DELPHINIUM — Order seed.

— Finish cutting back.

— Fertilize to encourage fall blooming period.

IRIS — May be divided from now until September.

LAWN — Give an extra feeding, taking a cool day for the job. Keep the grass weeded. When cutting, don't set the blade of the mower too short. About an inch and a half is right. If you note chlorosis (yellowing) of the lawn or plants, feed with iron sulphate. Never throw away grass clippings. If you don't have a compost heap, at least use them for a light mulch around plants.

ORIENTAL POPPIES — Order plants.

— Finish cutting back to encourage fall growing period.

PANSIES — Order seed.

PEONIES — Feed, to improve clumps for next year.

ROSES — Keep faded roses cut. Leave as much foliage as possible on the plant.

TULIPS — Take up bulbs where they are too thick. Store for fall planting. Keep varieties and colors separated.

July

ANNUALS — Pull up early ones that have finished blooming.

ASTERS — Hardy should be sheared a second time to keep them bushy.

CHRYSANTHEMUMS—Sprinkle leaves frequently.
— Fertilize.

EVERGREENS — Wash with strong spray of cold water to combat red spiders, now at their worst.

GENERAL — Keep cutting faded flowers from bloomed-out plants.
— Scraggly and unwanted growth may be cut off climbers.

PERENNIALS — Cuttings from house plants can fill in bare spots along border.

SHASTA DAISIES — Cut back after blooming.

TUBEROUS BEGONIAS — Sprinkle leaves frequently. Feed.

VEGETABLES — Plant for fall.

August

CHRYSANTHEMUMS — Feed. Don't let buds remain until late in month on any except azaleamum variety.

FLOWERING SHRUBS
AND TREES — Unwanted growth may be pruned away. Gently now!

IRIS — Order and plant new.

LILIES — Plant.
— Make divisions where necessary.

ORIENTAL POPPIES — Plant.

PERENNIALS — If weather is hot wait until September to plant seed.

ROSES — Feed.

September

CHRYSANTHEMUMS — Disbud and feed. Give more water.
— Wash off aphids.

COLD FRAME — Plant pansy and delphinium, along with other seeds, if weather is cool.

COLEUS — Root cuttings to take indoors.

DELPHINIUM — Plant seeds in cold frame.

GERANIUM — Root cuttings to take indoors.

LAWNS — May be planted now.
— Reseed bare spots rather late in month. Fertilize.
— Don't cut grass too short for winter.

PANSIES — Plant seeds in cold frame.

PEONIES — Plant.

PERENNIALS — Set out new.

ROSES — Use fungicide for possible mildew.
— Wash foliage about once a week.
— Feed early in month, as too late feeding will produce soft growth.
— Cut down water supply.
— Longer stemmed roses may be cut.

October

ANNUALS — Scatter-plant hardy annual seed.

BEGONIAS — Dig after first frost.

BULBS — Plant after leaves have started to fall.
— Plant daffodils as soon as received.
— Pot for forcing.

CHRYSANTHEMUMS — Put up cloth protectors for exhibition chrysanthemums, if you have decided to give them extra care. Feed every week until color shows in buds. Do necessary disbudding.

DAHLIAS — Dig after first frost.

EVERGREENS — May be planted.

GENERAL — Attractive dried materials and berries make good indoor arrangements.

GLADIOLI — Dig after first frost or later.

IRRIGATION — Continue, but not as generously as before, since soft growth might be encouraged.

LAWNS — Still time to plant, but the earlier the better. Fertilize.

LILACS — More successful if planted now.

PERENNIALS — Plant seed flat.
— Don't allow leaves to cover borders too deeply.
— Keep leaves away from delphinium and oriental poppy crowns.

SHRUBS — May be planted.

November

BULBS — Still time to plant but hurry.

CHRYSANTHEMUMS — Cut before severe frost. Put in cool place in water.

HOUSE PLANTS — Check. Give extra food, since they will be your gardening plants for the next several months.

ROSES — Hill in colder areas.

— Cut tall canes that might whip around in the wind; also trim off soft growth.

SWEET PEAS — Plant in damp soil but do not water.

December

BULBS — Watch pots being forced.

— Check to see if they need water.

— Examine stored bulbs, tubers, and similar items, checking against freezing temperatures.

COLD FRAMES — Watch.

— Water when necessary.

— Lift off cover on warm days.

EVERGREENS — Prune around Christmas time using the clippings for house decoration.

— Remember they like their foliage washed.

GENERAL — Plan holiday decorations and entertainment, forgetting gardening until that mid-January slump.

IRRIGATION — Remember to water every few weeks, on warm, sunny days.

ROSES — Hill up.

Plot Plans

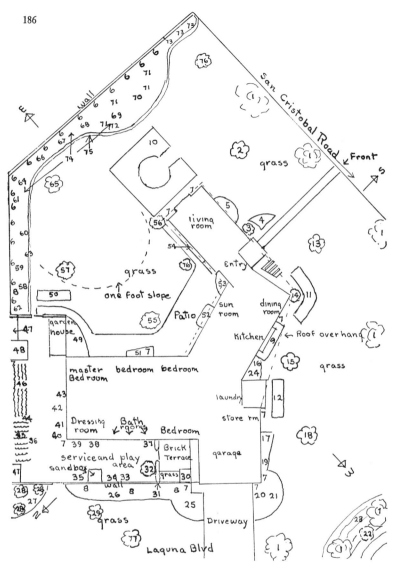

THE AUTHOR'S DREAM HOUSE is built on an odd-shaped lot with streets facing three sides of it. House and planting had to be shaped to conform. Each year finds small changes or added plant material, which, after all, is what makes gardening fun.

1. Cottonwood tree
2. Tree wistaria
3. Mahonia, Oregongrape
4. Bulbs, coleus, petunias
5. Fashion roses, dustymiller border
6. Climbing roses trained on arches
7. Climbing rose
8. Shrub rose
9. Floribunda rose, Circus
10. Hybrid tea roses, border santolina
11. Hybrid tea roses (yellow) border of lobelia
12. Hybrid tea roses (rose) edged with nierembergia
13. Prunus triloba
14. Spanish broom
15. Plum prunus cistena
16. Grapevine trained under eaves
17. Peonies edged by tulips, petunias
18. Flowering peach, Crimson Brilliant
19. Austrian Copper rose
20. Cydonia, Stanford red
21. Daffodils, campanula, hardy chrysanthemums
22. Yellow moss rose
23. Rows of ground cover
24. Kitchen garden
25. Michaelmas daisies, daffodils and peonies
26. Roses, lilies, and delphinium edged with strawberries
27. Iris and old-fashioned roses
28. Cercis, redbud
29. Weeping crab
30. Garbage area, with brick wall
31. Euonymus hedge
32. Apple tree
33. Hansen bush cherry
34. Dwarf Bing cherry
35. Peach tree
36. Apricot tree
37. Spirea, Anthony Waterer
38. Musk rose
39. Mockorange, Belle Etoíle
40. Euonymus
41. Pyracantha
42. Prunus cistena

Doolittle residence

43. Dogwood, Tatarian
44. Apple, "Five-on-One"
45. Vegetable bed
46. Exhibition chrysanthemums
47. Cold frames
48. Compost box
49. Bulbs, perennials, edge of alyssum saxatile
50. Pink roses, edge of lobelia and ageratum
51. Petunias, bulbs, edge of nierembergia
52. Bulbs and flowers
53. Camellia, hydrangea, amaryllis, caladium
54. Tuberous begonias, tulips, Wilson's holly, aucuba
55. Hopa crab
56. Photinia
57. Flowering apricot, Rosemary Clarke
58. Poinciana, Bird of Paradise
59. Laburnum vossi
60. Redleaf peach
61. Flowering peach, Iceberg
62. Forsythia
63. Weigela, Bristol Ruby
64. Hawthorne, Paul's Scarlet
65. Bechtel crab
66. Norway Maple, Crimson King
67. Smoketree
68. Flowering plum, prunus pissardi rosea
69. Flowering peach, Helen Borchers
70. Flowering cherry
71. Lilacs
72. Caryopteris, Blue Mist
73. Moss roses
74. Perennial border
75. Three borders, early pansies, later sweet alyssum and latest dwarf red chrysanthemums
76. Redbud tree
77. Howard's miracle plum

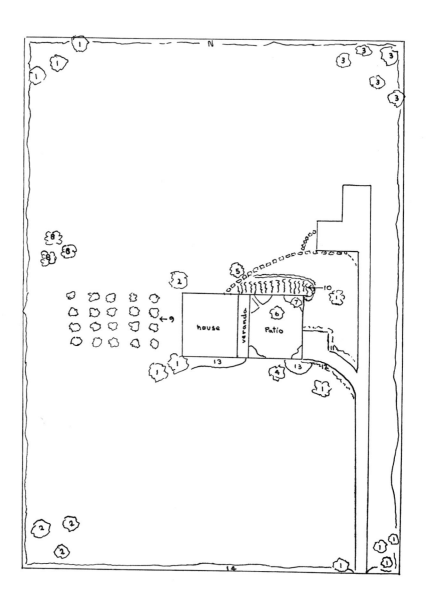

For the Ranch Home

THE VARIETY of trees mentioned here is only a suggestion, since trees native to the area would be suitable. Evergreens, too, might be used to advantage. Closer to the house itself, the patio trees and others may be those that require more care. Roses and perennials could be patio plants. Stone, brick, or cement could be used generously about the patio to reduce lawn care and conserve water.

1. Cottonwood tree
2. Siberian elm
3. Lombardy poplar
4. Mountain ash
5. Weeping willow
6. Bechtel crab
7. Redbud
8. Arizona ash
9. Orchard
10. Vegetables, surrounded by hollyhocks in early spring, marigolds later
11. Hedge of daylilies
12. Hedge of iris
13. Hollyhocks and native plant materials
14. Windbreak of Russian olive or tamarisk

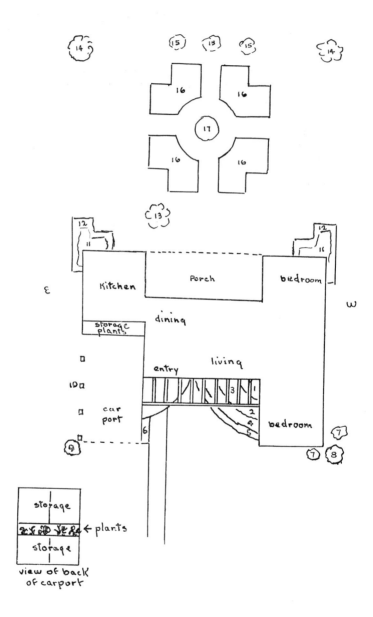

Modern House and Garden

SIMPLICITY is the keynote here for the gardener who does not have time for elaborate plantings. Roses, and the circle of flowers in the rose bed, are the only flowers sketched, making the care an easy task. To make it even easier, floribunda roses are suggested in the place of the hybrid tea varieties.

Edgings of coleus and centaurea may be purchased from a nursery. Daffodils are used in the place of tulips, since they do not require to be "taken up" as often. An edge of brick is laid even with the lawn to simplify the task of edging the lawn periodically. The "planter" in the carport may contain geraniums, coleus, and philodendron, all of easy culture. Evergreen branches may replace these in the winter.

1. Euonymus
2 and 3. Three mahonias
4. Coleus
5. Centaurea
6. Euonymus
7. Juniper, Spiny Greek
8. Juniper, Red Cedar, Virginiana canaerti
9. Photinia
10. Climbing rose, Paul's Scarlet
11. Daffodils and coleus
12. Centaurea candidissima
13. Arizona Ash
14. Arborvitae, Rosedale Blue
15. Arborvitae
16. Hybrid tea roses
17. Bird bath or flowering tree

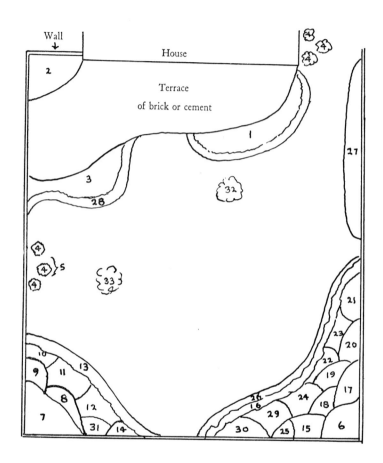

An Economy Garden

THIS PLAN creates a garden of mostly annual flowers that will provide glorious color and effects with a cost of less than five dollars. The plan would be good for a new home owner who cannot afford permanent planting immediately or for the temporary residents, such as residents near our army posts, and government employees. Often trees can be brought home free for the digging from river banks.

1. Pink verbena edged with ageratum
2. Korean hybrid chrysanthemum (easily grown from seed)
3. Purple single petunias edged with white sweet alyssum
4. Castorbeans
5. Three castorbeans, Crimson Spire
6. Cosmos, Pink Sensation
7. Tall yellow marigolds, Riverside Beauty
8. Orange marigolds
9. Yellow zinnias
10. Nasturtiums
11. Marigolds, Glitter
12. Anchusa, Bluebird
13. Marigold, Butterball
14. Shasta daisies
15. Burpee's Super Giant zinnias
16. Alyssum, Violet Queen
17. Zinnias, Fantasy
18. Larkspur
19. Snapdragons
20. Asters
21. Imbricated pompon asters
22. Arctotis
23. Bachelor's-button, mix
24. Dahlias, Unwin's Dwarf Hybrid
25. Feverfew
26. Babyblue-eyes (*Nemophila*)
27. Petunias
28. Sweet alyssum, Carpet of Snow
29. Pompon zinnias
30. Anchusa, Bluebird
31. Tithonia
32. Cottonwood tree
33. Russian olive tree

Pueblo House

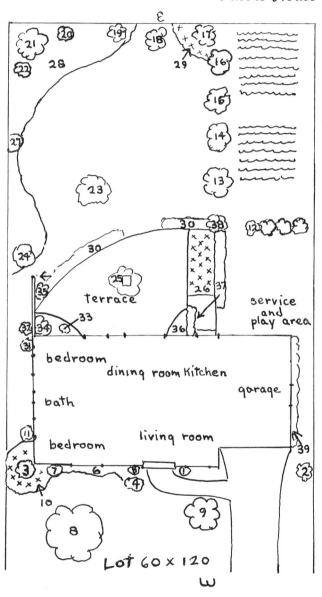

Lot 60 × 120

Border Plan

KEY TO PUEBLO PLAN

An edged rose bed that may be designed to grow alongside a garden wall, with a path between wall and flower bed.

1. Alyssum saxtile, with front border of lobelia
2. Forsythia
3. Spanish broom
4. Mahonia
5. Paul's Scarlet rose
6. Petunias
7. Hollyhocks
8. Russian olive tree
9. Flowering crab (Crimson Brilliant)
10. Fashion roses
11. Pyracantha
12. Variety of lilacs
13. Dwarf apple
14. Dwarf cherry
15. Dwarf Bing cherry
16. Dwarf apricot
17. Peach tree
18. Laburnum vossi
19. Caryopteris, Blue Mist
20. Vitex macrophylla
21. Sycamore
22. Buddleia, Flaming Violet
23. Cottonwood
24. Cercis, redbud
25. Hopa crab
26. Hybrid tea roses
27. Climbing rose
28. Perennial border
29. Floribunda roses
30. Spring bulbs, petunias later
31. Cornus alba Tatarian
32. Climbing rose
33. Lavender
34. Crapemyrtle
35. Spanish broom
36. Begonias
37. Euonymus hedge
38. Juniper, Spiny Greek
39. Chrysanthemums

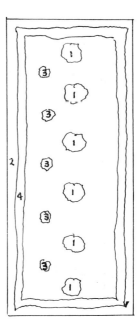

1. Floribunda rose, Floradora
2. Babyblue-eyes (*Nemophila*), replaced later with ageratum Blue Cap for late summer
3. Veronica
4. Pansy, Sea Blue

Note: Veronica is placed next to the walk and is higher than the pansy border, since the bed is viewed more from that side.

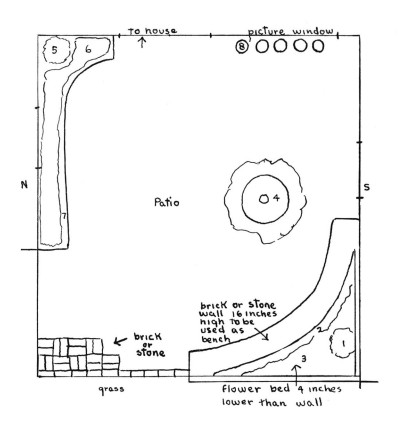

Plans for a Small Patio

CURVES are used to break lines in this small patio plan. The brick "bench" makes a raised flower bed and at the same time provides extra seating spaces. Flowers that do not grow tall will be effective in this bed and will create an attractive view from the opposite windows. In fact, all planting is done to provide a pleasing view from opposite windows.

1. Crapemyrtle
2. Alyssum saxatile
3. Tulips, followed by petunias or geraniums
4. Flowering crab, Crimson Brilliant
5. Silver juniper
6. Tuberous begonias and columbines
7. Pansies
8. Potted geraniums

Ribbon Flower Bed

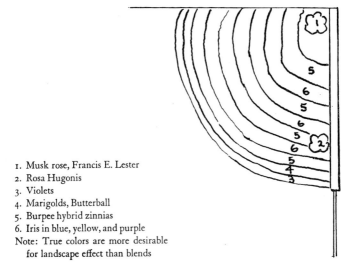

1. Musk rose, Francis E. Lester
2. Rosa Hugonis
3. Violets
4. Marigolds, Butterball
5. Burpee hybrid zinnias
6. Iris in blue, yellow, and purple
Note: True colors are more desirable for landscape effect than blends

Perennial Border

BULBS AND ANNUALS may be worked between these plantings for early spring and late summer bloom. Number after each flower indicates number of plants used.

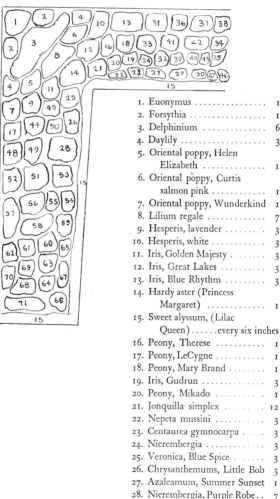

1. Euonymus 1
2. Forsythia 1
3. Delphinium 6
4. Daylily 3
5. Oriental poppy, Helen Elizabeth 1
6. Oriental poppy, Curtis salmon pink 1
7. Oriental poppy, Wunderkind 1
8. Lilium regale 7
9. Hesperis, lavender 3
10. Hesperis, white 3
11. Iris, Golden Majesty 3
12. Iris, Great Lakes 3
13. Iris, Blue Rhythm 3
14. Hardy aster (Princess Margaret) 1
15. Sweet alyssum, (Lilac Queen)......every six inches
16. Peony, Therese 1
17. Peony, LeCygne 1
18. Peony, Mary Brand 1
19. Iris, Gudrun 3
20. Peony, Mikado 1
21. Jonquilla simplex 12
22. Nepeta mussini 3
23. Centaurea gymnocarpa 3
24. Nierembergia 3
25. Veronica, Blue Spice 3
26. Chrysanthemums, Little Bob 3
27. Azaleamum, Summer Sunset 1
28. Nierembergia, Purple Robe.. 7

29. Button chrysanthemums,
      Pink Jewell   1
30. Aubrieta leichtlini   3
31. Lythrum, Morden's Pink . .   1
32. Sedum Sieboldi   3
33. Phlox, Rose Blue   3
34. Phlox, Mary Louise   3
35. Iris, Blue Summer   3
36. Iris, Sable   3
37. Iris, China Maid   3
38. Hardy aster, Survivor   1
39. Hardy aster, Redrover   1
40. Hardy aster, Violetta   1
41. Phlox, Columbine   3
42. Peony, Longfellow   1
43. Tulip, Clara Butt   12
44. Iris, Ola Kala   3
45. Daffodils, King Alfred   12
46. Alyssum saxatile   3
47. Centaurea candidissma   3
48. Delphinium   3
49. Shasta daisy   3
50. Oriental poppy, Indian Chief   1
51. Peony, Frances Willard   3
52. Leonian hybrid daylilies   6
53. Tulip, Golden Age   12
54. Grapehyacinths   12
55. Gaillardia   3
56. Columbine, Colorado Blue . .   3
57. Iris, California Gold   3
58. Snapdragon mix   6
59. Pansy   2
60. Korean hybrid chrysan-
      themums   3
61. Tritoma   3
62. Rose, Austrian Copper   1
63. Baptisia   3
64. Pyrethrum   3
65. Triteleia   24
66. Nepeta mussini   3
67. Saponaria ocymoides   3
68. Sweetwilliam, Newport Pink   3
69. Daylily, Hyperion yellow . .   1
70. Delphinium   3
71. Pansies

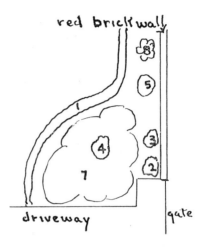

Corner Plan

red brick wall

driveway   gate

1. Strawberries
2. Climbing rose
3. Rose, Frau Karl Druschki
4. Berberis, red leafed
5. Shasta daisy
6. Cecil rose
7. Mixture Michaelmas daisies—
    a. Survivor
    b. Mt. Everest
    c. Beechwood Challenger
    d. Violetta
    e. Blue Gown
8. Cecil rose

Driveway Border

A MASS PLANTING here is more effective than a straight border along the edge of driveway and garage.

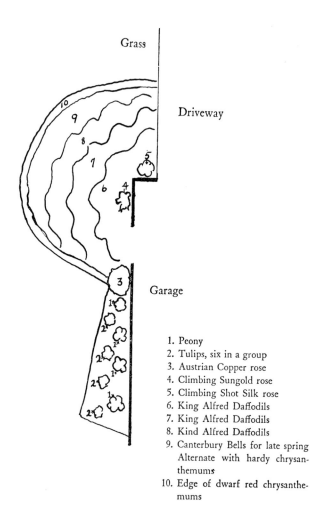

Grass

Driveway

Garage

1. Peony
2. Tulips, six in a group
3. Austrian Copper rose
4. Climbing Sungold rose
5. Climbing Shot Silk rose
6. King Alfred Daffodils
7. King Alfred Daffodils
8. Kind Alfred Daffodils
9. Canterbury Bells for late spring
   Alternate with hardy chrysanthemums
10. Edge of dwarf red chrysanthemums

Shady Bed Plans

A BED for a very shady corner planted with material that thrives on such
a situation.

1. Azalea mollis
2. Bleeding heart, Dicentra
3. Columbine, Colorado Blue
4. Pyrethrum
5. Tuberous begonias

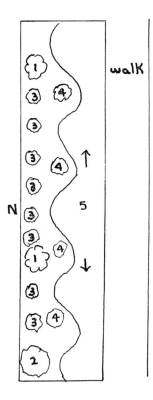

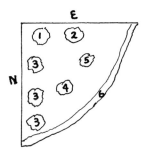

1. Camellia
2. Azalea
3. Azalea
4. Hydrangea, Domotoi
5. Camellia
6. Tuberous begonias

Plan for Continuous Bloom

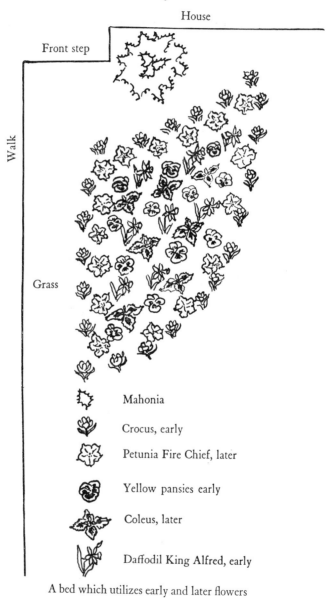

House

Front step

Walk

Grass

Mahonia

Crocus, early

Petunia Fire Chief, later

Yellow pansies early

Coleus, later

Daffodil King Alfred, early

A bed which utilizes early and later flowers

Vegetable Garden

PLANT MORE VEGETABLES in empty rows about July for fall use.
Beans may be planted with corn and allowed to climb on corn.
Small gardens may be closely planted if well fed.

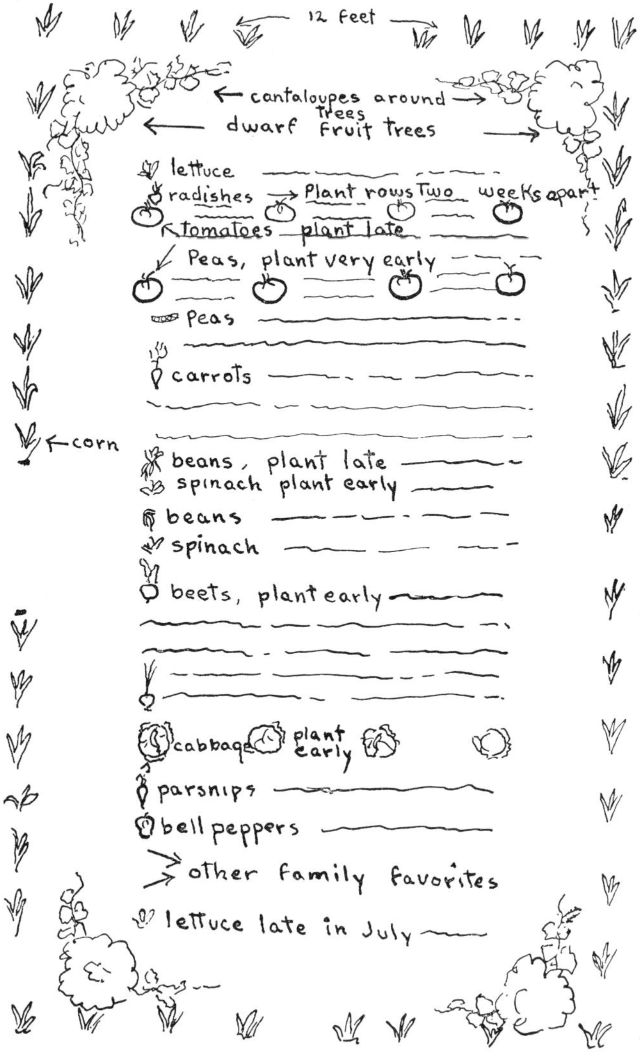

12 feet

← cantaloupes around →
Trees
← dwarf fruit trees →

lettuce

radishes → Plant rows Two weeks apart

tomatoes plant late

Peas, plant very early

Peas

carrots

←corn

beans, plant late
spinach plant early

beans

spinach

beets, plant early

cabbage plant early

parsnips

bell peppers

other family favorites

lettuce late in July

Bibliography

BEFORE YOU KNOW IT, you, as a beginning gardener will find yourself collecting books, magazines, and pamphlets on your favorite gardening topics or on general information. No one book is enough. In fact, I have found new and exciting books regularly on all aspects of gardening. Books on compost, on perennials, on roses and lilies, and, most recently, a book on orchid culture which I am now following diligently as I pursue this newest garden hobby of mine.

By no means discard any copy of gardening magazines to which you are subscribing. Eventually the articles within them will interest you. Some magazines provide easy index guides for future reference. Make a habit of saving leaflets and booklets, issued by reputable garden supply firms, on new techniques and methods in pest control, and other topics. Some of the better nursery firms send out gorgeous catalogues which I save through the years for reference and comparison.

Books listed in this Bibliography are in alphabetical order according to title, rather than by the name of the author, in order to be more helpful to the gardener unfamiliar with garden-expert authors.

African Violets, Helen Van Pelt Wilson, M. Barrows and Co. 1963.

All About House Plants, Montague Free. The American Garden Guild, Inc., Doubleday and Company, Inc., New York. 1946.

The American Horticulture Magazine, Daffodil Handbook, American Horticulture Society. 1966.

American Rose Annual, American Rose Society, Columbus, Ohio. Issued annually.

The Art of Home Landscaping, Garrett Eckbo, McGraw-Hill Book Co. 1956.

Better Homes and Gardens Garden Book, Meredith Publishing Co., Des Moines, Iowa. 1951.

Bulbs for Beauty, Charles H. Mueller. M. Barrows and Co., New York. 1947.

Climbing Roses, by Helen Van Pelt Wilson. M. Barrows and Company, Inc., New York. 1955.

Color and Design for Every Garden, by H. Stuart Ortloff and Henry Raymore. American Book-Stratford Press, Inc., New York. 1951.

The Complete Book of Chrysanthemums, Cornelius Ackerson, Doubleday and Co. 1957.

Daffodils, Outdoors and In, Carey E. Quinn, Hearthside Press, Inc. 1959

Flower Family Album, by Gretchen Field Fisher and Gretchen Harshbarger. University of Minnesota Press, Minneapolis, Minnesota. 1941.

Flowers of the Southwest Desert, Natt N. Dodge. Drawings, Jeanne R. Janish. Dale S. King, editor. Southwestern Monuments Association, National Park Service, U. S. Dept. of the Interior. 1951.

Flowers of the Southwest Mesas, Pauline Mead Patraw. Drawings, Jeanne R. Janish. Dale S. King, editor. Southwestern Monuments Association, National Park Service, U. S. Dept. of the Interior. 1951.

Gardens Are for People, by Thomas D. Church. Reinhold Publishing Corp., New York. 1955.

The Gardeners Bug Book, Cynthia Westcott, Doubleday and Co. 1964.

Garden Flowers in Color, G. A. Stevens. The Macmillan Co., New York. 1933.

Gardening Without Poisons, Beatrice Trum Hunter, Houghton Mifflin Co. 1964.

Gardens in Color, Richard Pratt, with color photographs by Edward Steichen. Garden City Publishing Co., New York. 1948.

The Handbook for Flower Shows, National Council of State Garden Clubs, Inc. 1966.

High Altitude Gardening, Los Alamos Garden Club. Southwestern Publishing Co., Santa Fe, N. M.

The Home Garden Self-Pronouncing Dictionary of Plant Names, Ralph Bailey, editor. American Garden Guild, Inc., New York. 1948.

The How and Why of Better Gardening, by Lawrence Manning. D. Van Nostrand Company, Inc., New York. 1951.

How to Have a Green Thumb Without an Aching Back, by Ruth Stout. Exposition Press, New York. 1956.

How to Have Good Gardens in the Sunshine States, George W. Kelly. Smith-Brooks Printing Co., Littleton, Colo. 1957.

Iris for Every Garden, by Sidney B. Mitchell. M. Barrows and Company, Inc., New York. 1949.

The Joy of Flower Arranging, by Helen VanPelt Wilson. M. Barrows and Company, Inc., New York. 1951.

The Judging of Roses, C. H. Lewis, Available from the American Rose Society, 4048 Roselea Place, Columbus, Ohio. 43214

Landscape Architecture, John Ormsbee Simonds, McGraw-Hill Book Co. 1961.

Lawn Problems of the Southwest, Howard J. Dittmer. University of New Mexico Press, Albuquerque. 1950.

Let's Arrange Roses, Emilia Burke. J. Horace McFarland Co., Harrisburg, Penn. 1951.

Let's Grow Lilies, The North American Lily Society, George-Little Press, Inc., Burlington, Vermont.

The Living Soil, by E. B. Balfour. The Devin-Adair Company, New York. 1948.

The Magic World of Roses, Matthew A. R. Bassity, Houghton Mifflin Co. 1964.

Manual of Cultivated Plants, L. H. Bailey. The Macmillan Co., New York, 1949.

Mrs. Foote's Rose Book, Harriet Riseley Foote. Charles T. Branford Co., Boston. 1948.

The New Book of Lilies, Jan De Graff. M. Barrows and Co., New York. 1951.

Ornamental Plants of Sub-Tropical Regions, Roland Stewart Hoyt, compiler. Livingston Press, Los Angeles. 1938.

Our Garden Soils, Charles E. Kellogg. The Macmillan Co., New York.

Pacific Coast Gardening Guide, Norvell Gillespie. Doubleday and Co., New York. 1949.

Pay Dirt, Farming and Gardening with Composts, J. I. Rodale. The Devin-Adair Company, New York. 1948.

Peonies, Outdoors and In, Arno and Irene Nehrling, Hearthside Press Inc. 1960.

Perennials Preferred, Helen VanPelt Wilson. M. Barrows and Company, New York. 1945.

The Plant Doctor, Cynthia Westcott. J. B. Lippincott Co., Philadelphia and New York. Revised, 1950.

Rocky Mountain Horticulture is Different, George W. Kelly. The Green Thumb Council, Denver, Colo.

Rocky Mountain Trees, Richard J. Preston, Jr. Iowa State College Press, Ames, Iowa. 1940.

Roses for Every Garden, Dr. R. C. Allen. M. Barrows and Co., New York. 1948. Revised.

Roses for Pleasure, by Richard Thompson and Helen VanPelt Wilson. D. Van Nostrand Company, Inc. New York. 1957.

Roses of the World in Color, J. Horace McFarland. Houghton Mifflin Co., New York. 1947.

The Secret of the Green Thumb, by Henry T. Northern and Rebecca Northern. The Ronald Press Company, New York. 1954.

Smith's Chrysanthemum Manual, Elmer D. Smith. Elmer D. Smith and Co., Adrian, Mich. 1930.

The Soil and Health, Sir Albert Howard. Devin-Adair Co., New York. 1947.

Soil Development, Edward H. Faulkner. University of Oklahoma Press, Norman, Okla.

Southwestern Trees, Agriculture Handbook No. 9, U. S. Dept. of Agriculture, Forest Service. 1950.

Standardized Plant Names, American Joint Committee on Horticultural Nomenclature. J. Horace McFarland Co., Harrisburg, Penn. 1942.

Sunset Garden Books (various subjects). Lane Publishing Company, Menlo Park, California.

Taylor's Encyclopedia of Gardening, Norman Taylor, editor. American Garden Guild, Inc., and Houghton Mifflin Co., New York. 1961.

A Treasury of American Gardening, John R. Whiting, editor. Doubleday and Company, Garden City, New York. 1955.

Trees and Shrubs of the Rocky Mountain Area, Burton O. Longyear. G. P. Putnam's Sons, New York. 1927.

Trees, The Yearbook of Agriculture, U. S. Department of Agriculture. 1949.

What Is New in Gardening, by Dr. P. P. Pirone. Hanover House, Garden City, New York. 1956.

Wild Flowers of America, R. W. Rickett. Crown Publishers, Inc., New York. 1953.

The World Book of House Plants, Elvin McDonald, The World Publishing Co. 1963.

 *Glossary*

ACID SOIL—indicating acidity under the neutral point of pH 7. An acid soil is sometimes called a "sour" soil.

ADOBE—A heavy, clay-like soil, used by natives for constructing brick, damned by gardeners encountering it in their back yards.

ALKALI—White, crusty substance seen on surface of dried-out river beds, arroyos, or fields. This is a heavy alkaline condition, containing too much lime, and unfavorable to most plants.

ALKALINE—Soil-designation of a soil above the neutral point of pH 7.

ANNUAL—Plant with a life cycle of one year.

BALLING—Failure of buds to open properly, often due to the tiny insect, thrips.

BALLED AND BURLAPPED—Shrub or tree lifted from ground for transplanting, with soil remaining around roots and wrapped with burlap to protect this "ball" from drying out.

BASAL BREAK—A shoot from the base of a plant.

BASE-PLANTING—Planting of shrubs and other plant material about the base of the house or building to carry out a landscaping plan.

BED—Area assigned in garden designs for flowers and plants.

BEDDING PLANTS—Flowers and plant material within beds arranged for color and mass effects.

BIENNIAL—A plant requiring two years for its complete cycle, being planted the first year and blooming the second.

BLUING—Slight bluish cast developed by petals of red rose as the bloom ages.

BORDER—Edging of plant materials designed to outline or to contrast, either with color, height, or texture. To separate garden areas, such as service yards and cutting gardens, or to define beds, lawns, to edge driveways, walks.

BRANCH—Offshoot growing from the main trunk, stem, or cane.

BREAK—New shoot developing from an eye or bud.

BROADCAST—To plant seeds with a loose scattering motion over an area, in contrast to planting in rows or at intervals. To spread plant food uniformly over an area.

BUD—The undeveloped blossom or leaf and its protective covering.

BUDDING—The process of transplanting a bud to other stock, generally to increase hardiness, promote a stronger root system, or general adaptability to soils, and the well-being of a plant.

BUD OR EYE—The point from which springs a stem or shoot. See illustration in rose chapter.

BUD UNION—The point where bud of a shoot and understock are grafted.

BULB—The best-known bulb is the onion. In the flower world, the tulip is the most familiar. Actually, the bulb is the thickened stem end inserted in the soil from which roots spring and which produces the flower and leaves.

CALICHE—A soil with an adobe texture and extremely high lime content or almost pure calcium carbonate. At times almost cement-like in hardness.

CANE—A main branch from plant base.

CHEMICAL FERTILIZER—Fertilizer whose components parts are chemical, in contrast to organic fertilizer composed of animal and vegetable materials.

CHLOROPHYLL—Green coloring matter in plants.

CHLOROSIS—Loss of color, pale and sickly in appearance. Due to lack of proper plant absorption, caused by unbalanced soil.

CLON—A mass of roots to be divided for propagation, such as those of the chrysanthemum and iris.

CLUMP—A group of plants or shrubs grown closely together.

COLD FRAME—Protective box-like frame with no heating device, used for starting seeds, cuttings, and other garden materials.

COMPOST—The term used in this book for a mixture of decomposed kitchen discards and garden refuse mixed with animal manures and soil, used for feeding the garden. Can be used in its simplest meaning as decomposed vegetative matter.

CORM—Short, bulb-like, fleshy stem, such as the gladiolus.

CROWN—Junction of stem and root, also used to describe the round head of a tree.

CROWN BUD—Generally formed first at the top of a plant, surrounded by vegetative shoots instead of other buds.

CULTIVATION—Stirring of topsoil to aerate, eliminate weeds, make a dust mulch, and improve general appearance.

CULTURE—The general care given to growing plant life.

CUTTING GARDEN—Section of the garden allotted to flowers that will be grown for indoor use. Here plants are grown in rows, with artistry disregarded.

DAMPING OFF—Fungus disease arising from a condition developed by too much moisture, which literally mows down seedlings or plants.

DISBUDDING—Practice of removing excess buds in order that one selected bud will develop with additional size and quality of bloom.

DIVISION—Individual plants springing from the parent clump.

DRIFT—Groups of plants massed for effect.

EYE (BUD)—The point from which a new shoot grows from stem or branch.

FERTILIZER—Plant food.

FOLIAR FOOD—Fertilizer that can be put into solution and sprayed directly on plant foliage instead of on the soil at base of plant.

FORCING—Providing conditions to force a plant to develop and bloom earlier than its natural cycle.

GERMINATE—The birth of a plant from seed.

GROUND COVER—Low, creeping plants used to cover areas of bare soil.

HARDY—Descriptive of plants that will survive general weather conditions in a prescribed area.

HEELING IN—Practice of temporary protection of plants by covering roots with dirt pending their position in a permanent bed.

HILLING—Soil mounded above the base of a plant.

HARDEN OFF—To gradually prepare a seedling, cutting, or other tender plant material for outdoor conditions or for cold weather.

HOT BED—Frame or low box designed, with artificial heat, for starting seeds, growing seedlings, propagating cuttings, etc.

HUMUS—Decomposed plant material.

HYBRID—A plant that is cross-bred to improve some aspect.

LEACHING—Movement of water through soil transferring its elements.

MESA—Flat land, in Spanish it literally means "table."

LIQUID FERTILIZER—Fertilizer in solution with water.

MULCH—Light blanket of leaves, compost, or other materials, used to keep ground surface cool and damp, to conserve moisture, to keep down weeds.

ORGANIC FERTILIZER—Plant food consisting of vegetable or animal substances.

PEAT MOSS—Peat is a plant substance derived from bogs long before it has had time to turn into coal. Peat moss is the plant material sold for the use of gardeners as a mulch, to aerate soil, and to provide humus.

PERENNIAL—A plant with a continuing life cycle, reappearing year after year.

pH—Term devised to measure degree of acidity and alkalinity of the soil, pH 7 being "neutral."

PINCHING OFF—The practice of pinching out the tip of a plant to encourage side shoots or branching. Synonymous with "stopping."

POTTING MIXTURE—Properly proportioned soil for pot plants.

PROPAGATE—To increase the number of plants by any of several methods, i.e., seeds, cuttings, divisions, and leaf rooting.

PRUNING—Removal of unwanted twigs, stems, and branches.

PUEBLO ARCHITECTURE—Following the style of Pueblo Indian dwellings.

RHIZOME—The fleshy root of certain plants, such as the iris, equipped with the eyes and roots for next season's growth.

ROOT—That part of the plant that gathers food from the soil, with a few rare exceptions where the root is exposed to the air.

SCATTER PLANT—To sow seeds broadcast, not in formal rows or spacings.

SEED FLAT—A box used for planting seeds.

SEEDLING—A young seed-grown plant.

SHOOTS—Small plants springing from a parent plant.

SHRUB—A bush plant, with many branched woody stems, used in landscaping for foundation and accent planting.

SPIKE—Upright stem bearing more than one blossom.

STAKING—Supporting a plant by inserting a stake in the ground next to it.

STALK—Stem of a plant.

STOPPING—Pinching out the tip of a plant to stop growth upward by inducing branching.

SUBSOIL—The layer of soil immediately beneath the usually richer topsoil. Often value-less in this area until combined with humus and other soil nutrients.

SUBSTANCE—A term denoting that intangible designation of a plant that shows good health and sturdiness in structure.

Sucker—A shoot springing from the parent plant, sometimes from beneath the ground as in the case of lilacs, and from beneath the graft in the case of roses. Tree suckers may spring from trunk and main branches.

Terminal bud—The central bud in a cluster of buds, a term used most commonly in the culture of chrysanthemums.

Topping—Taking off the top of a plant, shrub, or tree to stop upward growth.

Transplant—To move any growing plant.

True Leaf—The leaf characteristic to the plant.

Tuber—Fleshy root or underground stem, with eyes, from which appear shoots of new plants.

Understock—Plant used for grafting.

Vermiculite—Mica product manufactured for an insulating material, adopted by gardeners for aerating the soil and for water retention.

Wilt—A virus disease attacking plants with very sudden and complete results. The plant literally collapses and "wilts."

Windbreak—Any planned obstruction to divert wind.

Winterkill—Loss of plants by severe winter weather.

Yellows—A virus disease causing foliage to turn pale and sickly.

213

Index

NAMES IN ITALIC TYPE ARE PROPER BOTANICAL NAMES.

NAMES WITHIN PARENTHESES ARE RECOMMENDED VARIETIES.

NUMBERS IN ITALIC TYPE ARE PRINCIPAL ENTRIES.